Visions of Byron

BYRON

authorHOUSE®

AuthorHouse™ UK
1663 Liberty Drive
Bloomington, IN 47403 USA
www.authorhouse.co.uk
Phone: UK TFN: 0800 0148641 (Toll Free inside the UK)
UK Local: (02) 0369 56322 (+44 20 3695 6322 from outside the UK)

Published by AuthorHouse   02/14/2023

ISBN: 979-8-8230-8053-8 (sc)
ISBN: 979-8-8230-8054-5 (hc)
ISBN: 979-8-8230-8055-2 (e)

About the Author

Growing up in Rock forth Kingston Jamaica, Byron needle had a rough upbringing, he was one of eight children for his parents. He relocated to St. John's Road, Spanish town. This is where he grew up attending primary and secondary school, however, leaving school at 15 years of age. He began learning trade with his father, then obtained a job on a construction site. This was where things took a turn for the worst. He was involved in a brawl with another worker and ending up in prison. Bryon was fortunate to have encountered many people, who shared their life experiences and told him things that happened with them. Some of the stories are from personal experiences also. Bryony has had many close misses with his life and has learnt many life lessons. All of which are contributing factors that brought about the visions of Byron needle.

Contents

Chapter one

ALL STORIES ARE TRUE TO THE BEST OF MY KNOWLEDGE.

I was born in the early seventies in a poor family with seven other siblings. I was the fifth of eight children, for both my parents. I was born in Rock forth Kingston, grew up on Sherrington Road and attend Oliver Road basic school and church in that very same community. Life was very hard for both my parents in those days. From what I can remember, my father was always working to keep food on the table he paid the rent along with other bills, while also sending my older brother and sisters to school. He was also a very strict man; he loves music especially (Bob Marley and the wailers). He would play them loudly when he's home and not working. My daddy also loves animals especially dogs, he always had a dog are two as pet. He was a kind-hearted gentleman; he was also a welder and mechanic by trade. He was born and raised in a place called Harvey River district located in Lucea Hanover.

My father was also an honest man, he keeps less friends, and was very careful with the little friends he has chosen to stop and chats with while he was traveling to and from work. He always has in his possession a little bag which contains everything that he bought on his way to and from work, for the household. From my knowledge, I can remember some of the things he would have in that bag. Such as feeding for my little brother, bread, eggs, sugar, flour, rice and fruits, like mangoes ripe bananas and oranges. He also had feeding for the birds in the cage better known as(coop) and also food for the dogs. He would feed all these birds, and animals' day and night, year in year out, and he has been doing this from we were all young. I mean all eight of us, until we are all grew up and started taken part in the feeding process with him in the mornings and evenings. We also benefitted from it too because the chicken would lay eggs, which we would eat sometimes, more than once especially for breakfast.

Visions of Byron my mother story

My mother was born and grew up in Dundee pen Lucea Hanover. She always told us that whenever she gets upsets and (cursing). Hanover is situated almost at the other end of the island, from where all her children were born and raised. My mother gave birth to all her children in the Victoria jubilee hospital in Kingston. My mother and father had met somewhere in and around Hanover from my opinion and the reason why I said that is because there are both from Hanover in the same parish. My mother would stay home while my father would go to work. My mother works hard around the house, she makes sure the house is always kept clean, and ensures that when all the kids went to and came home from school, we would get a proper meal. Whether its lunch or dinner time. My mother was also a lover of music. I can remember her singing when she is washing clothes and dishes. you could hear her singing out her favourite songs, that's a song done by (Marcia Griffith) and it's called a peaceful woman. She also loves and is a big fan of (Bob Marley), you could hear her singing loudly one of his popular song called (no woman no cry) while she washes the clothes. She would prepare lunch at the same time while my two older sisters and brothers make their way home from school. At the time they were all attending Windward Road all Age School that's in Kingston, and only a few minutes away from our house. In my opinion they would take about fifteen minutes, to walk home from school.

The house we were living in at the time was very interesting, it was owned by a very popular funeral directors, and was used for what we called a funeral parlour for making and storing coffin, washing and preparing the dead bodies for burial.

It was locate near to a popular supermarket, at the time known as Jon r Wong super market. In that yard was very scary because its inside that same yard, that they would wash all the sheets and clothing for the dead. From all the other undertakers around, all the clothes from all the dead bodies from all the accidents, from local hospitals and all the morgues in the vicinity .

2

From what I can remember there was a lady, that occupied the yard with us she is the one that does all the laundry for all these funerals parlour around. The person she was working for owned more than one funeral parlours and mortuary around. Therefore, the clothesline in the yard was always filled with bloody sheets and bloody clothes. The coffins were also made in the yard and put out on display at the front and back of the yard so that customers could come and view and choose their orders.

For some reason my mother and this lady could not get along. My mother could not stand the way she hangs the bloody sheets all over the place, and when the lines were full, she would then spread them on the fence and on the ground and walk way too. Now in the back of the yard was a very big, big tamarind tree filled with all kinds of birds. Like pigeons, black bird john crows, better known as (vultures). They would perch in the trees and keep on looking down on the ground. These vultures are always there because the smell of death is always lingering in the yard because of the dirty blooded sheets and clothing that came there to be wash from the other mortuary.

The clothes and sheets aren't wash straight away; this lady would leave them for days sometimes weeks, so the smell of the dead is all ways around the yard. You can even smell it from in the house. This also cause some big flies to linger in the kitchen we used to cook. The flies can be seen on the sheets that is piled up in what she would call a storeroom and you could hear them singing Also. (zoon zoooo zz) from anywhere you are around the yard.

The kitchen was also filled with big giant rats, big flies, and the john crows we talked about earlier and the black bird that we would call duppy birds were all sleeping in the kitchen at nights. When we would open the door in the morning you could see them fly out the kitchen or flying off the roof of the kitchen.

It was very bad living in that yard, horrible. The lady that did the washing, for the undertaker and looks after the yard her name is Mrs v. she was always drunk and swearing cussing loads of bad words she always has a cigar in her mouth. she smokes with the lit part inside her mouth meaning the part with the fire she was a terrible woman, very awful, but she has some really nice children, but for some reason they all died violently. The people within community would always say she is cursed.

one of her daughters was stabbed to death, in a dance by another girl. The other sister that witness the killing of her sister was shot to death before the trial started. The accused person walked free. Police killed her eldest son on a robbery on a Christmas Eve. Her next son was killed, in a cave by soldiers in Worricker's hill. By this time my mother and father started looking for a different house to rent so we could leave this yard. One day I can remember walking in the yard and my foot just touch on something on the ground when I look down, I saw something shiny on the ground looking like a marble. I picked it up and started playing with it I never knew what I had picked up until I show it to someone older than me. They told me to throw it away then told me what it was, I was so shocked to learned that it was someone's false eye ball. False teeth, what's known as dentures or even false legs, false hands can be seeing scattered around the yard like normal toys. Laying around the yard from back to front were prosthetic body parts and large pieces of human flesh can be seen, sticking onto the sheets that came there to be washed. sometimes you can even see maggots in it moving too, and this was clear to see and I was small.

I learned from that yard that the smell of human flesh is the worst you can ever smell when it's decaying. It was the stinkiest thing you could ever smell, that smells also lingers with a raw smell. the smell of human blood is also in a class by itself. Even the belongings of the dead people were scattered all over this yard, you could see rings earrings watches chains, bracelet and bangles. Another thing I must say that holds the stench is money. I saw this lady washes several blood-soaked monies to be precise, and when they're dried the smell is still unbelievable. She uses bleach, disinfectant, and it makes no difference. The coins also with dried blood on it she would give to us as children, to go and buy stuff from the shops, like cigarettes and cigars for her. Her son and I also share the same first name, Byron. He and I get on really well. He died also; he was one of the brothers that was killed in the cave R.I.P in respect. The smell would also stick around on the coins, also it leaves a smell in your hands, that was very awful. No matter how much you washed your hands, or how much bleach and disinfectant the coins were soaked in, it still leaves that disgusting smell that won't leave easily either. This lady has the stomach of an animal.

She is about five feet five inches tall with thick body. funny looking eyes, like lizard or cat eyes. She is always bare foot, her feet are big and broad, and her toenails all dug out. Her big toe is really big and the head of it looks all bruised, like she kicks out the nail on a stone. Her hair cut short like a man, and she wears only trousers and ties the waist of the pants with a piece of cloth. She doesn't use a belt she would rather use a piece of the cloths that wraps the dead to tie her waist. She herself smells stink sometimes. When she was having a shower, she would do it under the big tamarind tree in a bath Pan at the front of the yard she doesn't care who is watching or who sees.

one day she was having a shower in the bath Pan at the side of the house. I went around there to my dog Mystro. I saw her naked as the day she was born. when I saw her and turn back she would say (weh Yuh a run back fah Yuh fraid of pussy Lok pon it it nah bite yuh). I never forget the site of that vagina until now she was pulling the tongue of it, the hair on it is pitchy patchy like she is picking them off with her fingers that pussy I'm talking about looks like it as alopecia on it. She has no shame, I was so frightened by the looks of that pussy, that it hasn't leave my head in all these years and I am fully grown and over forty years old.

She would also cough up some phlegm what we call cold, sometimes when she is smoking the cigar with the fire in her mouth when she spit it out on the ground its black or browny in colour you can also smells it instantly and it would sticks on the ground. You can see it days after with flies all over it stuck to the ground.

My father comes home and told us he got somewhere, and we will be leaving by the weekend. Now where we would be moving to is in a class by itself. As I already told you there was not much money around and it was only my father alone that was working. We are going to move to a place called Ralington town not too far away, but we would be coming out of this effing dead yard as my mother would say.

I noticed my mother is getting really fat and fast at that time I am thinking because we are going to leave this yard, she his happy and putting on weight but little did I know she was heavily pregnant, and she really can't stand this yard anymore.

Finally, the weekend has arrived, and my father turned up with a big truck and a few of his work friends to help him move the stuff from the house unto the truck. Things like the furniture and other stuff that were pack in boxes. My mother would lift the small ones and put them aside while the men and my father would put them into the truck. From the minute the truck reverse into the yard, it was not turned off. You could stay outside the yard and hear the truck trackling. A test of the horn from the driver sends all the birds from the big tamarind tree flying to the sky. The sounds the horn makes it goes like (paaaa paaaa) then comes Mrs v running, asking questions about the truck in the yard making noise. By this time the sky is littered with pigeons, vulture, black birds that is called duppy birds.

Mrs V always have in her position a lighter and a pack of cigarettes known as Craven A or a big cigar when she finishes cussing and swearing. She has a short chat with my father known as marrow to her and all his friends from work. The truck is almost finished packing, and my father would take a final look around the house and the yard, closed the doors give her the keys and a small amount of cash. Under his arm he would have his friend and pet that's his dog called mystro. His pet was the last thing he put on board besides him in the front. The truck is now full and everyone is now on board the driver test the horn again and ready to move off again (paaa paaa) Mrs v shouted (unuh tap the noise an cum out yah) meaning come out here with the noise, my mother shouted (fuck off you ugly like sin) as the driver drives away.

All my sisters and brothers or on board and sleeping, we reach less than half hour I am sure. I remember the fire station in front of the house very well . The truck then pulled up in front of the house, one of the men jump off the truck and move straight to the house door and open it with the keys. Everyone gets busy again taking everything off the truck to inside the house. Insides the house was clean and empty, you could see and hear everything inside the house from top to bottom but there was no light in the house meaning no electricity. The gentleman that opens the door knock the neighbours and asked them to give us some current for the night, so we would be able to see. My father would be going to the JP's that's the Jamaica public service to get the electricity reconnected. It seems as if it was disconnected after the person or persons living there before us moved out.

The Ralington town story

THE NEIGHBOUR GIVES US ELECTRICITY, SO WE CAN HAVE LIGHT IN THE house, to be able to see for the rest of that night. Everything was going well, we arrived safely at our new home thank god and started unpacking the stuff from the truck. We made temporary beds on the floor to sleep on, all of us were packed in one room including my mum and dad. The House is Filled with cracks all over the walls, you can also see a few holes in the roof over our Heads. I was only small at the time, so nothing bothers me. My father will be fixing those holes in the roof first thing in the morning when he wakes up. We all wake up well the next morning. I don't remember if my sister and brother did attend school the next day which I doubts because the first Monday after we leave windward road, my father will have to take them to school and pick them up for a few days until they knew their way. Anyway, that was done, and everyone was settling well. However, before we get our own light from the J.P.S. the wire unfortunately plugs out from over the fence where we gets the electricity from and nobody wanted to gets up and call the man next door. We wait until in the morning because it was too late and he might be sleeping as well.

Now out of nowhere comes Mr croaking lizard with a loud Sound. showing he was the man inside here he goes (crack crack crack crack) and that makes everyone sacred as hell. Everyone is crying, it can be heard all over the house. My dad jumps up and grab a broom stick and begins to lash out at the lizard. It runs away under some board in the roof and disappears for the rest of the night. Now we have a lizard on our hands, that is making everyone nervous as hell, trust me this lizard looks like he will jump down on you from off the ceiling. My father makes several attempts to kill him but was not successful. This lizard his moving like it has some sense I am wondering. My father killed quite a few of them, those ones were small and it's wasn't him, the big guy who scared every one and makes the loud cracks that makes all of us in the house trembles. My father was a country man, so he began to do some old tricks that he knows from the country. My dad started looking for

7

empty bottles, now this bit is very very funny. My father goes outside the house, in the bushes that grows in and around the yard, searching for empty bottles to make and sets trap to catch this lizard. He ran into what we called a ground lizard, this lizard has blue, green and silvery look, and slides on its belly like a snake. People always says that if you hurt a ground lizard and they squeak out, means (cry out) for help, loads of others lizards will come running to their rescue. I don't know how true that is but from I was small I heard that saying and I don't want to find out if it's true or false either. My father was very frightens at the time, I could see him flashing his hands, and runs back inside, shouting "shit shit he almost bites me".

Now this bit is getting really interesting, when my father wakes up in the morning, the first thing he does after praying is gets his machete, sharpens it a bit and then he would proceed, to chop down all the bushes in and around the yard and burns it. This makes all the lizards runs away from outside the yard to find somewhere else to hide. My dad is now back inside the house again, trying to kill this big head croaking lizard that comes out in the wee hours of the nights, when everyone is fast asleep in bed. He would make the loud creepy crack sounds that scares all of us, as children even my mother who gets frighten of it sometimes. You know women in general are scared of lizards, it doesn't matter how small it is they will scream (haaaa). Whenever they see it they don't care, where it happens either, their eyes and mouth will open wide, they will be grabbing or holding onto anyone in sight, picture it in your mind except there are no screaming. Whether they knows you are not, they are grabbing onto you, or the closest person to them, males or females it doesn't matter trust me on this I have experienced this type of frightened behaviour many times with women. Not just with my mother or sisters but with most of the females I have come across most of my life. The only person who is not scared, of this big broad headed lizard, with his rusty looking body, that takes the colour of the zinc on the roof above our heads, with his long thick crusty tail hanging behind him in my household is my dad.

My daddy did patch all the holes in the roof especially the one you could look through and see the sky. There were no more leaks from the roof now. also, he mended all cracks on the walls inside the house.

My dad went out and bought a thing called molasses, he then poured it insides all the bottles he collected. He poured about a quarter of all the bottles he had, and then sets the bottles all over the roof of the house, with no lids on them. He would make sure the bottles were firm anywhere he puts them, to prevent them from falling or moved easily.

He would check the bottles every now and then throughout the week. You would be surprised, when you look and see what's insides the bottles. I mean we were shocked it was filled with all types of insects inside. The molasses was a quite thick and sticky liquid, its similar to honey, but much darker almost black in colour and a lot thicker and very very sweet. When the insects goes inside and comes in contact with this sticky liquid they are trapped inside because of the heavy substance coating their bodies making them unable to exit the bottle after they entered. There are also unable to remove their mouths, so they would eventually, fall in the sticky molasses, and ending, up dying insides the bottles. At one point my dad shows, me inside one of the bottles, wow I shouted it was amazing, what I would saw dead, insides the bottle. (Roaches, mice, butterflies, crickets, grasshoppers, snails, flies, wasp, bees, big and small lizards) insects of all sorts inside. My father's booby trap is working, but until now we still can't see this big guy who keeps coming out in the middle of night and making the loud unusual croaking sound over and over again. Looking on this lizard in the roof, his head is about one and a half inches in length and width, also and his eye are shiny, like how a cat or dog eye shines in the darkness of the night. Trust me my father sets bottles upon bottles, but he was never caught dead inside any of these traps.

My mother was becoming restless, getting fussy and worried, I think it's because she don't want to stay here anymore either. Her tummy is also growing bigger, and I think she might have the baby soon, based on how she was moving. After moving here my father still goes to work at the same place, and my sister and brother are still attending the same school. I can remember my mom leaving and when she returns there was now a baby was with us in the house. The baby was always crying, my dad would hold him up sometimes, and shake him while singing some song for him to sleep. My daddy loved children and I am just like him trust me on that.

My father was always working hard, and somehow, he save some money, and manage to make a down payment on a house in Spanish town. He's making payment to man called Mr Roberts. This house was a two bedroom board house in St Catherine Spanish town, in a place called St Johns road. We did not relocate until my dad finished paying for the house. It took almost year before we were ready to move to the new house in my opinion. I think that's how long it takes him, to pay off all the money for the house. My father told us we were going to be moving very soon but we were still there for a couple of months. I know for sure my father was a very serious man, and he means every words he says from his mouth trust me·

One evening he brought home lots of empty boxes, and start building up them up, packing things inside of them like we did from the previous address. We will be moving in a few weeks and times is running very fast. The weekend comes even faster. I can't believe this, for some reason I don't know there is someone around the same, area we are living, that knows Mrs v the very same lady from the dead yard, as my mother would say. Who told her we were living around here and that we will be moving to Spanish town soon. Mrs v send a message telling my mother "God go with unuh Spanish town". I find this weird for her to say and have no idea what she meant by that at the time, but it doesn't sound good to me knowing the type person Mrs v, is and the relationship with her and my mother it's definitely not good.

My father came home and starting to pack stuff into the boxes. A moment later a big truck turns up outside the gate and the driver blows the horn to let us know here there. My father goes outside to speak to the driver and the other men on the truck who came to help loads the furniture unto the truck. Everyone is getting busy packing and it is going well. Night is quickly coming so they need to move even faster because it will be dark soon and we have a far way to go. The trucks is almost full now and they having a cigarette brake, everyone looks quite tired. I have noticed that my father always have his pipe with him, so whenever he wants to smoke its always ready to be used. He fills it with tobacco and have a smoke really quickly.

The truck is now finished packing and everybody is on board ready to be moved. My dad takes one final look around the yard by now it's already dark. Crack crack out of nowhere comes the goes the big lizard again.

This time one of the men in the truck I' reached over for a stick and struck him out of the roof, he falls to the ground you can see him clearly. We all started screaming my siblings and I, when we saw how big this lizard was lying on the floor on the ground.

It was just pure screaming this lizard is about ten to eleven, inches long. It's head one and a half inches, in length and the width his body about two inches wide. When he landed on the ground, the same man lashes him in the head again. Splashing everything out of its head. he's now turned over on his back with his four legs in the air. He looks scary, my skins crawls just by looking at it. He now dead, the man used the same piece of stick to pulled him outside the house and threw him into a cut off drum that was used as a rubbish bin to burn stuff out in the yard . My father looks around again pick up his dog and put him in the front of the truck besides him. This is his new dog Chaw fine, I think mystro has pass away, he was hit by a car and died, a few days before. My father gives back the keys to the man next door the one who gave us the light, when we had just moved here. The driver blows his horn and off we go. I'm not sure how long this will take but, we are off to Spanish Town St Catherine.

I woke up in the night in our knew home things was a bit better. We had our own electricity and water here. We all got up the next day checking the roof of this house because everyone still remembers what went down with the roof of that other house, in Ralington town. My father gets up early every morning as usual and goes outside. At the back of the yard behind our house there was a open piece of land that was long and wide. I don't know how much in measurement it was, but I know for sure it was a huge piece of land. It's in the Middle with two sets of houses on both sides. There's about a hundred houses on both side, with the back fence facing the open land. This area is call common. We are all getting settled meeting new friends and other neighbours, everyone is happy. My father began planting crops in the yard. Things like cane, calloo, pepper, scallion, onions, cabbages, cucumbers, pumpkins, okra, garden eggs among other things. He made a big coop for all his birds, such as pigeons, ball plates, babble doves, chicken and ducks. My father feeds all the birds and animals every day, I started to help doing this with him too. The chickens began laying loads of eggs.

A man by the name of (sunt) starts bringing him more and more chicken. On Sundays when my father his home, this man comes around trying to sell him all kinds of things. I don't know where he is getting these things from, but he comes with pigeon of all colours. One Sunday, I could hear him telling my father he has two nice puppies for sale and asking my dad if he's wants to buy them. My daddy said yes. The next day the man returns outside the yard early with the two puppies waiting on my father until he comes home from work.

We already have one dog (Chaw fine) and this man was able to sell him four puppies instead of the two. We now have five dogs in the yard which means a whole lot of shit to pick up. Chaw fine is a fairly big dog mostly white with a bit of black on his face, he's a lovely dog. The yard is now like a barn, everything you can think of is there. From animals big and small to the crops planted in the yard. The soil is good, so everything is growing fast and thriving. Again all is going well, we've been living there for a while and getting close to the neighbours. One day one of them started a conversation with my mother telling her about this strange place she use to live with coffin and things in the yard. It only took my mum a second realize she's talking about the same dead yard that we lived at. She had live there prior to us moving in. Now she's living here in the to the same lane as us in Spanish town St Catherine. As I listen the conversation between them I realize what she is telling my mother the same thing that happened in the yard with Mrs V and how she dislikes her because of her dirty ways.

This woman talking to my mother is called Mrs Ava, she has six kids four boys and two girls. They come to see my sister almost every evening to play school and ask my sister to assist them with their homework.

My two sisters are still attending school in Kingston but our parents are planning on moving them closer to home. As a matter of fact, all of us will be attending Friendship all age school. My father still has his garage in the city, and still working every day. While he's working in Kingston, we get to know other kids around the area. We don't stay in the yard when he's not there. One evening we came home after being out, my mother had gone to meet our two sister and left the baby in the house sleeping. We heard the dogs barking like crazy and jumping up on the side window. My mother rushed inside to check on the baby and made a loud scream, (Jesus Christ). We all run to see what was happening. You'll never guest what we saw, a big black cat had climb through the window and was on the bed with the baby while he's asleep. The cat was licking the baby's nose and mouth.

The loud commotion made the cat jump back through the window and over the fence. He ran into the bushes in the common and disappear. My mother started crying, all the neighbours have gathered talking some scary thing about the cat, saying a duppy puss and that is (obeah) the cat keeps coming back, every now and then. The dogs wanted to catch him, but he keeps on the roof. This cat is dangerous, he's killing the chickens and the other birds in the yard. Sometimes in the evening we see this cat staring over at us from across the fence. He is making my daddy upset and he really want to catch him. He's asking around for the owner, but no luck so far.

Anyway, we started visiting the common every Sunday to race with other children and fly kite. We would make box truck from the milk box and Juice boxes. All the kids in the area started gathering over common on Sundays. There was a guy we call Carol or lavvy as he prefers. He's the one that made some really big kite for me send them far away when he is flying them in the sky. He always comes out to train and run over common every Sunday.

(Carol or lavvy) as I called him will soon become the Jamaica four hundred metres champion. However, we later found out that his correct name was Berth land Cameron. The last time I can recall seeing him on TV was sometimes in the nineties competing in race. I never saw him again. I think he was a past student at St Jugo high school. We used to live about ten minutes' walk from each other. Also, the way he uses to runs and train and exercise really hard I knew he was going to do great.

Friendship all age is known for having many talented students attending there over the years. My mother took me to get registered into friendship school. However I didn't get in, the administrator said it was full at the moment and give my mother another date to return to speak with the principal.

Now Spanish town and the country is about to erupt. There was an announcement that the country's general elections is on its way, loads of motorcade started and violence is on the rise. I finally got a place in school and starting to attend but for me to get a space in to the school, I was put in a year back until space was available in grade two where I should be. I was a bit old for that grade but thanks to the principal at the time Mrs Edwards and vice principal Mrs Harris I was given a place. The school is referred to as all age because it starts from grade one up to thirteen from what I can remember.

The nineteen eighty elections as I mentioned is now at its peak. I could see green coloured painting as far as my eyes can see around john's road and beyond. A few red flags were about but you could hardly see them. At the time the peoples national party was in power (PNP) led by the right Honourable Michael Manley. The opposition party was the Jamaica labour party (JLP) its leader Right Honourable Edward Seaga, both are now decease Rip in respect of both prime ministers. Several shooting and murders was reported, school was interrupted a few times and closed students were sent home.

Friendship school was in the middle of all this situated about five miles out of Spanish town, or just a little bit more or less. It's on the right-hand side of St Johns Road, heading towards Frasers content better known as red pond. Just a bit further was the popular dovecot memorial park, the school is on the right-hand side of the road, after a section of the road known, as cross road which is a four way junction which runs (feather bed lane, Jobes lane, Fairfield road, and Johns road as locals call it. The school can be spotted on the right-hand side after passing over the bridge of a canal a few hundred yards. There is a big open land besides the school and an even bigger piece, of open land In front of the school also. Still with directions coming from dovecot, and red pond (Frazer content) directions, or the green acres housing, scheme the school, will be on the left hand side of the road after passing ebony vale housing scheme on the left. a few hundred yard down was a property owned by the Smiths, something like a mini plaza with a meat shop and a few other business.

Just after the shops, you have a little lane, which is called friendship lane and then the school. In front the school on the opposite side of the road is a very big open property which has a massive house on it. It was once a rice and cane field, filled with coconut trees mangoes, guavas, and loads of other stuff can be seen on that property, also animals, such as donkeys, cow goat, sheep, pigs can be heard, guenia chicks, ducks can be seen. There are also two large fishponds on that property. you can see people moving around, trucks and tractors can be seeing going in and out the other side of the school. Just as you past the school on the left there is an open land Which have a few abandon fishpond and loads of cows can be seeing feeding.

I have given All the directions to find the school, I hope it helps. The school was painted in dark grey and white with a little bit of other colours here and there a touch of black and a little bit of dark brown too. There were always spooky rumours that I heard Surrounding friendship school like mermaid inside the school toilet, and duppy (ghost)on the school compound. Apart from that some popular students were attending the school like the twins from Frazer's content (red pond) p and p, was known to be the rude boys in the school. looking really identical, you can't make them out, if you don't know them very well. I have seen the police comes to school and talk to them more than once. Now Mrs Edwards, was a woman with high complexion real strict. I have never seen her with any kids of her own. I don't know if she has any kids either, but I have never seen them if there was any. Mrs Edwards lived on the school compound, around the back of the school where the six form classes use to be. In front of the house, was a few trees and at the was a big silver water tank, and that was, at the back of the six form classes. There was a dwarf mongo tree at the front also you could see the mangoes, pulling the branches to the ground. The mangoes on that tree, was very big. I think they called them (john belly full). I don't know if am right about the name but that's what I was told. She also drove a cream-coloured rover in those days from what I can remember.

Mrs Harris was the vice principal at the time she also very strict but she was a very understanding and nice person. Mrs Harris have a few kids; I think she has about four or three girls from what I can remember they were lovely girls. Mrs Harris also lived on St Johns Road. One of my sister and Mrs Harris second daughter was really close, her name was

Gee. Now Gee and my sister Remi were good friend and classmates. They would study together both at school and home. They will soon sit the common entrance exam to move on to higher education. They graduated from Friendship all age school because they both pass for another school. My sister passed for St Catherine high school and I think Gee pass for St Jago high school. St Catherine high is not too far away from friendship school. It is located on St Johns road about a miles up the road heading towards Spanish town. St Catherine high is also next to another popular school called St Johns primary school. St Johns road is known for these popular schools and shops, also the owners of these businesses were some well-known people from what I can remember. These shops and owners can be used as land Marks to find street and directions for people in around St Johns road.

I will give you a few of the shops names and location, starting from Frazer content is the red shop which all taxis will empty out and pick up passengers coming are going from Spanish town. Just a little further down the road heading towards Spanish town, exactly in front of ebony vale housing scheme on the opposite side of the road, is a shop called Claris. This is shop was named after its owner Mrs Claris. Most students living in Frasers content (red pond) would stop there to buy food. That shop was well known to have in its glass case (fried fish, fried chicken, fried saltfish, fried dumplings, fried plantains, roast and fried bread fruit cornbread, bulla and cheese bun and cheese). Loads of other stuff was in that shop it was well stock. Mrs Claris was a nice lady likes children too. Continuing down the same road on the other side is the Smith groceries where older and more upper-class people did their shopping. Still on the same side of the road coming towards the school were a lot of venders selling outside the school gate. Plenty of the students attending the school parents sold outside the school gate. I myself know quite a few of them that is outside there selling. still traveling on the side of the road going over the bridge of the canal now heading back to crossroads.

On the right sides of the canal, lots of boys would gather there to race board horses in the water. There was also a big gambling spot, and they washed car outside some of them did this for a living. Another thing on that same sides of the road was a small farm, there were many mangoes and ackee trees. Soursops, guava, sweetsop trees and bread fruit trees. It was a very fruitful land owned by some people called Macule. There was a massive upstairs and downstairs board house on that property right at the front of the road, at the junction we called crossroad. That place was later run down terribly, after the passing of those people. (RIP) in respect of these legendary people. To the left of the road on the other side were a lot of bushes, where they fix tyres that roads was called Fairfield road.

Running alongside Fairfield Road is Jobe lane, a betting shop was there, on the left side of the road was a lawn where they use to keep dance every weekend. That place was later Owned by some Indians who is well known until today. Continuing down on Johns Road on the right-hand side of the road was some chicken farm, loads of large chicken coop that holds thousands of chickens inside. It was owned by a prominent family, one of them was also a teacher at Friendship school that teacher was well popular in the school. Well loved by all students, her name was Mrs Wells she would later leave teaching and take up politics beginning a new political career. She worked as a counsellor for the people's national party (PNP) sometime in the nineties. She was married had three kids and was a nice lady.

Further up the road was Mrs Ferdy shop on the left, then you have Mrs Winnie shop and bar. Mr Moore shop was on the right then you have Aston shop, then Keith liqueur store, which later became white house cinema. In front on the right was Mrs Matty shop across from Aston at the beginning of ninety one lane. The list goes on to clayton heights. Mr and Mrs Henry shop on the left then sister super market, then Mr Wright at the top of Valdese road, which is bar and betting shop for horse racing. Those were the shops all the way to the highway. After passing Mr Wright shop and bar you can find St Johns primary school, and next to it was the St Catherine high school. The current Prime minster the right Honourable Andrew Holiness was a pass student of this school. Many who attended that school became lawyers, doctors, nurses, teachers and police and soldiers. Back to Friendship school and the eighty elections. The (PNP) lost the general election that year to the (JLP) in year 1980. Leading the PNP was Honourable Michael Manley and the leader for the JLP was the Honourable Edwards Seaga. Friendship school was in good hands at the time my sister left the school.

My sister Remi heads on to St Catherine high school and my older sister known as Sadie move onto CC college in Kingston. After they left, my brothers and I were still there that was in the early eighties. I must tell you some of the things I witnessed.

As a child in the eighty election I see loads of things a child shouldn't see. Like men chasing each other with machete and long gun up down, dead bodies, burnt houses and shops. Shooting like crazy police and the JDF busy up down. It was mayhem in those days. Winters pen, red pond, Jobes lane, Fairfield road, feather bed lane, Willowdene, Johns road, hold harbour road, homestead all these areas violence was on the rise.

People was advised to stay indoors you could hear the sound of bells. All over you could see drawings of bells and fits drawn on the wall as a representation of each political party. The bells symbol represents the JLP and was painted in green and yellow the party colours. The fits represent PNP and was painted in orange and black. Red and black could be seen in certain areas too just showing their political preferences.

I became very popular in school and made many good friends. From I was in grade one at school until today. I am fifty years old. Sometimes we use to hide from school in those same bushes we talked about in the school directions. We could a pick mangoes, apples and canes along the canal. We would also swim in the canal. I almost drowned a few times and was saved by my other classmates. We use to cook some kids food on the canal bank like roast breadfruit and ackee, thing we found at the canal. We would eat about two to three times. Sometimes adults would find us and take us back to school. They would inform the teachers that we are hiding from school and we would all receive a flogging for not being in school but at the canal bank. Quite a few of my classmates migrated to the United States, and never returned. Some went to England and Canada also. In school I was good at Reading, Spelling, English and Religious Education. With Maths I was rubbish the teacher always pay special attention to me when it comes to maths, they all tried to help me.

I myself know that was my weakest subject in class. Somehow, I tried improving myself with maths, but it just never works. I tried very hard Knowing that was a weak point for me. I did some evening classes years later for maths and English, but it still never works. I was never a sports man at school either. I can't play football, but I love watching it. I tried running for sports day it never happens. if ten person was in a race, I would finish seven or eight in that race sometimes even ten meaning (dead last). I was helpful in school and my classes in any way I can, school was fun in those days. I had a lot of friends from Fraser content, red pond which I use to visit their homes, like Kirk Morgan, younger brother of popular dance hall artist or DJ Charlie Chaplin. Keith Morgan better known locally and internationally as Junior Kelly younger brother of the late Jim Kelly. Students and teachers would think most of the times Keith and Kirk are related because of their surnames that's (Morgan) sometimes they even think they're brothers. Back then no one knew Keith would become the man he is today, because he never showed himself up as a singer or DJ from what I can remember. So far, I heard his songs playing and saw him singing here and there but no surprise. That's shows that no one knows what the future holds. In class Keith was known as the strongest Man. He had big hands with big veins visible in his hand. We used to ask him to muscle up just to look at the big veins under his skin, he had a few competitors, but they were no match.

Red pond was known back in the days, for big sound system. Around Red Pond there were lots of good DJ too. Artist such as Jim Kelly, Charlie Chaplin, Branner ranks, Ricky Chaplin, Ricky stereo, a friendship past student also. Loads of international, and local artists could always be seen in red pond Frasers content because, certain sound system was there like marathon, and a sound also called no limit. I don't hear or knows too much about it anymore but loads of Artist was always hanging, artists like pinchers, junior demos, lecturer and a DJ known only as Fullerton, lots of other Artist were there at the time. There was a resident sound there by the name of Marathon owned by a man known as (Tommy or O). I am not sure but that sound system was the thing in those days late eighties. I don't know what became of marathon or its owner today from those times I mentioned.

Frazer content become a place of beauty at one point, for the rich and the famous with some big houses and loads of pretty cars. A lot of big event and parties took place all the time from what I remember. Back to friendship school when school was over in the evening, we use to walk through a place called site which takes us into red pond quite quickly. Site is now ebony vale housing scheme and fear view park housing scheme. It's also very near to winters pen. You can walk winters pen and head into to red pond too. Winters pen was known for some real rude boys as well, that was one of the place that was real bad during the eighties election. Violence in that area was out of hand, then to match the ruthless rude boys were the even more ruthless police officers of those days. Killing them like bird as people would say. Officers like (Smalls, Amin, String beans, Mackey, T. Fry, bad Indian, Robocop, and others). These officers were the ones who drove fear in these ruthless rude boys. Sometimes you hear the sounds of gunshots and few minutes later you would see the green jeep or the Jump out passing you with somebody legs, hands or even their heads hanging outside jeep. Blood trails can be seen on the ground behind the jeep draining from the decease.

The Gruva Story

I remember one Sunday my friend and I was coming from the canal after just having an early morning bath. Coming from jobs lane canal, on entering a lane called Ackee tree lane we saw a large crowds gathered and people talking. We overheard someone say, "police have one of Johns Road most notorious rude boy". On the front he was known to me as Gruva. He was always feared because of his ugly looks. He was a very ugly man known for rape and murder. People feared even his name especially the females. No woman wants to be rape trust me.

As we walked through Ackee tree lane we entered the front of Johns Road, then turn and cross over the main road onto the left-hand side of the road of St Johns garden. We walked down for a bit, past a place called big yard. Then approaching the next lane, we saw more crowd gathered at the lane mouth, we turn left into the lane and walked down a bit on the right-hand side of the lane.

We were now closer to the crowd and saw a man that turns out to be Gruva, with loads of board on his shoulders. Bringing them out of a yard on the right-hand side of the lane with a police officer known as Amin. A big black man with a gun hanging out of his waist, with a long magazine visibly hanging from under his shirt clearly to be seeing. He used a piece of board to slap Gruve a few times over his head, you could see blood running from the side of his head. At the time he was carrying the boards to pack them where the officer wanted him to put them, for them to be taken to the station so they can used as evidence in court, that's my opinion.

Now Gruva, has a lot of family on St Johns Road, I know this for a fact. Everyone was there watching the event unfolds, a few of his family members were at the front of the crowd. They were shouting and calling his name, some were even crying. One of his female family shouts out "Gruva" and said, "run boy". I could hear her clearly her name is Mrs Eve. When she said that he looked at her, she slightly shadows the policeman a bit by blocking him to make Gruva run away. Hell breaks loose that Sunday morning. Gruva has cuffs on one arm his left arm to be exact. The hand cuff was swinging, in those days it was the silver bangle, the ratchet one with the teeth. Gruva takes the opportunity and drop the board from his shoulder and took off. He shoots off like a rocket, down the lane with Amin running behind him and pulling his long big black magazine hand gun from his waist.

Screaming start as Amin gets his gun out of his waist the sound of people screams (murda, nuh kill him). The officer lost his balanced a bit, but he finally got his gun out. The sound of bullets going off as he runs and fires at Gruva, who kept ducking and running. The crowd behind is running and screaming murder when gun shots litters the air. I am running behind them too. Looking ahead I saw him jump a few fence ending up in an Open land heading towards St Johns garden. The officer is not leaving him a bit (pie pie pie pie pie pie) bullets like crazy. Gruva run insides a house on St johns garden and run into a room and began screaming "kill me kill me and dun the". The officer ran into the house behind him. Gruva falls on a bed and the officer points his gun on him straight in his face. People screaming "don't kill him, murder, murder Jesus Christ".

The officer was trying to get everybody out the room chasing them away he really wants to shoot him in the head. I can see it in his eyes. Gruva was bleeding, it looks like he's been hit but I'm not sure. The officer uses his radio and call some other officers who respond quickly. Gruva is asking for water everyone is saying don't give him water to drink. The officer looks like he need water himself. It was one heck of a running that Sunday. This was about nineteen eighty-two over some sixteen-gun shots fired that day.

Gruva has a long mouth and a long pointed head also he as some fine teeth in his mouth, and all the hair on his head is looking like baby hair. You can see all is scull the hair on his head his red he was short in height, and he as really fine voice you can hardly hear him speak. He was black meaning very dark in complexion. his shoes always look bigger than is foot. The clothes he wears is always bigger than him. He is always wearing some big khaki-coloured pants and one big green long sleeve shirt all the time. He was taken back to the Spanish town police station, tried and charged and then sentenced to about four to five years in prison.

After serving about half his sentence he returned home. When he returns home from prison, he was more vicious, more ruthless, with an even more serious and dangerous intention, he had murder on his mind. After coming from prison Gruva was hanging around Johns Road areas. The ladies were getting worried again because he was very scary, little kids would see him and start crying they called him quite a few names like (does he bite, and scissors) but all in his mind is to get a gun to carry out his execution. A man that goes by the name cabbage came to visit one of his friends by the name of long. Long was also born and raised here in St Johns Road and is close friends with Gruva. His friend is from downtown Kingston. Whenever he visit Long, Long would always take this guy to Rob people coming from work on weekends, people from in and around the community. I was told he has with him a Revolver of some kind. All his friend knew about the gun, and they would all talk about it.

One day they were talking about the gun and planning a robbery. Gruva overhead the conversation. He listens carefully and tell himself he wants to be on this next robbery. His intention was to get a whole of the gun he heard them talking about. The man cabbage was already there with long waiting for the weekend to arrive. They were planning to rob this lady coming from market. Gruva told them that money coming from the market is a small change and he knew where bigger money is. The guy took the bait and ask him where, he then start a conversation with the guy telling the guy something. This is all happening at the front of the ackee tree lane on the main road. The guy then goes in the front of his pants and take out a 38 Revolver and hands it over Long. Long then check it if it's loaded and puts it in his pocket. Gruva was there watching all of this ask to take a quick look at it. Long gives it to him. Now this was what he was waiting for, he takes a look recheck the barrel if it was loaded and gives it back.

Immediately Gruva asked to see it again. Long thinking nothing of this gives it to him again. Gruva looks at it and said it looks nice and fat, both men responded yes. Gruva then look at them saying "Yuh know how long me want one a dis ". The two of them stared at Gruva, then Long said "pass it". Gruva shouted "pass wat, A one yuh want outa it, left yaso". Now the sound of a shot (bow) could be heard. Gruva had fired a shot over their heads. Long started running with his friend behind him. This is now St Johns Road worse nightmare. That same day he went and searched for some guy he had an argument with. He didn't see him, so he went back the next day. Again, he didn't see him that day too, so he went back the night and found the guy. He shot the man three times in his head killing him on the spot. Now he's wanted by the police. He went and killed a girl in the scheme according to witness they saw this ugly looking man in a big green shirt same type dressing that matches his description.

Gruva is now wanted for two murders, everyone is scared and worried. At one point he even shot at his dad. His father is a well-known drinker around Johns Road, he sells crab and mangoes. He's always drunk from what I can remember. Gruva goes on for a while like this robbing and killing he never stop. he had a sister in the lane where he killed the guy. The guy's friends are going after his sister. His sister was going out with a warden, and they were having problems. Gruva didn't like how the warden roughed up his sister, so he tried killing the warden. He fired at the warden but missed. The warden ran away scared as hell. This is getting on the police nerves. Every minute there's a shooting. The same police Amin, that arrested him before comes searching along with all the top CIB in those days. They looked for him all over the area. The main place Gruva would visit is winters pen. Sometimes he's in Jobes lanes or he's in feather bed lane.

A few years earlier this incident happen before Gruva took the gun. There was a church convention taking place, everyone was attending. Some men went there to chase after women and women went to get a man. There was this Indian man from Feather bed lane, people called him Indian. He had an argument with Gruva because of some misunderstanding, I don't know what started it. It could well be over one of these girls at the convention. Getting a girl from the convention is like winning some money you feel important. In those days it use to be a challenge every man wants a church girls so loads of men turn up from all over at this convention girls like wise. No one remembers the purpose or the reason for the convention no one is thinking about God. During the argument between Indian and Gruva, Gruva spoke less but had his right hand in his pocket all the time during the argument. When Indian turned his back to Gruva, Gruva took the opportunity to take the ratchet knife out of his pocket. He then uses it to make a massive cut from the neck to the shoulder and then the side. He also gave him a long cut across his chest, from the left breast to the right and slanted it down towards his belly. He then stabbed him three time in his belly and cut him in his face multiple times. The cut to his torso was so bad his intestines were hanging out. He almost died; people rush with him to the hospital he was there for a month. When he came home, he looked different with all these cuts all over him. This was another reason why people feared Gruva the way did.

Feather bed lane is in a class by itself, mainly because of how lonely it was with no street light. It was in utter darkness which made it an ideal spot where women and men were getting Robbed and rape. They targeted Christian, people who were going church and even taxi drivers. The drivers were afraid to drive a certain place at certain time trust me. The police were on to him, they knew everything. This guy was getting out of hand. There was even a rumour about him saying he wants a bigger gun. He is now wanted by the police dead or alive. Yet, he still goes around doing this over and over again. He's becoming more ruthless by the minute. There are sound of shooting and reports of murder every now and then. Police is visiting his home every minute. They even picked up his father on several occasion for questioning, then let him go after few hours or a few days.

St john's road his known for a bit of violence. Everyone is on edge because they are scared of this ugly man. In one of the yard in the same lane where is sister use to live, he is going out with a mother and two of her daughters at the same time. It so happens that one of the daughters got pregnant and because of the situation the child was given to her boyfriend. However, when the child was born it was a different story. The child is the splitting image of Gruva, ugly same way. Everyone is gossiping behind her back, saying the child could not be for the man claiming to be the father. This baby could not hide and bears no resemblance to the man known as Eddie. I think they will break up eventually. At some point he will know and sees that that's not his baby, it will happen sooner or later and that's just my opinion.

The whole community is talking about this disturbing situation. How can one man be sleeping with a mother and her two daughters.

Worst of all they can't say anything because they were scared of him. Sometimes they'll watch him goes with each other and can't say anything at all. His gun is always visible and he's always playing with it. He calls it Suzie, it is a black blue steel Smith and Wesson slug nose six cylinder 38 Revolver with a broken brown handle. He gives it to all the little boys around him and plenty youth like him too. They don't even know their own danger, because if anyone of those police men that I mentioned before even glimpse them with him then there would be a shootout I'm sure. Things can go really bad I know this very well. In situation like that where he and the police are in a shoot-out, his family would send him away to the country. They would beg him to stay there but as soon as he goes there, he comes back saying he can't stay in the country. He said it's a bit strange and he can't stay in one place to long and he don't trust country people. I will tell you about the rest of Gruva story later.

Let me get back to my time in Friendship school. I've been attending Friendship for a year now. I am about to go in grade two in about a month are so. I have adjusted well and made a lot of friends both boys and girls and was loved by quite a few teachers. I was popular in school as I said before. About the second day in grade two schools dismissed about minutes to five in the evening. I was on the evening shift me and my older brother ran out the gate heading home. We went through the gate turn left my brother was in front of me running heading towards crossroad. All l can remember is the loud sound of a car and saw myself flying in the air. I felt a heavy bounce in my back I was only small, so the impact of the vehicle threw me high up in the air, l felt like I was in the sky for a bit before falling on the ground. I was thrown further out then the car ran me over. I stuck underneath the car and dragged some yards before he eventually stopped. I could hear people crying out "him dead, him dead". I remember loads of people looking under the car. I was taken out by someone who shouted "him nuh dead", bring him to the hospital. Meaning he's not dead.

I was put in a vehicle and rush to the Spanish town hospital. By this time my brother went home to inform my mother about what has happen to me. I was in and out of consciousness, I could hear voices and sounds. I also remember being in the arms of my teacher Mrs Will, she was one of the persons who took me to the hospital. She stayed with me until my parents arrived. While at the hospital I was examined by a doctor. I was asked questions, like my name, my address and parents' information. I was asked to closed my eyes, I did while he's touching and squeezing me. I was asked to move both feet left then right. Next, He asked me to move my arms, the left one moved but my right arm couldn't. He asked me to do it again only this time I should touch his forehead. I did and all five fingers on my left hand moved. However, when I tried this with my right arm only the fingers could move, and it was swelling really fast. I tried again but I couldn't the pain was too much. The doctor touched just below my elbow, and I screamed out mama, mama. Now the doctor is saying he sure the arm is broken but I need and x-ray, to see how badly its broken or if it's broken in more than one places. My head was also swollen and I needed additional tests to make sure I didn't have any head injuries. Even though I didn't have any head injuries I still sustained other injuries, like a broken arm, cut all over my body and my skin all rub off because of being dragged under the car. I was put to sleep then taken to the theatre to fix my broken arm and stitch my cuts. I was Look after very well at the hospital. I can remember special teacher, the one who brought me to the hospital never leaving me until I was released. She was a nice lady in and out of school.

I wake up later with my hand in plaster and a sling around my neck to hold my arm in place. I was told by a nurse that I'll be going hone soon. My father came to visit me and said "waah gwaan, them fuck yuh up Mystro". He gave me a hug and told me I need to be careful and watch out for cars. He asked if I was hungry. Mrs Wills and my mother was there also with a few other people. The gentleman that was driving the car that hit me was there in the hospital too. Even the police were there to ask some questions.

Nothing came of the accident, the driver of the car Mr Elly was known by my mother and father, they get one well. He lives somewhere on Nugent Street and has a business there from what I was told. I was only eight at the time and survived by the help of God. I was discharge and sent home from the hospital. My parents were happy, Mr Elly and Mrs Wills were happy too. After eight weeks and a few follow up appointments, it was time for the sling and plaster to be remove. I was sent into a room and told to sit beside a table. On the table was some kind of electric looking ox saw. I just knew from seeing it that's what he'll use to cut the thing off my arm. In minutes my arm was free, it looked white and dry, but it was not itching anymore. Eight weeks of scratching and discomfort gone in minutes I was glad.

I'm feeling better and is excited to get back to school as normal. Everyone in school took notice of my arm and saw that the plaster was missing. It might have looked different to them. I go all around the school and around the surrounding area. I go everywhere I have a classmate 1 even visited their homes from Winters pen, Fairfield Road, Jobes lane, Irish pen, Belleview heights, Willowdene Green acres Brunswick avenues and many more places I didn't visit during eight weeks.

I have Missed death a few times because of some bad incidents I've been in. I remember going to the canal by Macule and climbing an apple tree. I saw this ripe apple way up in the tree, I was a skinny boy so I would climb anything, go through any small space, fit though windows, go underneath bridges and culbuts and could swim like a fish. I went up in the tree and kept going higher trying to reach the branch the apple was on. I reach the branch and was stretching for the apple when the branch broke from under my belly. Now I'm falling headfirst from the tree and fell into the canal. I dropped into the water with a splash, but I hit my head at the bottom and was knocked out. I nearly drowned, someone jumped into the water and pulled me out. I was drenched and unconscious. It took a few minutes to regain consciousness. I was bleeding from my nose, dirt in my eyes and my body was filled with pain.

Life is a bit up and down; you must take the good with the bad it never stops. There was this other time on the canal bank but from Jobes lane side on the bank towards reservoir at the examination depo. My four friends and I Raphie, drew and two others. Raphie was living in that part of Winters pen called Mac Island. We went swimming in the canal, we used to run from the top of the bridge on the road and dive over down into the water. You have to run really fast and pick up speed to go over the bridge and then go over the barrier made down in the water. Everyone is doing it from the road. The road had become wet when it's my turn I start off running. When I made that leap my leg slipped. I barely made it over the bridge. When I go over that barrier in the water the top of my foot banged into the barrier made of solid concrete. The top of my foot was white before it started bleeding. It was so badly bruised, only my instep hit the wall hard. There are few more instances where I can remember something going wrong, and I have to thank God for making me be alive today because no man knows what the future holds. Life has always been a challenge for me, but when I reflect back on my life I have more than one thing to be grateful for and be happy. I just celebrated my fifty birthday and I'm honoured to be sharing this with you.

Now back to Gruva, he's on Spanish town most want list for multiple murders and shooting. He will not give up easily, according to him, he's not going down without a fight or bring one with him. Strong words from a man like that. Everyone knows what he's capable of doing because of the bad things he's done before. He's moving from lane to lane, the police are crawling all overlooking for him. People has asked him time and time again to turn himself in, but he never listens, it just goes through one ear and out the other.

Once he was involved in a robbery where some truck was robbed an argument broke out over the money, at least that's what I heard. You know how Jamaican are they'll give you a basket to carry water. Any way he and these set of gunmen kicked off and they are trying to kill him over and over but he's like a ghost. He hides around the area in lanes and places they won't expect him. He always surprises them, some of these men that are attacking him are from community like Homestead and Toys pen otherwise called, Horizon. In Spanish town these men are the town's most notorious, trust me on that and they are wanted by the police for serious crimes. They are involved in several shooting out and murder just like Gruva. Sometimes when the police are successful in finding them its fatal, nothing new. Every now and then there's a funeral, they shoot at the police ever so often, but they always end up losing their life. These gunmen dresses and look like the police, they look exactly like the C.I.D hunting them.

Let me give you a brief insight about how these men operate. One day my friends and I were all at the ball field playing in my lane as you know it's on Johns road. Little before midday three men came to kill a man, they took this man by gun point and was carrying him away to murder him on the canal bank up by cross road. On their way to crossroad, here comes Gruva out of nowhere. In fact, they were in search of him pushing and slapping the man with the gun and asking him questions about Gruva's where about. Gruva spotted them because of how they were dressed, he thought they were the police. Then he heard his friend begging and crying for his life and pleading with them not to kill him. He told them he doesn't know where Gruva is, Gruva hearing all this came upon them like a thief in the night to save his friend. That night he'll be rated as a superhero with his 38-slug nose. All the others were armed with 9mm pistols and 45 calibres auto.

A shoot out began, Gruva first fired (blow blow). They let the man go because they have to defend themselves. The night lit up with gunshots, now Gruva has to be careful how he fires his Revolver. He has only six bullets and each one of these men have ten and over plus there are four of them. All you could hear was the sound of relentless gunshots blow, blow, blow pie, pie pie, blow, blow, blow nonstop. The men ran away they all went in different directions, they can't pass back the way they came because Gruva is there. Two of them entered a lane to try and exit but here comes Gruva again pie pie, another round of gunfire began. They ran like crazy but don't know the area as well as Gruva. They returned a barrage of bullets on Gruva who jumped over a fence, rumours has it he's been hit. Police comes asking questions but no knows about the shooters they were all gone by the next day. I saw a guy asking for antibiotics, said that Gruva been shot in his toe. You could see where the bullet went through his shoe bottom and went between his little toe. He was wearing a brown Clarks that looks bigger than his foot. He has to dress it himself he can't go to the hospital, or he'd be arrested by the police.

The person that shot him on the toe heard that he was shot and can't move properly. They are trying to kill him before he's well but Gruva has loads of family and friends on Johns road so he gets information quickly and someone informed him of this plan. We are all at the ball ground and heard shots being fired on Johns Road. Everybody started running towards That direction because we heard them screaming him dead, him dead. These men I'm telling you about jumped out of a taxi and approached a group of men standing up at the front of the road just after big yard, Gruva was not there at the time. The gunmen opened fired causing everyone to scatter in different directions with some of the gunmen chasing them firing shots. One guy ran into a lady's house and ran under one of her kids bed holding onto the child. The gunmen run into the house after him and saw him with the child and pointed the gun on him. He began crying out and shouting the men's name and saying you know me(murder, murder) while under the bed clutching the baby to him thinking that would deter the man from shooting him. The gunman shot him a few times even though the baby was in his hands and walked away. Another of told that it was Gor. By this time Gor was still alive even though he was shot multiple times. He was still holding on to the baby groaning. Several other gunmen returned one shouted him nuh dead and looked under the bed. They dragged the mattress from off the bed and pulled the baby out of his hands. They all open fire at him firing rapidly loads of bullets, now he's really dead. They also wanted to kill the lady and her son but everyone shouted out that a man was already dead. The men ran through the house and bushes jumped over the fence to make their escape. All this time Gruva was in another lane further down the road by the time he reaches its done and Gor is already dead. By the time my friends and I got there the yard is filled with onlookers. When the police arrived everyone is gone, no one knows anything, no one saw nothing and that's just the way it goes.

The gunfight continued between Gruve and these other me. He is now wanted like no body's business he keeps clashing with these other guys night after nights. Police keep coming and searching and sometimes he spots them from all the way at the top of the lane and disappear in the yards nearby. He never knows that the police are setting a drag net to take him down and out. We will get back to that bit shortly.

Feather bed lane was known to have the Vick sparrow cane field, when we were feeling peckish (hungry)we use to go there after we swam in the canal. Sometimes more than one group of youth use to go there that was where some people have their tea, lunch and dinner. Sparrow was looking more like a European because of his complexion. In those days the sugar cane industry was huge business. As you know the cane field make sugar and white rum. You had Sparrow's, Inswood estate and Burnal lodge estate. All three were big cane farmers supplying Jamaica with sugar, rum, vinegar and other stuff like molasses even honey. They supplied loads of other stuff you can get from a farm like coconuts, papayas, sweet potatoes, pumpkins cabbages, callaloo, onions, scallions and peppers. Some even supplied live stocks like pigs, goat, sheep, rabbits and cows. Most of these factories are closed down and turned into housing scheme. The Vick sparrow cane field is now Inswood village housing scheme and Inswood estate is under construction right now this minute. A police officer was killed on site there sometime last year. All these famous cane farm are now turning into housing scheme, anyway this is still a good thing. God bless all those farm owners they fed plenty of hungry youngsters like me in those days and may God bless the ones mentioned. If they are still here or if they'd past away (R I P) to them in all respects.

Inwood Property Story

I CAN SHARE A FEW STORIES WITH YOU ABOUT THINGS THAT HAPPENED over on Inswood property. Some serious happenings and few narrow escapes too. One day me and my younger brother and two more of our friends. One of them who had migrated to Connecticut USA from early out in the eighties. His name was Brown. His mother has been travelling to the states for a long time. He has two sisters and a brother. We are good friends, but we see each other as family. His mother also became one of my mothers. We usually go to Inswood to catch fish and eat sugarcane, drink coconut and ride on the back of the trailers that carry the cane to Burnal lodge. This trailer was similar a train with a lot of carriages. The top was open and at the side you had iron pole going across, so that the sugarcane could be loaded onto of each other. Another thing about this trailer is that it only run on a farm. It has massive wheels it's called a (Gonna Gonna)

We would pick ackee and bread fruit while the men are in the field cutting cane. We watch until the Gonna Gonna is full and ready to leave. Everyone would run behind the trailer and hop onto the back. We ride as far as we feel like came off and walked it back. We would do this again wait until the next one is filled with cane again and start the ride all over again, until we got bored. I found out that other boys were there waiting like us to do the same thing. We met some little boys out there waiting for the trailer all in their school uniforms it about six or more of them plus one little girl she could not keep up with them, so she went back to school. It was their lunch time just to make it clear to you. Inswood estate had a school on its compound as well, which is still in operations right now. After running and riding the trailers one left just before we reached so we started chasing it down. One of the boys in uniform is behind me, he is about ten or eleven years old. I was so tired I felt like was running out of breath. I wanted to stop but my friend Brown is on the trailer and so is my brother. The driver slows down to go over a little bridge, so I catch the trailer and hop up on it. The little boy who was behind me struggles to catch up.

He still can't reach the trailer, so we began shouting run run run. Brown decided to help him by jumping off the trailer and hold out his hand. The second the boy held his hand he stared running down the trailer. Brown was older than all of us and bigger in body too. Something wrong with the trailer and the driver stops. They both reach the trailer and is waiting for the driver to fix it. When the tractor starts again and the trailer start rolling, Brown jumps off and run behind the trailer and hop on again. The little boy in uniform follows. When he reaches the trailer, he grabs on and jump. Now the trailer falls into a ditch and went up and down with a loud bang bang noise. Suddenly we heard a loud scream from the boy, but can't see him. The screaming continued but he's not where he's supposed to be. We all looked on each other. When he screamed again, I looked over and down I almost shit myself with what I saw. He is under the trailer his head next to the wheel his legs stuck and he's being pulled. He's crying like hell from between two of the adjoining trailers. The good thing is that he is holding onto the bottom of the trailer if he lets go, he is finished. His leg is stuck so I tried pulling it, but Brown said no. I came down further to hold his hands while still holding on myself, so I don't fall. All this time the trailer is banging like crazy. I felt like his life was in my hands. As soon as I touch his hands, he lets go you can see he could not hold on much longer.

I cannot let him go, I held his hands and Brown held his feet. He's crying and we're all worried about him. The driver is upfront and oblivious to what's happening. This little boy is crying to us begging us not to let him go. When the trailer finally stopped to cross the Old Harbour Road we shouted for the driver, the driver drives across the main road then stop by this time his leg is free. The driver starts cussing and swearing he's mad as hell. We ask the little boy how he's feeling, he said he ok but his feet hurts really bad. The driver drove away and left us there with the boy. He needs to get back on the school compound but when we checked on him, he we saw that he had some minor bruises. There was blood on is uniform especially his pants. We lift the pant leg but there were no cuts so told him to take his shoes off. Now we are in for a surprise when the shoes came off everybody cry out at the same time(blood claat). The top of this feet was split in two the shoes filled with blood. He just starts crying again gripping onto me and said don't leave me he was crying for his mother too (mamma mamma). The shoe is rip opened at the top and the top of his feet is split the bone completely crushed. When he looked down and saw his feet he fainted. When we saw how badly he's injured myself and Brown started carrying him. A man came on a bicycle and ask what happened we told him, and he show us where the clinic was and we head off in that direction. When we arrived at the clinic and explained what happen. They attended to us then call an ambulance to take the boy to Spanish Town Hospital. He went home after a couple days at the hospital. Thank God he didn't die.

I was a skinny boy with brown complexion loved swimming and climbing trees, flying kite was a sport. I was fun loving and have always liked cooking. I used to cook for plenty of people at a time. My friends and I would always go Inswood and catch fish and cook we use to look in the gutter and canal and see the fishes swim under the bridge. We sometimes came back with buckets what we called kegs and bail out all the water from under the bridge and take out the fishes big ones and small one. I'm usually the one who go under these bridges, that's my job. There is a bridge up in Inswood where we throw our fishing line in it and catch big fish, so we said we are going back there to bail out the water. There were loads of bushes and we look and saw a huge fish, I said to myself shit we need to catch it, so we judges the sizes of the fish and came back with my friend's mother and father. We block the water to stop it from going under the bridge. We packed loads of mud and lilies a couple of feet from the mouth of the bridge making sure the water is running in a different direction. Or we'd turned off the notch as we would call it.

We saw more big fish running under the culbutt. We are all excited Mr and Mrs Willard their two sons and I. Everything is going well everything is looking good. My job is to get the fishes from under the bridge so when the water is low we catch some in buckets. Once the water gets low the fishes started to head to where the water is going. You could hear them fluttering when it gets too low. This happens when the water is bailed from the bridge. We can't let the workers or the ranger a man called Hard who rides around on a horse patrolling the estate catch us doing this. Furthermore anyone he sees on the estate he stop them, if you have no reason to be there you are turned back and search before you go, if caught with anything you're in big trouble. Now the water is low enough so we began using the buckets to bail the water and throw it on the bank, every time we do this a few fish is throw on the bank. We pick them up and keep them in another bucket. Sometimes we even caught a few shrimps too.

We heard this heavy splash under the culbutt, at first we all started laughing thinking that the fishes are going crazy. The Willard's started looking under the bridge, one of the son said that he could see an eye and that it might be a frog. However the sound keeps coming towards us and the fishes are swimming rapidly towards the mouth of the bridge. Everyone knows it's my time so they shouted for me Prentice, I came with my bucket to catch more fish, but listen what happens next.

The same son looks under the bridge again said he saw two eyes this time. I was going to walk at the front but changed my mind and entered from the back. The fishes swim to the front so it's easier to came out at the front and pick up the fishes because I'm now behind them. There are numerous fishes at the front now and I need help to pick them up. The Willard's are helping but the Mum keeps instructing me to go further under the bridge. The son repeated that he saw two eyes to this the mum replied that it's a big frog. Just as I'm about to enter the culbutt I lie flat on my belly where I can see through the bridge and told Mrs Willard to peek and tells me what she sees. She bends down and look under the bridge the only thing I heard was her screaming wooi wooi wooi blood claat. She came face to face with a crocodile.

She took off like a rocket running away with her husband and two sons running behind her. She even dashes the bucket of fish away. This lady was very slim she reminds me of olive from the cartoon pop eye. We heard a growl like a big dog would make craaa craaa. I jump back out what I saw made my heart tremble. I saw a crocodile about 16 feet in length under the bridge. He flashed his tail and bared his teeth like a dog. You can see he's upset he was switching his tail and began climbing over the mud bank we had make to stop the water running. He jumps in that bit of water and dived under no one could see him at the moment because the water is dirty. He stays under it for a bit. I ran to catch up with the Willard, when we are all together we saw and told this Indian man. He went away and come back with a group of Indian looking like they're all family in an old land rover jeep. They had ropes and long sticks these men look like they do this all the time. They asked where the croc was, and we show them the water they got the sticks then the ropes. He started to push the long stick into the muddy water. The croc flashed his tail and made a run for it, this time he is doing heading for the main canal. The Indian not leaving him. The croc snap his jaws trying to bite the stick, he starts spinning. He's long and wide just imagine me and him under the bridge I would have no change.

This operation to catch him now is getting intense. The Indian manage to get a short piece of rope over its mouth but it's not enough and it's not safe either. I overheard one of the men talking to another and he is saying they're quite a few crocodiles living around here, the other man saying that they are plenty in the area and that I'm lucky the crocodile didn't fuck me up. Which I already know he would tear me to pieces. I am not even in the mode to go to anymore bridges; I just want to go home. They managed to get more rope around his mouth he is spinning like hell. They continued to throw more rope around him and because he's flashing he tangled up in the rope. They pull him out the water, when they did, I got a real good look on him. Jesus Christ if that thing catches a man under that narrow bridge no luck or anything can help because you can't turn back.

You would probably end up on his back then he would ease up and you might be lucky if he frightens and runs away from, he heard someone behind him or something touching him too just saying. I am not sure about that either. After a hard fight the men managed to tie him up properly put a bag over his face. And cover his eyes they tied his mouth and tie his four feet behind him. Then they use a tape measure to measure his actual length. He is seventeen feet in length and three and a half feet in width. He can't fit into any of the vehicle, so they send for a bigger truck to put him in.

His tail his long and hangs off the truck. The Indians said it's a male croc and they are going to take him to the zoo or a place for the wild life where he would be protected and care for. Shortly after the leave a man told us that he saw some men killing and skinning a crocodile in the bushes. They were Planning on eating him the entire time. The man also said those individuals were known for catching and eating crocodiles they eat lots of them that he knows for sure. He also mentioned that there was a rumour going around that they even eat dogs. My days of going under bridge is over I am yellow as a traffic light. you know the saying if someone says you're yellow it means you are a coward. The only water I am going into now it's my bathtub Trust me. That incident has plagued me for days, months and years. Mr and Mrs Willard had since pass away. May their soul rest in peace.

Another drama I witness heading home from the canal one day, I saw a man runs past me faster than a jet plane. Few minutes later I saw a group of about seven to eight men running sweating like hell asking me if I saw a man runs past. I said no, they knew he had passed there so they continue looking in the bushes searching and swearing all kinds of swear words. These men I realized I knew some of them. Gruva 's dads were among them. He's always drinks and get drunk. He goes by the name of Rump. Now Rump has a big round belly, whenever he ate any food he would use the Gravy from the pot throw it in is hand middle and wipe it on his belly. His belly rival that of a pregnant woman. He drinks rum and rubs it on the same way. The search is on I heard someone said they catch him.

This gets more interesting I heard this man crying don't kill me please. I realized I knew this man. This is the same person that sold my father the chickens and puppies when we just move to Johns road. I can't help him but that's not the point. They started beating him that's too much for me right now. Soon after the alarm is made that they hold him, I realized I knew a few of these people beating him. I could hear one of the men said (weh mi anti cow) mean (where is me aunty cow). Now this is getting even more interesting he has been accused of stealing a cow. A few of the people beating him are people from our same community, just by the front from the same lane Gruva was chased and shot at by the police. They beat him, cut him, chopped him with a machete. They hurt him really bad I thought he's going to die he stand no chance against this angry mob. Some only wants to kill. You could hear whispers from a few on looks saying every one beating him is a thief. He keeps crying to Gruva dad.

For some reason the man leading the mob was a man who was always seen together with the man they are beating. It's not looking good from what I can see, I feel it for him. The crowd gets thicker and thicker and no one is pleading to the mob of angry men to stop. Gruva dad is his friend and doing him the worst thing you can think of, he is bleeding badly he wants to kill him quickly.

From what I can see people are whispering and chatting loud saying he didn't do it but no one speak up or tries to stop them from beating him. He's look as if he's dying. I walked away leaving them with him I consider him dead trust me. When I reach home I saw everyone busy this looks like the words is going around about what took place today it is not easy to watch how horribly they are treating him. I can't believe what I've heard and seen it's scary. Listening to what these people are saying, you don't know what's true or what's not. They are saying the ones who are beating him are the ones who stole the cow, or they all stole it together. I am wondering what's going on, it looks like it's a case of thief beating thief. Listening to and watching the behaviour of others I now come to terms with what I have seen and realized life is not fair. Just a few days later they found the cow, the find was unbelievable because it was in the possession of Rump Gruva's dad the one leading the mob. He had the cow trying to sell it and was caught trying to load the cow in the back of a truck on the highway.

This situation is so fucked up, just the other day he was beating a man senseless. This is really unfair to me and the worst thing is no one can say anything to him or beat him like he did the man because of who is son is. He beats this man nearly killed him and he was the real thief, or they both did it. That's the reason the man was calling on Rump for help and Rump showed him no mercy. He was trying to get rid of the man because he doesn't want it to leak out that he played a part in stealing his own aunt cow and it came out anyway because he was caught red handed. It's not the first time a cow goes missing. The thing about Johns Road is a lot of mysterious things keeps on happing every now and then. All these things I have mentioned it occurred in the late seventies' early eighties. As I've already stated I was born in the seventies, and it's written about the history of Johns road and the surrounding communities.

Now back to Gruver's story. One of my sisters had a boyfriend that comes from one of the lanes on Johns road known as ackee tree lane. He was her first boyfriend his name is Davie he is better known as Buks. He is close friend to Gruva, so we get to know him even better. Gruva always shouts my sister whenever he sees her going or coming, he follows her home, worse if it's late and he see her walking alone from work. She was a bit conscious of his presence, but he will never hurt her. I won't swear for him but it's clear he had a lot of respect for Buks. Thank God Buks was always kind to Gruva and us. We love Buks because he would share anything thing he had with us no matter what it was he just kind. He would smoke a spliff at times or a cigarette. He was very funny always telling jokes. Anywhere he's going he would take us like to the canal, cane field, mango bush and fishing.

He loved my sister too but he wasn't a soft guy either for example he was very jealous over her until it became dangerous. There was this guy who came from Old Harbour Road, he always visits next door because he had a school mate there that he followed home most evenings. He kept coming over my yard and chatting up my sister Buks tell him stop and warned him not to come back. He won't stop and won't take no for an answer. Now I can see this from a mile off this spell trouble and the ending of this will not turn out good in my opinion. He started by telling the man that he was a bad man. One Friday Buks was with us he was smoking a joint (spliff) and chilling. Gruva was not about that day, he was wanted so he had to keep moving. Every single police in Spanish town living and working in St Catherine knew about Gruva I am sure.

Back to Buks saga

BUKS WAS CHILLING AT THE HOUSE, NOW HERE COMES MR MAN FROM next door walked through the fence he came straight over shouting out my sister's name after he was told repeatedly by Buks to leave and not come back. He didn't 't care, he stood in front of Buks, ignoring him. Buks went (bup bup) two solid punches in his mouth. All I can see is blood, There was a few fist exchange after by the two of them but the two first blows landed solid in the face which slowed him down. The fight was parted and he left never to return or visit either his friend or call out my sister's name.

Now all this time the police have taken on a keen interest in Gruva. There is a lot of police presence up and down in every lane. They search everywhere he goes, they're in constant pursuit of him. He's looking a bit different sometimes you see him but he always wearing a big green shirt and a big brown Clarks. This guy looks really weird, sometimes you can see he's a bit lonely too. He always comes to our house asking for Buks even when he knows Buks not there. He wants to sit with the other boys around the area, but no one wants to be around him. They can't shun him either because they are scared of him, but he doesn't like it he doesn't want them to be scared of him but no matter what they are still scared. He is trying to live normal but it can't work whenever he see the boys playing football he wants to play too, he always wants to go on to the field with the youths but it's dangerous for them. Whenever he saw a car or any vehicle approaching, he hold onto the gun it's not safe to stay around him because he is ready to draw his gun and fire. Loads of rumours started going around about him most of which are true, like he robbed a man who use to drives an ice truck. Back in the days when Ice was driven around on trucks and sold to shops, he was very famous Mr Davis he uses to come out early every morning and start the truck service it a bit and drove out for the day delivery. One morning early before five am the community was lit up by loud explosions. I heard loud noises and sound of voices there was a large crowd of people crying. It's not normal for those types of crowds moving in the morning, I was on the morning shift I overheard someone telling my mother that they have killed Mr Davis the Ice man. Everyone was whispering about it, they started to call names straight away of who they suspect Gruva's name hit the top of the list. I remember from long ago his name was calling on murders around the area. They said he killed a policeman somewhere in Spanish town and he killed some men in winters pen too.

The police decided to close in on him, a girl was killed in Willowdene someone said they saw him. I don't know if it's true but that's the talk. This is around the ending of eighty-three coming to eighty-four. The police are keeping a close check on him every time he goes somewhere the police visit there, sometimes he reaches at spot and was told the police Just left. They are keeping him busy, he's on his peak being vigilant. The police are coming regularly so he starts to keep away for a bit, but as soon as he returns the police are on him again. He start to link up with Buks my sister man he want to stay where ever Buks is, but we don't want the police to come see him here because it can gets messy, because Gruva is always saying if he goes he's taking one with him. The police keep coming and coming, one night we heard a loud gunshot the sound going through the still of the night. It sounds close too we heard fences shaking he is good on jumping fences he is like a cat, trust me. He his swift on his feet. I am on the edge now worried and afraid because he keeps coming to our house and Won't leave whether or not Buks was there. He's coming to keep a low profile, but word is going around that he is harbouring in our house. The police began watching our house too the word is everywhere that he is in our house hiding at night times when he is in the area.

He goes to his house in the day, and he also goes there to have a shit most of the time. Now the police have studied his movements. They've turned the heat up on him, pressuring him every day and every night, he was constantly running. I saw him one morning after they chased him. When I look at him you can see his cheek bones sticking out, he's looking bony and different. The constant running and hiding was taking a toll on him. I can see time was closing in on him. Around the fourth of January the police moves to him in a lane called (eighty three) he was going to his sister's house and they came to catch him. But Gruva is always on guard, he jumped some fences and disappears leaving them to wonder where he could have gone. He runs to his father's house the police went there the next day he leaves them again. He has the police going around in circles. The next morning he came to the lane, we saw him with some ackee he said he wanted some flour and salt fish to cook ackee and salt fish over by his father house. This time though the police set a real bubby trap for him. He told us he was on a quick move because he needs to shit really bad so he moves off toward his yard.

The police have circled all the yards around his house bending down and peeping through the fences. By this time the police have a jeep driving down in each lane. Gruva is now over his house and in the toilet. The police in the surrounding yards get a close one on him. They saw him and he hasn't seen them, they saw him pulling his trousers underwear down quick and move to the toilet. As soon as he sat down on the toilet the sounds of the rifles go off (blab blab blab blap blap blap blap). The place gets busy the other boys from around the area start firing shots in the air. Gunshot salute in the air like fireworks. The police start driving and searching for the others who were firing the bullets in the air. When we went outside and look, we saw Gruva dead on the ground mash up with his pants down, he shot himself, his head mash out like a smash up water melon. One of the police take out Gruva's gun Suzie and said feel your own gun and fired three shots in his head from his own gun they pull him by his two foot and throw him in the back of the vehicle. That's the ending of Gruve, after he died his father takes a turn for the worse with drinking.

The Oily Man Story

GROWING UP AND LIVING IN SPANISH TOWN YOU SEE AND HEAR THINGS that only happen in movies, trust me. I knew of a girl that was walking home from a party, she was going to Valdezes road, all the way from crossroad, all by herself. Walking down Valdezes road by herself she saw someone and tries to catch up with them. However, she never managed to catch the person when she reaches where the person turned off its a bit dark there. When approaching the spot, she slows down she said she felt a bit scared but she continued to walk anyway. After leaving the dark she starts to feel better because she is going back in the light. But that feeling was short lived, out of nowhere a big hand just covered her mouth and started strangling her. She said his hands was rough and crusty and he smells sweaty and stink, he smells like oil. She tried to scream but he held her mouth and give her a few punches in her belly. He told her to walk in front of him and not to make any noise or she's dead. He had a long pointed knife pressed against her throat, that he keeps pressing it in her skin. He instructed her to lay down. She was begging him don't kill me she beg and begs but he just kicked her in the tummy several times. She said she couldn't breathe her breath had stop and she was gasping for air. He then gave her a big blow to the back of her head and she don't remember Nothing more. She woke up after naked her hands tied with her clothes, she screams out for help, but he is long gone and she don't even know that because she was knocked out cold. She went to the police station and was informed that she was the third one to come forward with the same story that morning.

Another party was held in Willowdene, it was a city rock party. The party was hype and nice as always. City rock was the hottest thing around town. At the time girls like crazy wanted to hear Eric on the Mike hyping up the city rock and hearing the sound effects (city rock city rock) if you want to party it must be city rock turbo crown, strike force, exodus, don Ruben, squad one at one point marathon. There was a variety of sounds with deejays that we couldn't resist going to these parties or dance as we call it.

These party drew crowd like crazy especially women. Plenty girls, anywhere the girls are you know the men always follow. You know the saying ants follow fat well in this case too much fat. The youths would walk from anywhere to have fun and the selectors must be on point. When you are here the duck rhythm and the bounce, the dance gets hot like fire. Ian, one of the selectors always put on a show and the girls went crazy until it has to stop because it's getting too late. That's when the ladies start to worry because they must head home.

They were worried because some girl got raped going home from one of these parties. She explained almost the same story that a man held her from behind he kicks her in her tummy and knock her on the back of her head knocking her out she woke up naked and tied up in her own clothes. She said her screams alerted the crowd and she was taken to the hospital then reported it to the Spanish town police station. Another girl had a similar story saying the same thing and the man smells of car grease he was sweaty and stink. He also has a big long pointed knife that he squeezed at her neck the same way the other girls explained he did to them. The police are now suspecting that a serial rapist is about, everyone want to know who he is and is desperate for him to be caught.

He sexually assaulted about fifteen to twenty women in a short while, he goes on for a few months almost a year and disappear into thin air. The police and everyone were on alert the tension was high. Everybody feared this new threat, everywhere in Spanish town you go the hot topics was on greasy or oily the name that was given to this new predator. It was rumoured that he got arrested, at one point we heard he was dead, but I don't know how true that is. However, the place gets quite for a while Oily, the man who bored fear into the female population. About a year or so later he pops back up but this time it was with a difference. He is even more deadly, his new rep was using a stone wrapped in a sock or pants leg to attack his victims. He is now known as the stone man, the havoc he creates in and around Spanish town was no was joke. The whole place is under sieged by this dude, this freak is sick or something he is also attacking men. No one is safe no matter who they are.

At one point he takes a mother and her daughter they said when the stone hits it's no joke. People get slap by the stones only to wake up in hospital almost dead in intensive care, the hospital is busy with this type of attacks. He had this in common with the other cases, he his stinks of oil one person said he has gun.

Witnesses said they saw him with knife and a gun some only report seen a knife, but all said he smells of oil. One Sunday evening on top of the bridge at the top of fear field road entering from cross roads a soldier man sits hanging out with his woman. Other people would sit down on top of the bridge hanging out too it was like a popular hangout spot where couples would just sit. Over the years you could see lovers hanging there day and night, some people even walk down the bridge to get a taxi. This bridge was a popular spot in the vicinity. The soldier's girlfriend was sitting looking down in the water. Night falls its now dark and other people have already gone home but the solider and his woman remain on the bridge looking down in the water. What they are looking for I don't know but that's not a good spot to be when it so dark trust me. Music was playing in the scheme a few people from nearby would stand up there for a bit, but they don't stray too far from their houses either. People feels more safer this way because of the way how things are going. Its 's best for them to stay indoors and don't leave their yard especially if they're a woman. Listen if a street light even blinks it sends everyone running and shouting that they're going home because the stone man is about.

Some take this for a joke but it's not funny we all know this is serious. There was once a power cut in Spanish town and the entire place was in darkness. The place get really quiet only the sounds of cars, trucks, motor bikes and the aeroplane in the sky could be heard. The place has becomes desolate only for people living in the area to hear screams. They don't know who it is but will find out in the morning when day breaks. We could hear the sounds of siren and police vehicles flying from Spanish town back and forth. The road sounds busy everybody want to know what's going on, people are speculating about the darkness and everything they can remember. They just want something to talk about. The sounds break in the morning that the solider who was on the bridge was hit on the head by the stone man and his woman taken and rape. The solider was taken to hospital and admitted in intensive care unit (ICU) with a fractured skull. Some people say he is dead some saying he is not going to make it. If you stand on the bridge and looks down by the cross roads where blight super market is, all you can see is police. For the entire week loads of police up and down asking for information. Again no one knows what has happen they saw very little, the solider is still in the hospital while everyone waits for the girl to return because people wants to have an idea or wants to know what this creature looks like.

Believe me I know this girl called Cleranet who lived in Homestead. She was walking home from a party she said she heard like someone was running behind her, when she looks back this person was right next to her in her face. She said she was so frightened that's she nearly fainted. She was sweating and out of breath, he suddenly swings something at her what we know to be the pants leg with the stone in it. He swung it at her head, she said but it never catches her head. if it did, she would have died, she said the stone missed but connected with her back (bup). She said it made her breath stop instantly, her ears began ringing and she could see specks of lights. She also said her tongue got heavy and she starts to cough up blood. From what she remembered he was rough, he grabs her and give her one more slap making her unconscious. She mentioned that he also smells stink of gas oil or engine oil and that when she woke up she was tied up in her own clothes and he was already gone and her back and her body hurt like hell. This man is like an animal because how the lady said he kicks them in their tummy. She was also raped what kinds of person is this. Where does he gets this behaviour from, he's a beast. I'm curious why is he always stink; does he have an infection going around with. Is he a carrier of something. This man needs to be taken off the Street.

No one knows who he is, he waits until these party dismissed and take advantage of the woman. One night a lady is going home from work, she works as a hairdresser. She said she saw a man following her, she starts to panic and began to walk faster. The person starts to walk fast too, so she ran into one of the lanes to hide from him. He quickly walked into the lane but didn't see her. He made a few hasty checks then turn away. She said she almost scream out in panic but didn't. She said she knew without a doubt that he was searching for her. She informed the police, who then search the area properly but couldn't find anyone. She said she knows he will come back again.

After a few weeks something similar happens, again this person was on her way home. He followed her down a dark road, she starts screaming and he runs away fast. A man came with a licensed firearm searching but he's long gone. His appearance and attacks are becoming more frequent. He attacked a lady in West more gardens when he grabbed her from behind she spins and bite him in his chest and start screaming for help. A man came to help but never saw him. he disappeared into the bushes nearby, seems as if he knows the area well. Everyone his on high alert again, he goes absent again for a while from what I can remember, he either as local connection or he lives locally and knows what's going on that's what I am thinking anyway.

The thing I am trying to understand about this man is why he can't stop what he's doing, it not good. It's appeared as if he enjoys hurting people especially females. This man or creature or whatever he was, seems like he had no mother, sisters, niece aunty or any female in his family. I seriously don't know what the fuck his problem is. I am just upset because he had made everyone scared I am thinking why he don't just go kill himself and leave people alone. Why can't he go about his business he is so damn disgusting he his messing up every body livelihood, he just need to put himself out of his own misery. I have two sisters and have two nieces on the way, so two more members will be adding to my family, and they are females. So, I don't and wouldn't like the stone man oily or whatever he's called to harm them. Giving you all these experiences, I have had you will have an idea of what I am talking about living in these types of community. However, it doesn't stop there sometimes you here things you say it's getting bad to worse, well it will get a lot worse. I will get back to stone man shortly.

One evening everyone was out in the lane and heard a barrage of gunshots, this sounds like war is going on. Plenty of bullets like sand, what is this. We are all looking towards where the sounds come from. Crowd starts running towards crossroads when we reach there, the crowd was very thick and everyone looking down in a car that is well shot up. In the car was three dead bodies they were some youths from Irish pen traveling in the car two of them wanted by the police. The police got information that these men were going on a move to do something bad. I think it's a robbery but it never work out well for them trust me. The police said they killed three and one escape in nearby bushes. The search is now on to catch the one who get away they search everywhere some take the canal bank, they go all the way to Inswood and came back. They said blood his on the ground somewhere down the road, there were crowd everywhere. We heard some people crying like it's their family in the car that get shot up. They don't see where this person had gone or heard anything about the other person. When the police finish Searching properly, they found two firearms in the car with the three dead bodies. The one who escape on foot is now missing and never to be found. Life around Johns Road is not easy sometime as a youth the things you see will either makes you stronger are weaker you have to be both Physically and mentally strong to overcome the perils of living in Johns road. There are a few good taxi drivers on Johns Road like (Stumpy, Festus, Mando, Thumpa, Stickie, Skinny, Bagga, Rex and Bull). You have loads of good people as I mentioned and bad people living on Johns Road. It's not somewhere to grow up too soft. In every family on Johns Roads, you have someone related to somebody either cousin, bread in-law sister-in-law, mother in law but some relation is always there and they also talk.

It was rumoured that obeah (voo doo) is a common methods use where I lived. I've come across so much of it and never know what was going on or what's happening, but I see it with my very own eyes more than once. Listen this, in my yard we have an outside toilet those makeshift one with no flush on it. One morning I went outside my house to use the same toilet I saw Mrs Tee standing outside her house on the top of a car and steering over my fence. She never saw me she had a white piece of paper in her hands which she threw over my fence. When I saw her doing it, I never said anything she did it again and again I never knew what it was. I was ignoring this lady doing this over and over only to find out it was parchment paper with people names on it. I was told by someone a few times that it's a ritual involving obeah. When I look on the object, she threw over my yard it looked like grease paper. This lady keeps doing this, I can tell you this from my heart with no exaggeration my father just left and never came back home trust me on that. One of my sister Remy start to get sick and my three other brothers start to sick as well. My older brothers Dean and Edward and my little brother Delving but I will soon come back to that episode shortly. I've seen this lady doing several unusual things it plays out even more to come. This place I've heard about is not a joke this is real. I used to visit a man with a hand cart every day just to push the cart and take it for fun. The man had about ten or eleven kids could be more or less but its somewhere around that amount. Everyone said this man was a reader man from what I know he was also called an obeah man so I asked him a few questions. He answered but always wants to know why I am so curious. I was witnessing things from time to time happening plus all my siblings were getting sick.

I am almost twelve and there's an announcement from my school. The principal Mrs Edwards announced that there will be no more friendship all age school, it will now become Friendship Primary School. So, with me going in grade six I will be moving to Spanish town secondary school soon more experience for me. Let's get back to the sicknesses and healing and the roll I played in this. I mentioned Mrs Tee unusual behaviour to my cart friend, he ask me where live and I told him where. Listen this, he said that place is not nice a pure dirty people live in deso let me tell you something about in (deso) meaning (there) he first asked who my parents are and where are they and if my parents are home. It just got real, after taking some of the papers thrown behind my toilet and showing it to him he started talking loads of things. This is just about time my sister Remy gets sick too real sick. I don't wish to say because of memories, and I never asked her if I can mention this but she was really sick. My older brother was sick and had to be admitted in hospital for months. Next brother similar and younger brother just the same. I won't mentioned for the same reasons. This woman keeps coming over an asking question and coming back asking what's going on. She the one doing the things that cause them to be sick and she's pretending like she cares. She has her motive clearly; she wants to mess us up. I have gained experience from this man I've been around and knew something is wrong. She thinks she is smart and behaving like she is helping my little brother Delvin. She keeps coming every time to spread the bed with Delvin on it, that is all she is interested in doing.

I told the cart man, Mr Weaver he said to not let her back in the yard. He came and met with my mother they start doing what needed to be done and he started visiting us frequently. Has I have said my father just up and leaves and never came back barely pass through form time to time. He's staying in Kingston at his garage, before finding a place in Spanish town and move over to Nugent Street where he started to work. Mr Weaver met with my father, from he met with my father you can tell my dad is cautious. You can't tell my father these type of things but they chat about what's going my little brother who was so sick we had to put him on a cart and take him to Mr Weaver's house for him to work on to work on him for a few days. My brother is a bit better now, this same wicked woman tried over and over to come in the yard she is dangerous trust me. My older brother Dean is back home from the hospital, it takes a while for things to get back to normal. My other brother Edward getting back real slow, and Delvin is up and running again. Remy is well and still going out with her boyfriend Buks. Now Buks mother was the same types of person like Mr Weaver she has a few children all boys her name is Mrs Henry.

My sisters leave school and are both doing well for themselves. That these people start with their Nasty behaviour with this obeah thing again. That even Mr Weaver and Mrs Henry says it because they were envious of my sisters why they are doing these wicked things. It's real my big sis use to attend a school called Citizens Collage and my next sister had graduated from St Catherine high school and started pursuing a career in nursing which she would become years later, I was at the graduation myself. My oldest sister Sadie was going to a hairdressing school she was doing good. She is a shy and quiet person, always stays by herself never having a lot of friends either. She started out by doing the girls in the community hair on Sunday and was fast becoming the perfect community hairdresser. Very quickly her clientele grew and people started to book appointment to get their hair done. She's getting so good now she started to learn more and begun working with a lady called Cint. Cint was located in Old Harbour Bay, from my recollection, she was the girlfriend of a well-known business man. From relaxing hair to weave, cornrow and braids she was getting better at it every day and started making a bit of cash for herself. Going back and forth between Old Harbour Bay and Spanish town doing her hair dressing.

My dad still lives in Spanish town same way, things are getting to a point where its rough. Sometimes it's up and down as we would say. My older brothers and I are heading to Spanish town secondary school and my two younger brothers are remaining in Friendship primary school, while my other brother heads to Jose Marty school. It not easy as it's my mother alone but are fighting on. My oldest sister decided to get a job closer to home and began working in Larisa Spanish town for a couple from England. My other sister Remy took on a job as well working for a factory called Thermo Plastic for a while. I was in secondary school at grade seven, I was placed in a room sit a placement test. I was placed in seven three on the morning shift. I will be seeing my father everyday now because his garage is just yards away from the school. My father told me that I needed to start learning trade, you know how these country men believe in trade, they want you to learn something have a skill to fall back on. I am on the morning shift, so I brought a change of clothes which stay at the garage. I stayed after school when I was on the morning shift and when I was on evening shift just the same. I started to learn how to weld and do body work on cars, as time goes by, I learn to do other stuff I never knew like how to turn the torch on and off safely. My father was very strict and careful about these things. It's been a long while since I've seen my father, so to get chance to be around him and learn from him something he loves was a joy. Anytime I go around my father he always ask me if I've eaten, even if I did he will still give me something to eat. On the weekend he would give me some money to give my mother and some for myself. Whenever my brothers and I are around our father he likes to ask us what we learn that day at school or ask us to spell what we ate that day at school. He was very serious about learning and love telling us nothing beats a trade, I never forget these things or his teachings.

My oldest sister Sadie is acting strange, I'm thinking there must be something wrong with her because she has fainted a few times. I not sure of what is happening but will later find out that she is pregnant and expected a baby girl. Everyone is excited and happy and can't wait for the baby to come. I use to follow her to the clinic for her check-up across Old Harbour road by the track in Sydenham. That clinic use to serve the whole area, most pregnant use to go there from what I can remember. I can see my sister getting fat and fatter but she still continues to work, doing hair on the veranda of our home and sometimes she will go to her clients home to do their hair also.

Attending school in Spanish Town was ok, we walked to school and back every day except for when it's raining then we might take a taxi. One day I was on the canal bank with a few other because the Willowdene football team were having a match that day. We walk all the way to Willowdene, we arrived early like an hour before the match began and sat and watch the players warm up for the game. The two side playing today is the Willowdene Division two and Homestead Division two that called Bazervac. Loads of spectators line up at the side line, the crowd that was gathering are from both communities. At one point both communities were rivals because of their political affiliation to opposing parties (JLP and PNP), but that's not the case today. This is a sports event; the match starts and is in full swing and everyone is excited and cheering for their team. As the game progress I notice this young guy looking at me, I'm now wondering if he knows me. I'm saying to myself who's this staring at me, he's looking and I'm watching. Then it's clicks, you'll never guess who he is. I signal for him to come over where I was, and he came. I ask him if he knows me, and he said no but not in a bad way. I then asked him where he lives and he told me, by talking to him more he's becoming more familiar. I asked him he used to attend a certain school he answered yes, now he's starting to really look good at me. His friends came over because my friends were there, and it looks as if an altercation was developing. However, that wasn't what was happening. I said to him you don't remember me, and he said no. I then looked at him and told him to take off his shoes. He's now looking on me with furrowed brows and ask why. I said to him you look like a little boy I saved years ago in Inswood who fell underneath a tractor. I told him to remove his shoes, when he did the scar was there from where it got crushed. It was the same boy who tried to hop and ride when we were younger. He much older now, he starts to tell his friends what took place in Inswood that day. He laughing and said thanks again, we all began talking with each other, I'm filling in bit of what happened for his friends about how he got that nasty scar on top of his foot the bit that's called the instep. He started getting emotional, we are happy to see each other we chatted for a bit then went our separate ways. I caught him watching me while I was walking away with a smile on him face. The game is back on and he over the other side because he came to support his team. That day the game was a draw.

About two or three days later my sister had her baby, she gave birth to a baby girl. This little baby was loved and treated likes a little princess, we all loved her so much. She grew up like a Tom boy her name Moreah be we all call her Mummy up until this day. She grows up fast and she fits in well with us and grew rough like a boy. Everywhere we go we would take her with us, my sister would leave her with us and go back to work. So Mummy grew up under the supervision of six boys, she was always in the middle of us on a large bed. We've had this bed for many years and it was beginning to tear apart. It had a hole in the middle of it where we would stuff it with old clothes. In the hole in the bed that's where we would put Mummy every time, that was her spot. She grew up in that spot, we were all little boys back then. Listen, in those days I'm talking about, she grows up around all boys. If we were going to the canal she was on my neck or my brother's sides. We going cane field then she's on my neck, we go to Inswood she is with us. We on the site working, we make bed with cement bags and put her on it. People always says to us that we need to be careful or the baby might get sick. We go Inswood Mango bush she is there, if we go swimming in the canal, we bring her in the water and keep her on our necks. When she get cold and starts trembling, I would take her out the water dry her off and use Vaseline to oil her skin then put on her clothes. Listen she would pee and poop like any other baby but we didn't care, we just clean her, wash her in the canal and oil her again and off we go again. Whenever she wakes up in the night and cried for her tea or milk, we would have what we called a Thermos that we kept hot water in all night we also had sugar and milk powder.

Once she gets her tea, she goes back to bed. One night she started crying I could hear her crying but I couldn't see her in the bed, so I jump up and called out for her, Mummy but no answer. Everyone got up where is she, we started looking frightened as hell. When we turned on the light and look under the bed, she was under there sucking her lips hungry. When we took her out, she was smiling and sucking her tongue, Mummy, we shout giving her the bottle she drank it all off. She is now crawling and starts coming off the bed. So, we had to start watching her more carefully.

One day I was in the house with Mummy and fell asleep with her on the bed beside me. I heard the grill knocking loudly when I got up and look who it was, I saw that it was a man known as Mr Allan and he had Mummy in his hands. He told me that she saw her standing at the gate crying. It looks like she woke up crawled off the bed pull opened the door and went around the front of the yard stand at the gate and start crying. She began crying because she couldn't go out and she couldn't get back inside either so she goes out to the front crying Mr Allan saw her and came to wake me up. Thanks to God she never gets out side, mummy was an active little girl always moving up and down and she was also well known too, a popular little girl in the community. Everyone knows her as the hairdresser's daughter.

Mummy will grow even bigger and gained more popularity, not just as the hairdresser's daughter but she can sing good and dance. Everyone loves her, she is well behaving and really smart. She is very good at reading and spelling. Her dad lives down the road a few hundred yards away from our home.

Mummy is a funny girl, gives a lot of jokes. Listen this one day my younger brother had a fishing line which he uses to catch fish. He puts a single Hook on the line and started to spin the line with the hook on it. I told him to be careful with what he was doing with the hook and line but he kept on spinning the hook. I only heard when Mummy cried out and held her face. She started crying, I runs over to the baby guessed what happened, I can't believe my eyes the fishhook was imbedded in her face. The whole yard burst out in tears; she fell to the ground. My little brother was so frightened that he let go of the line and ran away. We tried pulling out the hook, but it won't come out. Thank God it wasn't her eye, we called a taxi and head to Spanish town hospital. I was there almost the whole night before we got through. The doctors and nurse were all playing with her and having a good time, she was talking to everyone until the doctors said he's ready to take it out. When the doctor touch it he said he will have to push it through or slit the area to take it out.

She was crying all the way; the doctor asked her name she told him. He held her and injected the area and let it stay for a while before slitting it. He then pushed the hook through the skin and take it out through the other side. He then covered the wound with a plaster. That cut is still visible today on her chin it was never stitched, something was put on it to hold it together. When the doctor finished Mummy looked at the doctor and told him, she is not going to play with him again, the doctor laugh. We left the hospital in the hours of the night and went back home. When we came back my little brother was nowhere to be found, until my mother called out his name. He answered in a tree beside the house, and this was my little brother Jay. My mother gave him what we called an arsing which is the same as a proper flogging. Mummy was always smart as we said before and quick in her head. She started attending Friendship primary and was doing good in school. The teachers would always tell her mother and father about her progress in school she is doing very well, and everyone knew of her improvements. Her attendance was always good, we brought her to school until she stared going by herself. She started going to Spanish town to Buy fish and cook for herself, she started visiting her dad's workplace. She was a bit mature for her age. She took the Common Entrance and passes all her subjects and moves onto St Jago high school in Spanish town. She attended for a few years then visited England and return back to Jamaica, then returned to England again where she studied law. She then quit law had a child married and became a qualified nurse until today, I still love mummy to bits.

I Will tell you a bit more later. I started doing lots of construction work, selling figurine, selling mangoes, gineps, breadfruit and cutting people's yards to make money. The older I got; things became harder in school. I was doing electrical installation, and still going to my father's garage. Sometimes it's rough on my father sides too, I knew this well because it was clear to see, he didn't have very much. My mother was looking after some elderly people in the housing scheme, she was trying her best. She worked hard to make ends meet. By this time my next sister Remy helped Buks to returned to England, it was discovered that he was born over there and got stuck in Jamaica for some time. I don't know the reason that cost him to be stuck here in Jamaica but I know he's back in England, they kept in touch for some years.

My sister Remy try a few things that never worked, like making figurines, baptised in a Poko church and throwing pardner. She always tries to help but the return is always small, or it never worked. My sister would always help people in and around the community where we lived. When Remy goes to work in the morning people would be waiting at the gate, they always wanted to speak to the nurse girl night and day. I wonder what is going on sometimes, especially with the ladies. They would asked all sorts of questions, for all kind of things, especially about tablets. I don't have a medical background and I had no medical experience, but of the somethings I heard them asking for, made me want to know what was really going on trust me. Remy moved out the lane and rented a house with this guy she was going out with for some time his name's Browny, but people called him Brown. He was around for several years then they started doing stuff together they moved to Willowdene and then they moved address again several times together in Willowdene. They were always trying all types of things together to make ends meet. Brown goes off and joined the Jamaica constabulary force, he never last long in it, I have never asked how he lost that job so quick, but I'm always curious about that. I would always go to the police academy to visit him, my sister and I on Sundays. He would come home with some of his friends from the academy for dinner on the weekend.

This get a bit funny to me, but I have never ask my sister what went on or what went down. He's from a big family of Brown's living in Linseed and Browns Hall in St Catherine. Brown has a bad temper and all the time we have to go around the house to settle argument between them. He had a lot of rude words in his mouth for a man to be honest. I'm the one who's always talking to him about his bad behaviour. Most of the time him and I start going around when he supposed to be in academy. I started seeing him at home regularly now, he couldn't get along with my brothers at one point they wanted to fight each other because he is always arguing with my sister. He has a lot of mouth from what I know and speak like he was ready for a fight. When it's time to fight he would always calls his police friends especially the ones he knows and trained with at the academy. There are times heard about. Until the child is born and has a birth mark, you will hear people saying the baby is marked for certain things the mother wanted to eat and never had it when they were pregnant. That scenario I have just given to you is for pregnant women in general. My sister started walking very slow getting miserable very easily. Her feet started swelling up, she is very different since she became pregnant trust me. My oldest sister started to bath her because her tummy got so huge, she could even see her own two feet. I followed her to clinic sometimes she was getting closer and closer to having her baby. She is still going work up until the last minute, Brown his there all the time but still arguing as usual. Now he's thinking about how to make some money.

Now because the baby about to born he was running some taxi business now and again. This he will have to take serious as it will become is profession. They move house again but still in Willowdene, he bought a car and sell it back and then bought another one. He repeated the same thing again and now he's starting buying and selling cars. He thinks he's heading that way and no turning back. he's doing good now, one night we got a call that my sister was taken to the hospital to give birth. She gave birth to a healthy little baby girl; her name is Shawny. I now have two nieces. Shawny grew up really fast, she's doing well she gives a lot of jokes and she walks really fast. Her dad loves her very much, also her aunty and uncles. She likes playing with the dogs in the yard also everything you asked her she would say buun buun now carry that name until today we still call her Buun Buun. Shawny attend a proper basic school she's always saying buun, if you ask her name it's buun, buun what your mother name it would be buun buun.

Shawny was never the rough type even though she was around all her uncles and aunties. She was and is still very polite. She attends church but still loves to whine meaning (twerk). Both her and Mummy, my other niece are first cousins and are also great dancers. Pause with buun buun for a bit.

From my mother and father left Hanover they have never returned, not one of the two but they both told us about the parish they and district came from. There was this minivan driver that used to run from Montego bay to Kingston who knew my mother's family and will soon pass message from them to my mother. This will link back the family to Hanover. They started sending food for my mother with this driver, his name Mr Dawah. He was a honest man he will bring anything they would send for my mother like yam, Banana, pumpkin and other ground provision, loads of plantains. The family are also glad to know that both my mother and father are still alive and well. This is great my mother and her family linked back with each other.

Now my sister Remy will be heading to Hanover soon, she did the journey and came back with all the news which is good. Now we will all be going to Hanover soon; my sister came back and the connection made was great. My mother cousin starts to rotate back and forth from Hanover to Spanish town. I went there myself and l loved it and will start visiting with them regularly. The family wants my mother in England which was good. My mother cousin started calling the other cousin. My mother was working for this family in the housing scheme, they loved my mother very much. This connection my sister made will soon land my mother in England with her long last cousin, nephew and nieces. My mother was invited to England and migrated; she was there for years. Now my sister Remy got invited to England too and was making preparations but not leaving her daughter (buun)she heads out with her daughter and within a short time she starts helping everyone over. My mother was not amused from my recollection but let me give you a bit more about Johns road then come back to that.

When we were small, we always heard about black Heart man. There was this saying going around that the black Heart man would kills woman and children and take their blood. We were told that a lot of people went missing and that the black Heart man kidnap them at one point. We were also told that it was a Rastafarian who was the black Heart man, which turn out not to be true. Life is like that, but sometimes you may never know what's in store for you or me. Hear this, one morning we woke up hearing some news that some goats and pigs went missing, every now and then this would happen. They have this man, beating him saying that he gave some pigs white rum to drink and they got drunk and he put them all in a handcart and push them away smiling, this is funny. The crowd were beating him until the police came and took him away.

On St Johns Road was a church known as pastor Bronson also known as froggy. When froggy preaches, the road would be blocked with people. At one point the whole place was filled with Christians because every youth was getting baptized and going church. We heard hurricane Gilbert is coming, the sky looks like gold and another time it looks black. You could see that something is wrong, the hurricane passed through and smash the place to pieces.

I saw house top flying all kinds of debris scattered over our house top. Zinc was flying all about and people going around looting and stealing. Plenty of trees fell on top of cars and on people's houses. A tree fell down and killed a man in his home, police shot and killed looters. All types of things were going on. The first part of Gilbert passes on, now it's coming back the other way or it's the second waves. Trust me I was scared as hell, the roads were filled with water, the gullies floated over, and the rivers broke their banks. Cows, goats and other animals drowned, cars got stuck in heavy muddy waters and big trees fell and block the road. Electric light wires fell, light post broke down, the place was in otter darkness for weeks. It's took some time to get the country back up to standard, but it did work out the twelve of September nineteen eighty-eight.

Jamaica took a battering from hurricane Gilbert that was my first witnesses of a storm. I have always heard my mother and father talks about fifty one storm, but fifty one storm I was never born. Now back to my niece Shawny or buun buun, as I said she would always say buun. One day I said to her, buuun come here and calls her over. She came I opened my mouth and tell her to touch the gap in my teeth meaning put her finger in the space between my front teeth. As soon as she done it, I lock my mouth on her finger acting like a dog, like I was going to bite off her fingers. I was making this sound (raaaw raaaw), she screamed out thinking I was going takes her finger off. She was always watching, after a few days I was with her again I called her and she came looking me straight in the eyes. I wanted to laugh she could see the smirk on my face I showed her my teeth again but this is how I know she was not a stupid kid, she is smart she put both hands behind her back. So,

I said Shawny touch my teeth this time she shouted out (noooo bite). I laugh until I nearly cried, she never said buuun this time around she only said two words (nooo bite). I tried her several times after, but it never worked at all. That's buuun story she continues in school until she migrated. There's a saying that chip never flies far from the block. Well, her father and quite a few of her aunties by her father's sides were in law enforcement. She is now also in that field of law enforcement in London England where she finishes school and work, love her to bits she is still called Buun Buun until today. Although she might not know how she came by that name, if and when she reads this book, she will get the full understanding.

As I have mentioned before, I started visiting Hanover by myself and getting familiar with everyone down there in Lucia. I got to meet most of my relatives, I stared going fishing with them I enjoyed every bit of Lucea, especially the fishing part. I could already swim, now I am an even better swimmer. Learning to swim in the sea is different from swimming in the river, in a pool, or in the canal. It's totally different trust me, the river water is flat and has no waves same as the canal even the pool is a bit similar but the sea keeps rolling and rolling. I always take a good look at the sea every time before I go in the water to have swim. I always try to see the bottom of the water before entering. I swim in a place called swallow hole in Lucia Hanover in a community known as Haughton Court otherwise called (hog bush). My families down there in Lucia is very friendly and kind, there are times when I look how living in Spanish town and inner-city Kingston is very difficult to live. Why I am saying this, is because the things that happened in the city regularly, I've never seen it in how many years I am there in Hanover you can take my word. For example, shooting, murder and robbery none of these types of crimes has taken place there. The things I have noticed over and over you are things like someone else drew another man fish pot petty stuff, or a goat might goes missing but apart from that it's ok you can live there. In my opinion life is a bit unbalanced, the people who you are kind to they are not the ones who will be kind to you or sometimes you feel like you love the wrong person, you love someone and they don't make you feel loved. Where I am from in Kingston or Spanish town I don't get treated like when I am in Hanover, the people in and around Hanover is totally different in every single way. I don't know but that's how I have seen it, but such is life you live and learn and that's what I am doing trust me. Start going and coming from Lucea I got more attached to my relatives in Hanover, I eat loads of fish all especially bonito, blue marlin and all kinds of other fishes. My favourite was the butter fish and the doctor fish steamed or fried. I get plenty hard food to eat yam as well, bananas, plantains breadfruits. I also got fruits like pineapples, melons and sugarcane. All these things were planted and grown by my cousin in Hanover. I even learn to cook certain types of food there or certain types of dishes like ital stew which is a favourite food among the Rastafarian in Jamaica. I learned to cook packassah better known as run dung. I started hanging out in Hanover with my family there I start going fishing with them. That's early in the morning, the first time I ever went fishing I was sea sick. I vomited like I'm going to die, my cousin who sold fish in Lucea market told me they are going to set and draw fish pots on Saturday it was the best thing I have heard in a while. She said this Friday morning before she goes to market her name his Mrs Elsie better-known all-over Hanover as Mim. I could not wait for Saturday morning to come because I really wanted to go out to sea and catch fish. Now the way how they bait the fish is a killer, they set good to lure the fishes in the trap. Early that morning one of her son and one of her nephew came with the boat to the back of the house in the sea, in an area known as swallow hole. This is about one to two hundred yards or less from the sea. Swallow hole is exactly beside Rusea high school to the left of the back wall. Most of my cousin attended Rusea high and that school is a very famous school in Hanover. The Jamaican champion sprinter Merlene Ottey attends that school, from what I was told. My cousin's house is also joined by the fence of Rusea high school.

I always sits on the wall of the school or go over the school to chased the goats off the school compound for my cousin Mrs Elsie or Mim. The school did hire some police to pound the animals or kill them, so we would chase them off the school compound. One day my brother and few of our friends came down to Hanover to visit, my brother likes fishing too. Let me tell you the fish pot story. Mim jump onto the boat behind swallow hole, before she goes into the boat she had about three buckets what we would called keg. I think they are the five-gallon paint buckets. She said it's the bait for the fish pots meaning the fish food. When we head out to sea with the buckets, I saw a yellow boie floating on the water I thought it was a football. they are in all different colours but mostly orange and green. When they reach the boie they used a tall stick with a sharp point hook and pull in a rope from under the water.

Lengthening down the pot to the bottom of the sea, the rope has to be very long for the pot to reaches the seabed. She pulls up a few pots and empty the fishes from them, she kept the empty pots in the boats at the front where they call it the stern. Now it's time to rebate the pots and set them back. She opened the first bucket and puts her hands inside it trusts me; it was pure maggots it was the stinkiest thing I have ever smelt in my whole life. My mouth started to be filled with water straight away, I wanted to vomit. She asked me what's wrong. You want to know what is really wrong the smell from the buckets, that's what making me sick. Maggots like sand and she just dipped her hands in it, worms stuck to her which made make feel even more me sick. She fills the pots and drop them back in the water, then said that will make the fishes smell them and come out trust me I started vomit.

I vomited she threw the stinking bloody water from the buckets into the sea. In a matter of minutes two big great white sharks started circling the bloody water. Let me tell you what was inside those buckets rotten fish guts from the other fishes they caught and clean and rotten fish heads. You already knew that anywhere maggots are like that, then you know it don't smell good, the stench will make your stomach roll. That's the whole thing I'm on about it's not normal trust me, your stomach must be strong to endure those types of smells believed me just to be on point you can ask any other fishermen you know about what I have mentioned and see what they'll say about this to confirm my story.

A gathering behind swallow hole

ONE SATURDAY CROWD WAS GATHERED AT SWALLOW HOLE, MY COUSIN and a few other fishermen were swimming and doing some exhibition on their boats. like going to the front of the boats and diving off in the water, when the boats is moving at full speed. It looked fun so I started doing it too. The boat picked up speed when it was my time to dive. The front of the boat had become wet and slippery, as I position myself to dive my leg slipped and down, I go. My life was on the edge right there, I went down flat to the bottom of the sea I could feel the propeller of the boat engine passing my foot, my waist, my back and my head. If that had ever caught me, I would be finished. I could feel the power from the propeller, which is a killer by itself and the engine, as the boat passes over me. When I resurfaced and look towards the land where my family were standing, I could see the surprise on all their faces. They were all thinking I'm dead or badly damage by the propeller. The fishermen would know what really happened there. Everyone was happy that I was ok, but as for me, I was in God's hands right there for real. The good thing I could swim, but not as good as those born Hanoverians, who lived by the sea sides and ride boats all their lives. That's not my thing, the most I ride is a bicycle. The sea is not my hubby not my piece of cake it's clear. Another shocker was, we went out to deep sea fishing. This experience is different and real I have realized the life of fisherman is in a class by itself in every way you can put it, it's dangerous. Let me explain this, my same cousin and I head out to deep sea, when I say deep, I mean deep past at least two different colour waters with different shades of blue. I meant the further out you went, some part of the sea water looks black to me it's real dark to be blue. It even looks dirty, the sun in the sky comes down in front of you likes it's on the water trust me on that. The heat is not easy to bare either, from my experience it's not an easy life. We stock up with water, bread, pear(avocado), bulla and some overnight food more on water. If you get thirsty out there, you'll experience what real thirsts is trust me. Driving the boat is my cousin he is the captain; he is doing the driving. They asked me if I can see, I said yes, I'm not blind. He said no that's not what he meant, if I can see birds, I said yes. When we reach out there, they said the birds were out there. I'm looking like hell; I couldn't see one damn bird but I they kept heading further out into the ocean. Then I said to myself but wait, when I look back land is nowhere to be seen now, I'm like what the hell is this and where are we going. What I've realised about fishermen are that, they are able to see things miles ahead on the ocean way before others can.

These men won't stop they are still heading out further and further into the ocean. Now when I looked ahead I saw the birds down on top of the water ahead of us. I heard my cousin said he's not going any further. We're heading in to Cuba's water, I said what, by this time we are in the middle of the Fishes, up down up down the lines kept going off (pie pie). We are catching fish like hell. Listen this, my cousin catches a marlin he's jumping like a mad man diving heading first towards the boat, like he's going to dive in on us. I am so frightened but the experience his off the hook. This fish is about a one Hundred are ninety pounds somewhere there in weight and is as tall as I am, with a long spear like a sword on its mouth. No joke, the spear on its mouth alone is about two to three feet, if it spear you with that you're dead or it would inflict a very bad wound. My cousin is wrestling with this fish for about forty minutes to an hour, but the fish kept launching itself. I thought the lines were going to break but it's holding. The fish got closer now it's on the side of the boat. To my surprise a big shark just came up and bite a massive chunk out of the fish, weighing about thirty pounds almost cutting the fish in two. My cousin used a munkle which is a piece of hard wood that is use to knock out fishes. He would hit them in the head and killed them. My cousin used the munkle to knock out the marlin and he and another cousin both pull the fish inside the boat. This shark was not satisfied and make a big bite on the side of the boat. I was so frightened but these men were used to this. Wow, that's an experienced. The shark continued to follow the boat, like he wanted the rest of the fish. We just continued on our way, eventually he gave up and went his own way. That's done, now it was lunch time. We all had lunch out there, they smoke, and they drank a shot of rum. Listen this carefully, both men said they wanted to shit now I am saying yes, we are heading back to land. However, what I'm about to witness, will make me face reality of the fishing, the sea life and fishing business. The two men pull their trousers down and stick their bottoms out over the side of the boat and over the water and shit like it's nothing. They didn't wiped their asses, just pull their pants up, didn't even wash their hands either and were ready to go again.

Just imagine that, when I asked how do you wash your hands, they just dip their hands in the water, that they just shit in and wash them. I was shocked, I have now learnt to give and take and accept life for what it is after that experience. I found out that the sea life can be dangerous at times and even harder than you think. When I see how my cousin had to pull down their trousers to do number two. I realised that this was their reality because there are no toilets or cubicle, nothing around for them to use. I wondered, what if we got stuck out here. How would we manage if we lost our way. My cousin had a son, who went out to sea and has never returned. From nineteen ninety they haven't seen or heard from him again. This very same lady setting the fish pots, both her sons were fisher man. Mim have a lot of faith and her nerves are strong. I respect her very much. Her son's last words, she told me or wherever she talked about him the day in question. It was raining and many other fishermen were going out to sea, but the sea got too rough, and they all turned back. There was a thunderstorm, all the other fishermen saw him and told him that they were going back and he said to them this is his own words to the others "you are going back to watch your woman Pussy" and started laughing. He said he's not turning back. His brother was there also, and he still refuse to turn back. His mother still cries after so many years, he's still remembered in Lucea Hanover. There was another guy by the of Rash, his house has been empty for a while after he went out to sea and never returned. For this I'm willing to pay any price the fishermen want for a pound of fish, because I am not going there to catch them. When you're on land or even as close as the seaside you don't know what's goes on out in the deep sea. I can tell you this from my experience fishing is not a normal thing, I take off my hats to fishermen anywhere anytime all over the world. In those dark waters no one knows what's under there or what challenges these fishermen face and I don't want to find out. I heard loads of wicked things happens on the sea and some of the stories are really gruesome. My intentions are never to be anywhere in the sea where I can't see the bottom. My mind is in a state when I remembered how the shark take out that chunk of the marlin and then bit into the boat. I'm thinking if that was a man lord God what would have happened.

From I went to Hanover, the cousins me as a man who loves to cook so I would cook anything for any one of my cousins. I don't know but for some reason they all asked me to cook or keep their children. My cousin came from sea and said he was hungry. He brought home a big barracuda; said he wants me to steam this big barracuda for him. There was a rumour about this fish, that it's not good to eat. I told him I can, but really I didn't want to, but he begged me to do it for him. I told him I would, I get fresh seasoning tomato's scallion, onions, garlic, fresh hot peppers and sweet ones too. I will give it my best shot, after cooking it with yellow yam green banana and dumplings. I asked him to share the food it smells really good I taste the gravy and it was nice I even ate a piece with one dumpling before it's finished cooking. After he shared the food for everyone the yard is filled with cousin both girls and boys babies too. About half an hour after eating it, everybody in the yard was now running for the toilets. They were all vomiting and shitting at the same time, one stared vomiting blood, others green stuff and other colours stuff coming out from them. One of them jumped on his bike heading to Lucea hospital and fell off the bike by Rusea school gate. Somebody picked him up and took the bike off him and brought him to the hospital. The hospital was a couple hundred yards from the house. The baby was the only one who didn't get poison from the fish. I didn't got sick or anything, I don't know what went down. Now, I don't even want to see a barracuda alive I don't was to stand near a dead barracuda, it's very dangerous trust me. I witnessed that with my very two eyes. Going back and forth from Hanover had left me in two frames of mind. I wasn't sure whether to stay there forever or just stay longer when I visited. I started meeting more people and heard more story about the sea, everybody story was different but almost the same. I spoke to this man who told me how many years he's been going fishing and this man cannot swim. I laughed because I found it strange that a fisherman couldn't swim. I am serious too, I saw another man with one of his arm gone I asked him what happened and he said he was spear fishing and a shark bit his hand off and almost killing him. He still glad he's alive. He showed me another man with both his legs gone and told me the same story about spear fishing, he spears a fish and a shark attack him for the fish and started biting him, took off both legs. It just goes on, I saw a man that shark killed his dad the fishing industry is not as easy as it might look. I love fish very much, but I will pay for it because going to catch them is not me. These fishermen has large scars over their body from congio bite, barracuda bite, one man even had a scar he got from when he got speared from a marlin, he's lucky to be alive. You are never too young to learn, most of the youths in Hanover are fishermen. They fish during the week and collect their money on the weekends. Funny enough what they do after is serious, the youths went out on the weekend in clubs and buy girls with their money. I am wondering what is going on with these men, they do this every week trust me. I don't say anything, they rent cars and bikes a lot, every now and then they'll have a tragic accident as well.

Now living in Lucea, I'm now in need of a job. I started working in Negril as a security guard. I worked at Hedonism and Grand lido hotels and several others. Now this is a world by itself, the first time I worked as a security guard I was posted on the nude beach. This his off the hook my mind was all over the place. For the first few hours before I got use to this work, imagine every woman nude from country all over the world. My job is to see to it that everyone stay on the beach nude. No clothes on, if you had clothes on, I'd asked you to leave off that beach, and go where they allow clothes and that's the prude beach. Everyone on this particular beach has to be naked because that's the rules of the hotel, or stay on the prude beach . After working at that place, it makes me strong so I can handle any situation with any women.

Let's go back down memory lane a bit this is very important. Back in the early eighties rumour start going around that my mother and father's favourite singer was sick. I heard lots of talks about this, but guessed who it was. It was about Bob Marley Noting to my mother and father like great Bob, I could feel the tension although I was only small but I understood everything well. They started saying all types of things. Bob was the man for everyone, he was loved world-wide.

Then an even bigger announcement came out that he has passed away. Shocking the world and the music industry. Everybody was saddened from this and made their own theory about what has taken the life of great Bob Marley. From what I can remember there was rumour that he had Cancer. The talks which stood out until today, was that he never wanted to amputate his big toe. That's where the Cancer was first diagnosed on him, rumour had it that if he had amputated that toe it wouldn't have spread and take hold of the rest of his body. Just to remind you readers again, I was only eleven years of age at the time so I'm giving you the best of my memories. It's also possible that some of my recollection might not be as accurate. Back to the topic, every day that passes by you could hear his songs playing on the radio, in cars an in public transportation. In those days there were only two radio station in the country from what I can remember one was called JBC or (Jamaica broad casting corporation) and the other one was known as RJR which means(Real Jamaican Radio). JBC was also the only television station at that time as well. You could only hear the news on one of these two stations. Telephone was about but not a lot especially cell phones, television operated differently in those days. It would sign off at a certain time of the night. You couldn't watch your television straight throughout the night like we do now. As time goes by the world and people evolved so much, it's really amazing. Looking back on where we're coming from when only rich people owned a computer or a cell phone with camera, it makes anyone having such a device looks very high profile and rich. It took a while before everyone started having cell phones like these. It will eventually happen but years later. Back to Bob's funeral. The announcement of Bob Marley funeral was made, and he is going to be buried in his birth parish of St Ann's. I overheard my mother talking about it and we were going to watch the funeral procession passes to his final resting place in St Ann's Bay. The funeral was set for the twenty first of May nineteen eighty-one (/21/5/1981). The funeral will be passing through the Spanish Town bypass, to flat bridge. The whole of Jamaica will be coming out that day, just to see the funeral. This was going to be the biggest funeral I have ever seen in my whole life from that time until now. It's approaching the day of the funeral, my mother was a lover of Bob Marley as I told you before.

By this time rumours were flying high, people speculating that he as fourteen kids, some were saying twenty one. Some people were talking about his wife Rita, some were talking about Cindy Breakspear. Plenty of other rumours were circulating about Bob. He was very popular, so you know women loved him, from what I knew. He also was very outspoken and straight forward from what I've learnt about him. Bob was not only the king of reggae, but he held the highest ranks in reggae music for Jamaica and Jamaican around the world. The rumours about his death came as no surprise to me. From he was sick this was the only thing that was handed down to man from God that is certain one hundred percent and that's death. Which is a surety for all Humans whether you liked it or not.

Some people love to talk just because they can, while some likes to talk because they have Nothing better to do. So they chat anything they can talked about even on his death bed people find things to say about his hair and his toe. They don't talk about the pain the he went through before dying as bob said in one of his song one bright morning when my work is over I will fly away strong words. Bob himself was a man of no fear, because he never allowed the amputation of his leg from the rumours I heard going around the world.

The day has finally arrived, and the crowd Began to move out in numbers, moving towards the bypass from early. Some people that lived near put stalls outside, selling all types of things. You could smell the scents of marijuana lingering in the air and saw the wisp of smoke that was visible all over. There were heavy police present as well. The bypass from top to bottom was filled with people from every community around St Catherine. From I was born I've never seen so many Rasta's in my whole life. Bob Marley's songs could be heard all over Jamaica, trust me. I was with my mother it took us a good half an hour to reach the bypass and find a spot to stand up. The crowd was thick, the day was filled with activities. Motor bikes and roller skaters, pure exhibitions taking place. I enjoyed the roller skater's performance, it was nice I loved it. The colours of red, green and yellow was all over as well. The crowd got out of control a few times and I almost got trampled. It was more of a stampede, my mother held onto me firmly. There were vans and trucks with loads of flags flown from their windows, trucks filled with people. The rollers skaters held onto the backs of any vehicle you name it. My mother was trying to lift me up, so I could see but it didn't work. Now everyone saying was it's coming, its coming and then the crowd got out of hand again. At one point I could see about fifty persons on the ground, my mother shouted out my name and held my hands even tighter than before. A big van passes and they said the coffin was inside it, but I was only small, so the thickness of the crowd prevented me from seeing it clearly. My mother was able to see but I barely saw the van, I couldn't see over these giant standing in front of me, and they didn't even acknowledged me as a minor. All I know is that this was the biggest crowd I have been in for a while. The funeral passed and people remained there to see it's return. I think it was because they were selling stuff, why they remained there for the day. I didn't knew when the crowd started breaking apart bit by bit, but the area is getting cleared. My mum and I took our time moving off a bit further down the road. I saw a lady crying, the way she was crying I thought she had kids for Bob Marley. Only to find out that they'd picked her bag and her money was all gone, along with her purse, house door keys and other important papers. That was an historic day for the island of Jamaica, as I've said I was only eleven years of age.

Life began getting Rougher and tougher each year for me and my family. The older you got, your responsibilities got bigger and harder. Still strolling down memory lane. After going up in grade at secondary school I was always visiting my father's garage on Nugent Street. I attended on the base on the shift I'm on morning or evening. My favourite thing was walking from school with my friends from Spanish town to Johns Road. Stopping at the bakery and getting hot Bread and bulla. We would use our taxi fare to purchase these items and then walk it home. Bulla and pear were the lick, especially if the bulla was still hot or the bread. We only needed water and we're all good. The walk from Spanish town became normal, it was like an everyday exercise, which was good and healthy too. The bulla and pear was so nice, the next day more friends will joined the group just to hear us chat about how delicious the baked bullas' and the hot breads were.

As I've mentioned before things were really rough and I eventually dropped out of secondary school in year ten. I started wondering

71

around construction sites, getting work as a labourer and digging the foundation. I worked on all kinds of site around Willowdene and the surrounding communities, doing any types of jobs I could find. From security to mixing concrete, helping to tie steel and doing anything else on site. Things got more interesting, if you had a weak heart, you couldn't do construction work. I've seen somethings I've never seen before happening on site, it's unbelievable. Listen to this, in Willowdene just after Mrs Jean shop a few hundred yards down, there was a house being built. There was this man called Cornmeal because he was known for eating plenty of cornmeal. He ate it in all forms, porridge, turned it with butter or sugar and in dumplings whatever. You had this other man on site by the name of Lucky. He couldn't speak clearly, because he had a little speech impediment or a lisp. What we Jamaicans called lisp tongue. People would make fun of him all the time, but he was like a brother to me. He could be really funny at times. One day Lucky and Cornmeal had an argument over who was doing the work from who wasn't doing the job. It was just a minor argument over the work. Listen up, Corneal started threatening Lucky, but Lucky wasn't having it. They began to get louder and louder, going up close in each other's faces. Then suddenly they began wrestling with each other. The loud commotion of the fight caused crowd to gather. Everyone was watching because they heard Lucky's voice and they liked to watch lucky because he was a joker. Everyone was saying to part them, but no one made a move to do so. This was becoming dangerous, two big strong men Wrestling like they were going for a trophy or some medal of honour. My eyes became watery when I saw another man took a machete and placed it down besides the two men. I was wondering what the hell is this man doing. Lucky now grabbed for the machete and missed, then grabs for it again. This looks like something terrible was going to happen here. I can remember the guy's face clearly and what I've realised is that this man wanted Cornmeal out the way or off the site, something. This was looking like a setup, why was he trying to make lucky get a hold of the machete. Yes, it was very clear, when Cornmeal tried to grab unto the machete the same guy moved it from out of his reach. Cornmeal quickly realised what was happening, he started shouting "yuh ago make him kill me". Seeing what's clearly going on he then tried to make a run for it. Lucky then grabs the machete, and this does not look good anymore. He gave Cornmeal one chop across his belly and another across his back. The sound of the machete was distinctive, I thought it was a bottle that broke. He fell on the ground holding unto the area that got red and was covered in blood. It happened about midday when outside was really bright. Everyone kept talking about what just happened, but not a soul was willing to putting him in their car or on a taxi. He just lay there on the road begging for someone to help him or take him to hospital, but that wasn't happening. The situation was more problematic, the cut Cross his stomach was unbelievable. I'm a bit shock but even so, I'm still trying see what's going on. When it was over Cornmeal was left on the ground holding on to his tummy, blood pouring from his wounds and turning is clothes red. He was gasping for breath, everyone said he was dying. When I took a good look at him, I saw all is intestines spilled out and shaking on top of him. Right in front of everyone eyes. Lucky just left the scene fast. They rush with Cornmeal to the hospital, we heard he was dead, some said he was in intensive care unit. That was all we heard about him, I've never seen or heard from him again. I don't think he was from around this area. I've spent all or majority of my life around this area, so I would know him or know where he was living, if he was from around here. Within a few days we heard Lucky got pick up by the police, placed under arrest and charge. He was there for a while until he got bail. I don't know what has happened to the case or how it went, but this happened on Willowdene through way in Spanish Town.

The Man That Raped his Mother

LISTEN THIS OTHER STORY I'M ABOUT TO SHARE. IT MIGHT MAKE YOU feel a bit sick like I did. There was this boy I always see on the front of the road by crossroad, sitting by the bridge while I was going to school. He would sit there every day, racing board horse in the canal, quite a few of them did it for gambling. It's an everyday thing so we got to know some of the guys by their names and knew their ages because some of them had smaller brothers and sisters attending my school. Any way this guy was very tall and had light skin what we would call brown skin. He was about seven feet tall or near that I would say and was called Chicken neck. One morning I was going to school, I saw some police officers taking him away. They put him in a police car and drove off, I haven't seen him for a very long after, like years. I'm talking about when he came back, he looked different he looks even taller than before. I found out he was arrested for stealing and breaking into some ladies' house and sexually assaulting her. He got bailed and went back to his same spot on the bridge, where he would gamble, wash cars and playing cards for money. All types of things started going on there, then his name came up again. Some house got broken into down the road, on feather bed lane. This time a lady was assaulted and badly beaten with a piece of pipe iron. One of her arms was also broken from what I was told. The police pick him up again, from what I was told. He was easy to recognised and described because of his height, his complexion and his full eyes which gave him a distinctive look. He went missing for a while but was released again. He did However, got sentenced and served sometimes in prison. This time when he came back, he came back as a monster. No one knew what happened to him inside there but trust me, he was a proper rapist when he came back. He was sick in my opinion, now here's why I'm saying this. He had a different appetite and a taste for his very own blood meaning his sisters and others family members. This was disturbing but it is getting deeper. One day I saw some of his cousin heading towards the direction of his house, they all had baseball bats. It was a big crowd with quite a few of them were blood cousin.

74

They caught him, tie him up and give him a proper beating trust me. By the time they were finished, he had multiple fractured bones. He was taken to hospital and admitted for a few weeks then discharged. He went back to his home that was on Fairfield Road. When you hear what he got the beating for, you know he deserved it. He made a move on his sister and got a flogging for it. He was warned by angry mob, that wanted to kill him but was spears with a good beating, trust me he was walking around on crutches.

When he got better, he went and did the same thing again, but this time what he did was even worse than before. Guest who he went for this time, non-other than his mother. He was trying to rape, yes rape his very own mother. He must be going out of his mind. Everybody thought his brother and the others would kill him because of his nasty and sickening intention towards his mother. They were planning to break his two feet and two hands but some people were suggesting that they cut his throat and leave him to died. It was his very own mother that saw him in pain and begged for his life, after he had violated her like that. It's not looking good for him or the embarrassment he caused this lady, his own mother. This guy is on a different level, he must have been mad or sick anyone of the two. I think he is really sick in his Brian, in all my life I have never seen or heard something like this. One of his sisters was going out with a soldier guy, he was employed to the Jamaica defence force. At the times his sister was also pregnant and had gone about six to seven months in her pregnancy. One morning he tried to hold his sister down in the yard and was trying to pull her in is room to have sex with her. Bear in mind he had done this before but it never worked out. What happened was, he got up really early every morning washed his face under the pipe, brush his teeth and sit down like he was meditating. I think he is sitting thinking of ways he could rape is family members. Real talks, this looney needs to be put him his place trust me he has gone too far. It was bad enough thar he was an already a rapist, but now he wants his sister and mother, I'm thinking he was troubled, something made him behave this because this is definitely not normal behaviour. For some reasons I think the prison grew what was already inside him, and that's just my opinion. The people around the area thought he was scary, this guy, I've already described what he looks like. Any man that wishes to have sex with his mother or sisters must be sick in his head. I know this because he made several attempts on his mother he does the same with is sister. I don't know what his problem was but I know he was seriously deranged.

Old people had this saying, when plantain want dead, it shoots. Troubles was around the corner because this man is a walking time bomb, he could exploded at any time. Looking and listening to all the things he was evolved in; I just knew he will do something soon. Early one morning, again in the same yard shared by the family. His sister got up early to have a shower and got herself ready for the day errands. Chicken neck tried again to hold down his pregnant sister, but this times her baby fathers was there in the house. He rushed out and gave him a few punches, shoved him off and roughen him up a bit. Doctor can't help this man, I don't know what can, because this doesn't look or sound good either. The baby's father his brother in-law always got picked up by his colleagues in the morning and taken to work. She was lucky that he was there that morning and hadn't left for work as yet. He tried several other times but hadn't succeeded. Chicken neck would always hang around the canal bank that runs long side his yard, and attacks anyone that passes on the bank. He could see anyone who came into his yard too. One morning the solider wakes extra early which was just a bit strange to his baby mother, but it is what it is. He goes to work as normal leaving early that morning. Everyone one heard an explosions it was low so nobody paid any attention to it. Everyone just carried on with their normal going and coming, until someone screams out. This was weird, Chicken neck was found lying face down in a pool of blood at the back of his yard. The police were called and up on the investigation it was said that he died from a single gunshot to his head. Chicken neck the family rapist was now dead. Different stories started circulating about what people thought had happened. There was also tension and speculation raised that caused the baby's father to come under fire, some saying he was the shooter. You know, in this world we live in people don't practice what they preach. Either way they were happy to get rid of him or it's the same old story of, see and blind hear, and deaf. There is this saying, you reap what you sow and what goes around comes around or if you can't hear you will feel. Well in Chicken neck case he had to learn the really hard way. Until today his killer or killers were never caught, I don't know what has happened with the baby father, but he is the man who everyone thought done the job.

Journey into Adulthood

HAVING GAINED ALL THESE EXPERIENCES ON THE CONSTRUCTION SITE, I was now beginning to see with my own eye the real facts of life. Like having a girlfriend learning about love and jealousy. If you've decide to have a girlfriend or girlfriends meaning more than one then it will become even more expensive and you will have to work hard to keep your girl or your ladies it all depends on you. In my time, I had a few lady friends not doing anything over the tops just normal stuff couples would do, you know what I mean. There are certain things I like about ladies and things I don't like. Likewise with me they might like something about me or don't like nothing at all or both and vice versa. I like a woman to be herself and carry herself like a lady, must be able to put herself together. The things she wears can be attractive but not having too much of her on display. Also, I like a natural woman especially with the way she wears her hair, it can be straighten that's ok. For me she must not be loud or vulgar and be easy going. She can also be out going but not eager to go to every dance, party and clubs not an all-arounder, I don't like common girls. I don't go everywhere either and dress like a man should. I like a normal shirt, t-shirt preferably blue or white with a black or blue jeans with a bit of room, not too closely fitted and a clean pair of trainer that matches the top I'm wearing at the time. I also like wearing a peak hat matching my outfit. I am picky about the size girls I date, I mostly fancy big girls not bashing a slim girl or anything but that's my choice and preference. When I say big, I don't mean over the top big, I like a bit of meat to hold into lol funny. I don't like a lady that smoke a lot and I don't likes a woman that's drinks too much either. I don't smoke, I only drink occasionally and that must be a Guinness and I hate gambling that's a definite no, no. My mother always says if you do these three things then you have problems ahead. Trust me they are problems, smoking gambling and drinking. These three habits are killers and I believe her because I've seen what it does to people and their family. The first female friend I remembered was Jay, she went to the states and she kept in touch for a bit and then goes missing for few years. Her family and I were very close. I tried to find her but no luck. However life goes on, all the best to her, we were only young not knowing what we were doing. Now we are older I heard she lives in Florida, is married had children and that's all I know.

Things began to get even tougher than before, my options were limited it was either choose between school and the streets. I was still learning trades with my father and doing a bit of construction too. Soon after I got to know a man known as Reds, or Redman. This man became a father figure and role model to me and many youths in the community. I began working with Redman, learning how to lay blocks and digging foundation known as excavation, a few of us did this types of work. Redman was known for his kindness towards the youths in Willowdene and the surrounding communities around St Johns Road. He was always travelling back and forth from the state to Jamaica. Every youth would gather around Redman when he was talking just to hear how it goes in foreign or the states. Everyone wants to go to America because of how its portrayed by people whenever they returned back to Jamaica. They painted a picture in people head, that once you reach the states, you're rich, especially when they return from New York or Miami. They came back driving rental cars and wearing big gold chain around your neck, gold chapparita and plenty gold rings. When you see this, it makes yearn to reach the Us by any means necessary. Redman enjoyed giving a lot of jokes and he was funny. One thing about him was that he could do everything on the construction site. He made sure that all the youths had food to eat and work to do, whether it was tying steel, lay block and digging foundation. We learned a lot from Redman, as I've mentioned he was like a father to every youth especially me. He was always thinking about the youths in the community of Willowdene and he was good with a lot of people in and around Spanish town. Reds had worked as a Construction contractor for years; he is also a license firearm holder. Whenever a youth needs help whether it be food or work or they needed someone to talk to, they knew they could rely on him, like wise he could call upon them to assist him with anything. He loves a hot cup of coffee in the morning or a hot cup of tea, from the time I've known him, I'd never seen him smoke, drink or gambles. Nothing to Redman like his blue pick-up van he cherished it, he said it has never failed him. Over the years I've watch and learnt a great deal from him, he was and still is a hard worker. He owns quite a few properties in Willowdene which made him well known. At that time, he was continuously travelling back and forth from United States and Jamaica. Reds was always encouraging us as youths to be fair in anything we do, he hated dishonesty. I've met a few of his family members, like his sisters and his nephew. When he is upset, you'll get plenty of jokes the things he says will crack you up. I will tell you a few things he'll say when he's upset. he said he doesn't want to go to heaven because when you want to go to heaven too many liberties are taken of you. He also doesn't like place where too much good things are happening; he just doesn't like it. Reds had travelled to the UK to attend a good friend's wedding. He's just a really good person. He makes Nothing bothers him, as long as it won't hurt him, he's good. He had quite a few children in the states both sons and daughters. I can tell you this for a fact he always encourages the youths to pursuit positive things never anything wrong.

Reds would always share with us some chilling story to about Bull Bay where he used to live. He would talk about his friend known as Brawdy who is now deceased rip. Being around a man like this was always good because you will always learn something big or small. I knew a few other guys like Reds, but Red is totally different. He's very honest and tells you How's it is, he was that straight forward. He would sometimes tell stories about Jones avenue In Spanish town where he grew up, his working skills made him wanted anywhere he goes and is roles are real important, plus he gets on with all youths except one who his known as Balk. Balk lives Further in the scheme, he always carries on likes he was a bad man trust me. He would make problem with most of the youths around and never wanted to share Nothing at all. His behaviour and just the way he acts will soon leads him in some shit. He was always doing things that causes offence to others and as I've said he is unfair. He had a girlfriend on St Johns road that he would visit night and day. He also had this bike, I don't know where the hell he got it from but whenever it started the old community smoke up like it's on fire and the sound the of the engine is like a lawnmower it's a really horrible. It was even mentioned on Mrs Barbara Gulden radio programme, I think it was RJR don't remember that well it could be another station as well if I'm mistaken. Back then people used to report nuisances and his bike was an issue that they reported. Anyway Balk being his regular troublesome self, went and started threatening Reds kids. Reds was informed of this, make no mistake Red was nice and good to everyone just don't fuck with him or his kids. It so happens that Reds saw him one day with his girlfriend and tried to sort the problem that caused the misunderstanding. Balk wasn't having it, he started carrying on with his antics from what I remembered. He told Reds he's going for his gun and that he was Coming back to kill him, but soon as he move towards his weapon, he was surprised by Reds who swiftly made his moves and discharging his fire arm a few times. Balk did not get the chance to make good on his promise, he just began running like a thief. Reds went and reported the matter to the police, the police then went in search of balk but was not successful in apprehending him. He was not arrested but had left the area for a while and then he returned. He had loads of family members living in the majestic garden area better as known as Rema. Reds had continued to reside in the area until he moved sold his house in Willowdene, bought a better property elsewhere and resides in an upper-class community near a popular beach in St Catherine. Reds has a good heart my kids love him like a father trust me.

In the community where I lived, there was this unfinished house on one of the roads about few hundred yards away from the ball field. It was partially finished the roofing was done but there were no doors or windows and it's been there for years. I don't know if the owner was aboard or sometimes people don't have the money to finished what they started, plus times are hard. We used to use that house for playing cowboys and Indians like in the movies, a lot of pretend shooting and chasing each other. You could hear kids making noise all day if was holidays or it was the weekend. That house was also use for whenever someone was walking by a needed a quick release of their bowels meaning taking a quick shit or to just do a wee. Listen, one day I was on my way home, it was late evening, and I was entering from Feather Bed Lane end from Cross Road. I walked across the ball ground where the house would be in front of me, I was heading straight towards the unfinished house. Approaching the house, I saw something or someone moving. I'm still walking towards the house entering the front of the yard. There were no fence or gate so anyone or anything could walk in humans or animals. Reaching the front of the house I saw a man came by the window, the man gave me a stare in my eyes I felt chills runs down my body. He tracked me with is eyes until I was out of sight. I was curious about his behaviour and why he would be staring at me the way he did, so I went back to the house after a day. I stood exactly where he was standing and steering at me from, to try and see what else he could have been looking at but there was nothing. So, I decided to have a look inside, I saw something looking like red liquid dried on the ground but not properly dried, so I follow the substance that I saw which led me into another room. I am now getting anxious just thinking about what this substance could be its causing me to become scared. I saw where the ground as been disturbed about six to seven feet in length and about three to four feet in width. The soil was not set, it was raised you know it had just been put back on like on a grave. This was the bit that got me really intrigued, so I decided to start digging. When I started digging the stick that I used to push away the soil touched something, I took off like a jet I was so frightened I've never said anything to anyone. I decided to never go back in there but anywhere me and this man saw each other we keep watching one another. I don't know but for some reason I was just not trusting him, or his behaviour and my heart told me to stay away from him. I heard he pass away now but even so I still don't trust him what he had buried in that house, only God knows but he was a creepy man. I don't want to speculate but the length and width fits the immediate image of a grave in my head, that have just been used in a cemetery after piling on the dirt on top of casket. This man watched me for years and I can't forget that looked he gave me that evening, it will forever be imprinted in my mind. He knew me well, I myself knew him very well also. I've seen in many times on the canal bank and in bushes with cows, he appears to be drunk to me sometimes. Whenever I've seen him, I instantly remember that death glare he gave me and I'm upset with myself for not looking under the rooted soil properly, to see what was buried there. In my head it was not something he wanted someone to see because of the look and the body language and years of watching me like I've seen something or knew something I shouldn't. Over the years I tried my best not to over think or assume anything because after so many years the what ifs won't make a difference. I contemplate this carefully before saying anything because assumption like this can have serious repercussions. I was about thirteen years of age when this happened. I can recall an encounter with this man, one day I was by the canal spear fishing, I had this feeling that someone was watching me and an urge to look up. When I look up, he was standing over my head. This old man was just standing over me looking down, he didn't say anything just kept gazing down at me. He kept on doing this like he was trying to be intimidating me, I didn't like him one bit. It's like he made it his duty to be everywhere I was, because everywhere I went, I saw him. He's on the cane field, in Feather Bed Lane with this sharp machete. I don't know what problem it was but this man did something bad and he believed that I knew something about it and that my honest opinion on that matter.

In order to have a bit of money I started doing all kinds of jobs just to make Ends meet. I started selling figurines that is sometimes called crockery. People use these ornaments for decorative purposes in their homes and offices. They're in all forms and were made from plaster polish and cement. They are moulded into various types of animals having different shapes and sizes. I try everything I could think of to make money, life was definitely not easy. Sometimes if you get in with the right company, you're good but if you get in the wrong crowd then you're in shit. My experiences thought me a lot and made me the man I am today. Learning from my mistakes and other person's mistakes, I'm far more vigilant around people and even family. Someone you don't deal with or someone you don't trust, it could even be an enemy, has less chance to harm you because they won't come around or you won't allow them to get close enough to hurt you. However, your family or the ones closest to you has the potential and are the easiest ones to hurt you and gets away with it because it's not expected, and no one would think about blaming them. My understanding of life and my outlook on life today is very different especially in a foreign country, those experiences and lessons learned are very different. I see brothers and sisters fighting over money and killing each other over land and other assets. Times are hard as we all know but there are lines and limits you just don't cross and things you just don't do, but seven brother seven different minds.

I learned trade with my father and how to weld, I learned construction with Reds. I did electrical installation in secondary school, and I did carpentry with a friend called Culture. Culture was a Christian and a man of God but curses a lot of bad words, gambles racehorse, bought sex, smoke weed and talks a lot of things, that's not compatible with a man of God in my opinion. He's ok though he has since migrated to America I was told. Anyway, going around a few trades man as I said didn't make much of a difference. Somethings I have mastered and some I didn't, but I can help myself. I'm sort of a Jack of all trade and master of non. My father started teaching me and my brothers, he was the one who gave me the first Guinness to drink on my birthday he said, "you're a man now". My father was a man of trade as I've already explained his story already. In my life journey there were a lot of phases, I went through to get where I am. I started selling figurines but that was for a short while, but I was still young. My mother was still working around the community washing people clothes then she got a permanent job looking after some old people. That however was still not enough because it was eight of us and as I've already told you my father story, how he left and didn't return home. I did a bit of construction as a labourer mixing cement known as mortar, cutting people yard, selling fire coal too and making the fire coal this was not easy. I liked to sing, but I would call myself a bathroom singer other person did it too sang in there bathrooms, I know of a few who've done so. I am all over the country anywhere I get some work on a site I go there and work. I've even slept there too that was a real challenge for me. I've had to learn how to live off nothing much or in some instances nothing at all, anything I got I learn to make it work. For example, someone I knew came from abroad and gave me a pair of shoes, I didn't care about the size I just make it fit. if I wore a size eight and the shoes was a size twelve, I'm taking it and wearing it I made it fits likewise if it was smaller, I am doing just the same. Just remember though, when you put on a shoe smaller than your size, you don't go around easy. It's completely different from when it's bigger than your foot. I can tell you this for nothing, tight shoes have an effect on your eyesight. The Squeeze you get from the tight shoes, even when you're grown you still remember it. I still have what we called corn still visible on my toes trust me, it makes you walked with your eyes dim and blurs your vision. You can't walk normal, and you always want to use the toilet, yes it weakens your bladder. Anyone who's ever worn a shoe a size or two smaller knows I'm telling the truth. This does not only happen to me, but others have also experienced this very uncomfortable and unfortunate situations especially female. I remember I had to cut off the point of the shoes just to free my toes because I wasn't seeing properly, it gave me shortness breath and made me sweat. Tight shoes are a punishment I would not recommend even for an enemy. Ask anyone about it who had this experience no jokes real talk. If you wear tight shoes, when you take it off the pain is even more than when you have it on. When you examine your feet, it has a thing called water boil on it like when you get burn by hot water or hot oil. I remember wearing this shoe that squeezed my big toe and my second toe together they became flat and white like it's water soak. I couldn't even touch my feet to try and rub away the pain. I had to sit down all blood flow to my feet was cut off I nearly fall, or I would have ended up walking into a wall. I am sitting now remembering what I went through when I was a boy. My father had brought home a shoe for me, God better on your two sides because he's going to call you to comes and try this shoe on. Even if it cannot fit you by all means necessary it was still yours. He used all types of tools anything he could think of to get it on your foot. He even used a kitchen spoon to get the shoe on your feet, If that didn't work he would sometimes wet your feet or rub cooking oil and Vaseline on it. By the time he's finishes, your foot feels like it was in an accident. He squeezed the toes together and forces them in the shoes, God help you if you even attempt to take a step. Trust me only people who have had this experience can relates to this believe me, if you suffer from migraine stay away from tight shoes it triggers it. Not to mention if someone ever step on your feet, while wearing a tight shoe, it puts you in a bad position. It causes you to become volatile and violent especially if you already have a corn or bunion on your feet. You will have a strong urge to hurt them and badly. I have learnt many lessons this was one, never buy or wear shoes smaller than your feet. You will experience nothing but torture and pain, now all my shoes are at least a size bigger than my feet. Similarly, to tight shoes the waist trainer is another killer. I have seen a few ladies put on a belly band or waist trainer to squeeze their tummies down in order to put on certain dress or certain types of clothing. When they take if of you see the marks and indents embedded deep into their skin. You can see the expressions on their faces it a shock to the system for the females. The belly band it carries bad pain also from what I was told.

Standing with my mother one day in the yard, my mother and I was talking about something. I suddenly heard a loud sound coming from my mother. I said what's that she blows off meaning did she eased her body or better known as fart. I can't believe my mother just done that big fart, I looked at her and said, "mamma did you just fart" she in return said, "mine you make my belly hurt me". It an old saying that if someone laugh when a baby farts, then it will hurt their tummy. I don't know if it's true, but I kept looking at her because I wanted to laugh. She said what she said and even out lined more argument to the story, this was what she said to me. "As the first you heard somebody fart, you an idiot". That comment made me laugh so hard, then she continued to say, "let fart be free because it killed Mary Lee". I nearly died with laughter, I don't know where she got that from, and I don't know Mary Lee either, so I have no clue if it's true. I kept hearing that phrase later time after time. My mother can be a joker when she his ready. One weekend I was on my way to Hanover, I was in a minibus traveling from May Pen to Mandeville and then from Mandeville to Savanna la mar. The minibus was so packed I had to stand up for a while and wait until someone got out before I could sit down. You know how Jamaican drivers do it in those days. Suddenly I heard an old lady shouting saying this to me "why your batty just up in my face like that, when you young boys ass don't have no manners", in a loud squeaky voice. All this time I was already trying to hold the pressure of a fart in my belly, all the way from May Pen. Looking at this woman face you can see she is a real miserable, this woman looks really disturb to me in my mind. I wanted to laugh out but I'm trying not to do so because any move I make may release the pressure in my belly. That didn't last, the devil is so strong a silent fart came out, you know the expression silent but deadly, well this was it. It wasn't loud but the smell was like I needed to shit. A shout from the old woman alerted the whole bus. She said, "hmmm in disgust what the hell smell so, see yah boy no tell me you just fart inner my face". She then gave me a sudden slap in my back and shouted move your stinking batty out of my face, damn nasty. Listen, let me tell you what happened. You know that big fart I was holding from so long, when she hit me in my back the entire thing, I was holding on to so long came to life. It just burst out in a loud rush of wind the sound was so loud and blaring poooooooooooop, one long non ending thing. I tried squeezing my bottom, but it just wouldn't stop. This lady was so dramatic, she started to shout even louder "Jesus Christ him shit up the whole a mi face". Blap, Blap in my back again and the rest of the fart just came out on her. The entire bus erupts in laughter some laughed until there were tears. The lady was saying something I couldn't hear because of all the laughing, the driver had to stop the bus for everyone to finish laughing and calm down. The woman didn't help the situation either, she proceeded to ask "a who a your parents". That's exactly what she said, I nearly cried. I told her I'm sorry but that was not enough to stop her from cursing. She made everyone cracked up even more when she said "weh you ago sit when we drive off, you can't set back like that". "Let me go in front of you and bend over and make my ass inna your Face, because I'm not going to fart, I'm not doing that. Lord God she said "you never knew you wanted to shit before you left your yard boy, see yah Jesus take this case and give me the pillow. "Me never see anything like this yet", said the lady. "Me ago mark you face, look if you shit you must have belly ache or running belly". When we reaches Savanna la mar and everyone was exiting the bus I said goodbye and the lady said to me "fuck off and don't chat to me, I don't like you and for a little boy how your fart stink so Gwen from me" she said "I have a whole lot of children and grandchildren and non a them nuh smell so, because them could not live in my house". "I've me smelled little pickney fart it nuh smell like so, I don't know what you eating, you need a wash out my god". I could talk trust me; I was in stitches she was funny. After she left I was still standing beside the mini bus, the driver came over to me and said "youth you made me almost piss myself, that was why I stopped the bus me nearly dead". "You really fart like that in the woman face", he said laughing his eyes out. I told him, yes, I farted but not wilfully and the slap she gave me in my back never helped the situation. It just released what I was trying very hard to hold back, it was a genuine accident. She wouldn't accept the one Hundred sorry I told her either. Every time I'm traveling to and from Hanover, I keep looking for her but I never saw her again.

Still doing a bit of everything to survive as a secondary school dropout, I try everything. I did a few other jobs like security guard work as well but construction was the main thing, It wasn't so bad. The labourer work was more easily gained for a day or two even weeks depending on you are and the area you get the work. Sometimes it's a problem working in a next person area which is not your home grounds or turf, that can sometimes cause a big problem. Working in construction you will meet all types of people on site, and you come across some funny guys on site too. This is a story about a guys called Giant and his greedy ways. Giant was also known as Hulk no jokes he wears about size twenty-four in shoes. He was always working bare footed, his two big toes looks like he had two different feet hanging on beside his other toes it was that big. He was about eight to nine feet tall. Each one of his teeth was about one and a half inches long and was stuck an inches out of his mouth. Just consider the rest of teeth in his gums, for every teeth there was a pair his mouths could barely close. His nose is about five inches wide on his face the nostrils just open like a gate, the nostrils almost an inch both ways in length and width. His eyes were as big as stadium bulbs as people would say, and had a wildness to them. His hands were big, wide and rough and looks like the feet of an elephant, all his fingers were long and appears to have two or three extra joints. This guy look like something from a duppy show (scary movie). Whenever he cooks, he would cook at least ten pounds of flour with half a goat or a whole goat for himself. He would ate a bread while he waited for the food to finish cooking. He would capture and kill people's live stocks anything he could get his hands on. It could be pigs, goats or chickens and he would eat this with a whole pot of dumplings plus other ground provisions. No jokes when this man eat chicken, he eats at least five or six five-pound chicken. Every morning he ate one tray of eggs, with two hard dough bread and drinks about a gallon of tea or juice. If he doesn't like you, you can't get a bite to eat from the food he was cooking. I have to say he works very hard and he was not lazy, he dug a pit and pack it back all by himself. He also worked straight through the night digging and watching the houses and have done this for years. Sometimes he was doing this for more than one house at the same time he was very strong. He had no woman, he bought sex every now. I heard that whenever he finishes with the woman they all had to go to the hospital and staying there for days. He had no kids either, but I know his brother too. Anytime he had a shower on the canal bank it gathers crowd, people watching him bathe or peeping especially women. Everyone heard about his third leg and wanted to see it for themselves. The ladies took it for a joke they compared him with a donkey or a horse no jokes. I once heard a few ladies discuss the size he is carrying, it not funny they all speak about the head of his penis that they said looked like a tennis ball. It was fun to hear them sometime, I wondered if they were exaggerating but I don't know. When the women looked, he didn't care he just continues to bathe in the water. They heard he pays a lot of money for sex, but after they won't enjoy the money or the sex because when he finishes they will soon end up in the hospital believed me. We use to watch him on weekends when we all got paid, to try and see which woman was hanging around him. When he's not with a woman and was sleeping in one the houses he cared for you can hear him snoring from a mile away (khoooo, khoooo) and some loud farts like thunder too (poooooooo, pooooooop) no jokes. Working on site we had to use make shift toilet, use the bush or sometimes a portable toilet is available. On a few occasions I heard hulk going toilet, not a word of a lie, you could hear the sound effects all around the site and hear shit dropping like boulders. When he was done no one could go near the toilet or even think of entering after him, the smell alone would make you vomit. I'm thinking to myself if he eats that much, the amount he shits much equate to about half his body weight. He and I are cool but I can tell you this for sure, you try to steal from him and that's a big no no. I wouldn't recommend it not even for someone I didn't like because if he hold onto you, he would rip you apart. You couldn't get away from him no matter how hard you try he was too strong, he wasn't only gigantic but he had the strength to match his size. From my understanding he used to live in Kitson town and up in the hills of Browns Hall on Point Hill. They said it was the residents of Kitson Town that chased him away. They said he continued to eat all their goat and pigs that were left in bushes to feed. I've seen him eats one goat and one pig like it was nothing trust me. He was a modern day giant eating the way only a giant could. When I see how he ate it makes me wonder how he felt after, I am thinking was this greed or was it because of his size why he really had to consume that much food. I'm thinking to myself how it is he eats like this every day, yet he is not putting on any more weight. It's unnatural for any one person to eat ten pounds of flour for themselves, this seems unreal but I've seen him do it every day so it's real as can be. Sometimes the other men on site ask for some of the food he wouldn't even pay them any attention, he pretends as though he didn't hear, wouldn't even budge. He cooks in a kerosene pan or cut a thirty pounds gas cylinder that is what he used for is pot. In my head I can remember him chewing his mouth, he is a serious man when it comes to food. I can tell you this man is like a machine when he boils the yam Banana and dumplings, he drinks the pot water after the food is cooked. He is something different, he was specially built trust me. God make him for a special purpose he is not normal and when he laughs that's another story. It was funny those teeth I told you about comes out for you to have a good look on them and when he laughed you had to crack up. Giant is always around Willowdene and Hopedale housing scheme he as brothers and sisters living there. I heard he passed away a few years ago I am saddened by his death, RIP Giant rest in peace hope you have loads of food in haven.

The older I gets and the more experience I gained on the construction site, it made it easier for me to gets more work on site and also allowed me to gets little things for myself. I can dig the foundation, mixed the mortar for the concrete, carry blocks and ties steel. I did a bit of pluming too and many more little stuffs around the site. I also worked as a security at some point. I met up with a long-time friend of mine know as Liam. He was a welder by trade, and he also fixes cars. We started partying hard our intention was to get a girl, you know what boys do, we are out looking for girls to dance with and have fun. It was a weekly thing for us to go to City rock. The selector Ian was the man, then you have Squad one sound system at the corner of Crossroads at a popular supermarket. Every weekend a large crowd would gather their people from everywhere would attend. That supermarket was called Mr blight, every Sunday was lovely. It was a good spot to hang out, girls like crazy with the same intention looking for guys it was the spot trust me. If you can't get a girl from this place, then you have a problem. My friends and I were friends with all the girls. Some of my friends were females that liked to laugh and were full of jokes. That was all we had we couldn't afford to even buy a drink for ourselves. This life will soon lead me in to having children and becomes a father of three, all three kids are from the Homestead community. I will give you the kids story in full. Rolling with my friend Liam was like a competition even with our other friends. Every one of us was looking for a girlfriend, if you didn't have a girlfriend in those days, you might not be called queer, but you will be called Tarzan meaning you haven't got a girl around you. Your girl must be good looking also and that's another story. You'd be a laughingstock if your girl is a ugly gal. It got real funny too, when we had to meet up with our friend to go out partying. There you will know what was going on, everybody's gathered there checking each other's girl out. If there was anything off with any of the girls, you'll catch your friends pinching the closest person to him or her pushing out there lips to make the signal, pointing without using their fingers. If your girl was nice and hot, then you will be greeted by a handshake or everyone there would thumping your fist. In all these boys will always be boys, you wouldn't dear to bring home a ugly girl to your yard to meet your parents or your siblings. Likewise, your siblings wouldn't bring home an ugly boyfriend or girlfriend either you had to be careful. I met a pretty girl at a football match at a school in Spanish town. My friend Garry was playing, he was the goalkeeper at the school. He knew her friend and I was introduce to her. She was pretty and fit perfectly for our required standards. She was in her last year at school we were are all teenagers and were either one or two years apart. Her name was Marks, she was quiet, very nice and soft spoken a cool girl overall. This was looking really good for me, a group of ten or eleven of us cycled to the match in Spanish town. At the school I asked her where she lived, when she replied it was somewhere I was already familiar with. It was a place call Kitson town just past Johnson pen, French man hill, green acres and Dovecot memorial park. That's where Kitson town is located up on top of the hills. This girl made me want to show off, now I felt ready for the good looking competition the girls had to be well dressed also and this girl was perfect, she just the person for the competition. Yes, I was over the moon, I was eager to take her to my home community. Everyone heard of her and wanted to meet her, all the other girls too no jokes. All this time I was still doing trade and working on construction site. I bought her nice things, for her to look good for the others to see whenever I took her somewhere. Wow, me and her were getting on well, she was willing to come and visit me in my community. One weekend my friend Garry was having a city rock party at his house. His older brother was a police officer and was well known all over Spanish town and St Catherine. I took a good look at my girl, her feet were small, waist small, top small and I looked for a perfect out fit for her. I love the colour blue, so I bought blue for both of us. I went shopping for these outfits myself everything I bought matches perfectly even the panties. I bought three of them, so she could choose any one she like or anyone that fits. It was approaching the weekend, and everyone was getting ready for the party. City rock was at its peak trust me; we were in for a great party that night. We all had to made sure that we had money in our pockets, all because we intend to show off our respective girlfriends. The crowd will be massive and I was afraid to be disappointed, so I asked her if she was attending the party for the whole month. It finally boils down to the day and her answer was still yes. I was already spreading the news about my pretty girl and there was now a look out going on from the morning until evening. Everyone was eager to see this girl, by these times I had already given her my sister's address for her to meet my sister. She had called and arranged with my sister when they'll meet. My sister was living at Lamington Drive Willowdene, she took at taxi that dropped her exactly at my sister's gate. When she got there, she rang my sister to informed her she was there. My sister then called me and let me know she had arrived. I walked away telling everyone I'll returned shortly. The day was still early, and phone calls are coming in like crazy. All my friends girls were attending, this city rock party was the thing you couldn't afford to miss. When I walked off, I took the first corner, I began to wonder what the hell I'm doing should be running like I'm in a race to go see my girl. I started running but to how fast I'm going I'll reach the yard in minutes. I decided to slow down and cool down, I didn't want it to look like I was running. I started to walk at an even pace to regulate my breathing because I was out of breath and that's not a good look. When I reach the yard, I went around the back first to take off my shoes and washed off my feet with soapy water, I used a soap called sudsil. I was just running like mad and wearing this shoe almost every day in the boiling sun, you know how that goes. It causes my feet to sweat like crazy plus my foot looks white like chalk. My big toes are burning because they are squeezed into the shoe. Trust me sometimes my feet smell like I stepped in dog shit. So, I washed my feet properly especially between my toes and dry them, I also washed the shoes and left then in the sun to dry. I'm going in my sister house where my girl was so I had to wash off that stink off my feet thoroughly because it could be really embarrassing for both of us. When I went inside I said hello, I needed a haircut at the time but my brother was a barber so that wasn't a problem at all I'll get one later when I'm ready. He was also the barber for the community. I went to greet my girl properly, when I saw her, I was like wow this is really real, it was going in the right directions for me. She was speaking with my sister, my sister was going shopping and wanted to take her along with her and asked me if she can take her shopping. I was so happy I said yes, no problem. I was thinking should I get my hair cut while she's gone. My sister liked her, she must do to asked her to accompany her on the road. This was going well it's like Christmas came in the middle of the year for me. Tonight, is going to be alright, this girl looks like she was Indian, with her pretty hair, red lips, looked neat in her clothes, had tiny feet, she wore about size four. Tonight, we were both wearing blue and white. My sister fixes her hair and start asking her lots of questions, I am listening but not saying anything. All I know she is my girl, and the party was on the way. My friends kept asking where she was and if she were still coming to the party. I'm not letting out the business, not saying a thing just yet. I wanted to surprise everybody, the night was all about excitement and I was well and truly excited. The feeling was over the top and I'm already over the moon. I got my hair cut in this style called kid and play, the top was high, and the sides faded which was the lick back then. My hair was cut and lined properly, I got a clean shaved and was feeling like a Star boy. The night was fast approaching, and we were all getting ready. I am the man tonight all eyes will be on me and my pretty girl, sexy girl. All the other girls in the family were on the lookout that was how we did it, every time over and over. The other girls and I were already good friends because they were my friend's girl. We always made sure that we look after the ladies, whenever we run a boat which means to cook, we gave them loads of food to eat. When we cook everybody would gathers together to eat, drink and chat all kind of rubbish until late in the night it was fun to just relax with our friends. Sometimes the girls enjoyed themselves so much they always wanted to come back. Those were the good days fun days. Now it's all about the party, we were getting dressed. I am watching her, and she was watching me. Both our outfits were matching, we were feeling happy. I wanted to go around there but not too early, it's only fun from time to time we meet up to share these moments. It was about ten o clock when we decided to head out and walk around to the party. When we arrived at the party had just started to fill up but this is the real moment and this is what I wanted, everyone started calling me over and asking loads of questions. I felt really important that night, I introduce her to the other girls, the other guys and I put our moneys together and bought drinks for them. We all started partying and enjoying ourselves, only for Liam to do nothing more than a big loud fart almost as loud as the sound system right in front the women. It was a shocker for her, but she just laughed until she almost drops. It was funny because he farted right in the other man face trust me, they were playing this farting game with each other, but we were neither at the place nor was it the time for that kind of antics. The other girls looked disgusted, my girl said she felt embarrassed. I told her not to be and explained that's how my friends are. The party had started to gather a huge crowd, both the road and the lane were blocked. The part was in full swing, you could heard City rock playing far away in the distance. We were all having a really good time, we dance and drink until we were drunk. All the liquor and food being sold were all sold out. Still, we continued to party dancing until we were tired. The party goes on until it was day light. My girl and I made our way to my sister house, when we reached we both fell asleep because we were so exhausted and drunk. We slept for the entire day, when I woke up my friends couldn't wait to start asking questions about my girl. They told me how pretty and nice she was. That was what it about trusts me.

The thing with life it that nothing is set in stone. You can have some really good time in life and have some real unfair sides too at some point. In spite of all the effort I put in to this relationship it was going to end prematurely. I was taking care of this girl to the best of ability but things are going to make a turn which I was not expecting. The mother of my girl was on a totally different thing from both of us and decided that things needed to end, whatever it was that was going on. I tried but I couldn't work it out, so I had to walked away the sore loser. I tried my best to get my girl back, but it wouldn't work, I hid and sent messages but still lose out. True love always finds it's ways through the darkest night. I think I was robbed, I walked pass the yard all the time looking but spotted nothing. This was life you win some and lose some. My heart has been broken but a part of me was still left inside her growing and in the years to come there was still a part of her that was left with me and that was magic shared between the two of us always.

It took a while for me to get over her, her mother has decided this was not happening so I decided to leave well alone and walked away. I won't be the first or the last person either to lose some one they loved. The both of us came up with a plan to run away but it won't work for long. We ran away but we ran to my sister house that wasn't far enough and that was just another wrong move. We hid in my sister's house but her mother was not having it and turned up at my sister's work place in half way tree. My sister was not amused, she was so vexed. She told me to give it up because she doesn't want the problem. It didn't stop there, her mother went back to my sister's work place a few times, making loads of noise and commotion outside her work place. My sister was trying hard for her not to come back, but until she got her daughter back it's not happening. We hid but it just couldn't work, we had no chance. We don't want to leave each other sides because of the love, if I had the perfect hiding place I would have definitely gone there and taken her with me. She was crying constantly she doesn't want to leave me, and I don't want to leave her side either. We were both happy with each other trust me but time always heal some problems but makes some gets even worst. After this happened, I was broken for a while but then I picked myself up and got over it.

I made sure nothing can make me feels this way again, from my experience that was a learning process. I am a well-built guy from this experience, my mind set is different and I'm more firm insides my body. I was a bit weak at first but now I am like a counsellor ready to give help to any one with problem like this my head is also in perfect condition. Lord thanks for making me with a decent size head so it can hold pressure and problems. This girl was all I had going on for me at the time, so I suffers a big lost, we were only young, but we have to move on. Life comes with some things in pairs if you understand what I mean take for instance in bracket (laugh cry. Happy sad. Live die). Some people on earth are hard to deal with as well but what can we do, people will be people. Some people will find it ok to disappoint you and go out of their way to do so every day. I got older I learn more each day now I'm at a point in my life to know the older you get the wiser you become. Once you're not ill and in good health life is what you make it. Sometimes disappointments are for a reason, I was told so. With me and my girlfriend separating not because of me or her fault but because of her mother's will for us to be apart. Anyway, I work with it I will have to try and fine another girl because loneliness won't leave me alone. I can't stay like this each day, so I had to dust myself off and move on. My life was always filled with challenges from I was young, but I realized that my intention were clear and I don't begrudge anyone over their stuff. I have always had ambition, manners and respect for everyone girl or boy man or woman. That puts me in a good place with everyone I encounter, I'm a very honest and disciplined man. Self-praised is no recommendations, but I can speak for myself.

Moving forward from the situation I've mentioned, my head was upsides down for a bit but god's not sleeping. When one door is closed many more are open. I met up with a girl who will become the mother of my children. She gave me three lovely children two girls and a boy. My mind is settled and calm but every now and then it's going straight back on the love of my life. This girl is nice but my heart still with my ex, worrying over and over about my ex- girlfriend. Watching these kids grow and stepping into the role of a father, is a task 1 now fully understand the importance of a having a father in the home. You can grow up a child without its father, yes mother alone but just remember his or her father is still missing from that Childs life. In saying that I must also say that these kids today are very different from the ones born in eighties. The kids born in the twentieth century are very difficult and filled with rude behaviours and very disrespectful to everyone. They don't care or matter who the person is, this also includes their mothers and fathers. These now a days kids as my mother would say are the generation of vipers. Meaning that they're very wicked and terrible. I believe it's true these kids today have no manners whatsoever and will assist in their parents down fall and demise. I love my kids, as a matter of fact I love all children, but it turns out sometimes the person or persons you love won't love you the same as you loved them. I find this to be quite unfair, but this is the reality of things. Kids today will even Envy their parents for their wealth, their properties and any other valuable assets or other monetary belonging that they can see or get a hold of. At the same time they think they are entitled or think they should be the ones to inherited anything belonging and owned by their parents. Even if their parents wanted or intended to give something to someone else, they will want that too. It doesn't matter what's the cost, life or death. They don't care, they just want it by any means necessary. I have seen this type of behaviour around lot and I believe it's a leading commonality with our youths today. Looking at these youths today their patterns are similar but what stands out the most is their laziness. That disgust me, they would sit beside a television and ask you to turn it on. I've had this type of discussion several times and it always caused a problems leading up to them calling you miserable or other things which is not nice. My intention was not to talk about this but touching on a certain topic left me with no choice but to address these behaviours of our youths today.

Moving forward a little to this girl I met after my ex-girlfriend. Everything was fine, she was ok for a time until she got pregnant and gave birth to a bouncing baby boy called Shay. He weighted ten pounds and four ounces. He was growing fine and doing well. Then my baby's mother was pregnant again, this time giving birth to a bouncing baby girl called Chiney. She weights nine pounds and about thirteen ounces growing and doing well also. However it didn't stop there, she got pregnant again for the third time about two years later giving birth to another bouncing baby girl called Grace. She was also doing just the same, growing well and in good health. Now this was even more serious than ever having three kids to look after and maintain. I had to Get moving get a steady job. I had three kids in a row, like counting 1 2 3 and it wasn't easy growing them up. Supplies were expensive and they needed milk pampers or nappies. Babies in general needs attention and are expensive to have. By the way my baby's mother shares the same name as my ex-girlfriend.

Working on the construction site as a security guards and labourer is another story by itself. In that field I got to know a few people as well, I was introduced to a few politicians as well. Meeting and working for the politicians is also in a class by itself, you needs to know this about the Jamaican well known politician. It's okay to know them sometime, but it's not a good thing for you all the time. It can help you sometimes but puts you in danger another time or even get you hurt. I had worked for a few politicians plenty of times, my experience with politicians is the reasons for me saying this. These people meaning the politicians will stop at nothing to win their seat or to beat their opponent. If it takes the sky to come down on earth, they would bring it down Knowing it will crush the earth and everyone beneath it they don't care trust me. Their main priority is winning, they are able to open a few doors for you opportunity wise but it's not safe for you and your family. Sometimes I would work in a rich politician store and in this store I realized the type of man I'm working for. He is a proper businessman who was kind also but you take no chance with these types of person. Listen to this one day I was on the job and he called me in his office for us to have a chat. In a time like that I was thinking it was something to do with the store yard. Once inside the office the boss said he is offering me a job and that jobs were the most shocking job offer I've ever had. I would have never expected to be asked a question like the one he asked, but I still listen to him carefully. I look him straight in his face like how he was talking to me and staring me straight in my face, with not even a blink from either of his eyes he was offering me a job off the compound. This was on another premises one of his other business place in Spanish Town. This was strictly confidential, he was about to give me another contract to secure another shop and also keep an eye on is wife. Yes, in our term to watch his wife and also one of is employee's, a youths he employed at the shop for some years. He said I should take a good look on this employee in the shop and take notes of him and his wife movement and bring anything I saw that looked suspicious to me. That was my new job this was no jokes either. I thought about it properly and told him I will try and get someone to fit the position for him, he then made an offer too which was very interesting. I am thinking about this move constantly, I began thinking it could have been me but no worries because I am not his wife friend so I don't even have to think about it. The point I am making now is to let you how some of these money men behave. Not only politician as you know but this was one I'm working for, so just letting you guys know what's was going on and it does not stop there. I take up the offer and sublet the job out I found the perfect person for the job he gave the information to me, and I pass it over to the boss. What he was saying to me was that his wife and this specific employee is moving strange, and he don't trust them. What he was saying to me was she doesn't let anyone drives her car, she doesn't even wants him to drives it eithers as her husband. Now he was saying that it caused an argument between them sometimes for him to drive it. He was saying that he was now getting to understand that this person he don't trust is driving the car frequently for the last few weeks. He mention that he found it very strange because the car is new and no one goes around that steering wheel for no reason at all. So, it strange to him and others at the workplace find it really suspicious. I wondered if it was the others staff that noticed this behaviour also and notify him. She only bought the car a couple of months earlier, so you know it's a newly bought car and she is very strict with it. So, he is thinking what's the hell is going on here, he needs to find out and soon. This is common behaviour in males or females with their partners I'm not saying I would or wouldn't have done the same thing if I had the money and suspect funny movements around my partner, but for now I can tell you this form my honest opinion if a person is capable of doing this then I think something can go terrible wrong. I think you can expect the unexpected even more if you understand what I am thinking and talking about. Having three kids to feed I need money, so any work I get I will take. The extra money would do good for me and the kid's mother. I'm around these people working in the store and on the construction site, at times I do some cooking on a Friday that brings in a little more cash too and this is even more helpful to me. I did all types of things I am sweeping the yard, lifting board, cement, zinc, steel and also loading sand gravel and other stuff onto the trucks in the Hardware. All these things I have mentioned was what customers order and paid for it to be delivered to their respective addresses. Things got quiet sometime in the shop, so I had to do construction work more often and that is the quickest job to get my hands on at the moment for some quick cash.

On the construction site there was always some loud talking going on or some form of funny jokes. At some point, sometimes on the site you had to fight for your work or even fight to keep your work because other youths just might need your job, so they will just come and take it away from you. I have now learned these types of behaviour and had witness a lot of fight on the construction site all over the community of Willowdene, where I spent many years. I learned a lot from this type of work and just remember one thing, it's not easy working on a site if you're not from that community where the site is located. Sometimes this cause a lot of tension results in stone throwing, machete chopping and sometimes even guns are used to defend one's community and the work site. I am all around doing what I can and there was a time when I had stand up for myself. I had learned stuff on site that made me appeared more manly. I can help myself, going around on these sites I never knew one day the same things I have seen on site would come staring me in the face. This means I will have to stand my ground, one day in the near future and this will soon lead me in a dark place. One of the darkest places I have ever been on earth from I was born. When you start having children sometimes you have to make decisions which makes you sometimes lower yourself to others. You will have the last money sometimes and have to give it up, not in a bad way but it means you have to prioritise, forgo certain things in order to provide for your children. Any parent would do it that's what I think anyway. I can tell you quite a few stories and raised a few scenarios from you say the word children and it's not made-up stories either. As times goes by, I learn the seriousness of having and providing for children. My intention is always to see them grow up in good health and past the worst.

My father had now build a house in a place called Dam Head and also occupied a garage on the main heading towards Flat Bridge. He became very popular in that area very fast because he was very good at fixing cars. It was quite a busy road so the garage there is very crucial especially for the taxi operators. Dam Head is known for a popular club called Riverside Drive Inn, which is like bar and club that caters mostly to men. It's a place where girls dances. Many men would hang out there because you all know by now that anywhere plenty women are, there will be men hanging around. Even in the animal world no disrespect to woman or men it just for raising a point, female attracts males. Dam Head is where the Rio Cobre River runs from Bog walked from the Dam where the water supplies all over. The water is processed and sterilized and runs all the way through St Catherine until it reaches the sea. Whenever the rain falls it sometimes cause severe flooding from this same river. Just to make it even clearer this is the very same river that runs the island most famous flat bridge. From I was small I heard loads of mysterious things about the Rio Cobre where Flat bridge is located. People always say it's an evil spot because every now and then the river comes down and wash away cars, trucks and killing loads of motorist and that is still happening today.

The river itself have its own history surrounding it and that stretch of road is known for lot of drownings occurring. Back in the days before I was familiar with the area, I heard about a sugar factory that was around that area and engineers were working on the old water dam where the factory was. There were loads of engineers under the ground in water pipes working on the dam. It's believed that someone had turn on the water, opened the floods gate and drowned every single person under there killing them all. So, this is one reason why everyone says that the river is haunted and filled with evil spirits and other mysterious things. This is what I heard but saying that I must say this to you, I have learned a few things from the area and things I personally knew about the river myself that occurred on the same stretch of road. I've seen loads of truck turns over in Flat Bridge over the years, vans and cars. I've also witnessed a few boys, trees, shop, houses and animals get washed away. When there are heavy rains fall and the river raises over its banks, it becomes very dangerous if you are in its path whether you can swim or not, you'll be in trouble because the current is strong.

I've always swim in that water and bath in it also, this was when I was about nineteen or twenty years of age, until I was a bit older. Hear this, I caught a fish in the river and pick a few ackee to cook on the riverbank for me and my friends. The river is filled with fishes like eel, perch, tarpon mudfish and shrimps. Catching these fish was fun for us and a bit of challenge, but we were ready for this adventure. Some people lived off the river, both the water and the things grown on the banks. Things like coconuts, breadfruits, plums, oranges soursops, sweets saps custard apples and many other fruits and ground provisions. Most of the fruits you could think of it was there. The bank was also littered with human and animal waste, used Condon, plastic bag, wrappers and many other things. People uses the riverbank for different reasons. I am going to share one of the mysteries that I personally knew about this river. People have always said that mermaid or river maid is in the water. Everyone has some strange thing to say about the river, like a place called Lock ness in England it's also a river that is rumoured to have a monster in the water known as Nessie. Try Google to know more about the Lock Ness monster are Nessie.

The Dam Head Mermaid Story

My story is about a fisher man called Kock who lived in Dam Head, anyone who is interested and needs any more information about this story can asked anyone who lived in Dam Head community of St Catherine. This happened in the early nineties from what I can clearly remember. This guy lived off catching fish from the river and selling them. Every day he would shoots fish, uses lines to catch them. He sets pots and fish traps all over the river included stuck nets. Listen this, at one day he shoots a long string of big fish and crawfishes he then walked and sold them all. He had done this every day or least every other day. He makes a living off these types of hunting, I am sure. He then goes out the following morning and does the same thing he had been doing for years repeatedly. He caught, cook and sells, this was like his job. He would wake up very early and sets off for the riverbanks, even when it's wet and dark and the dew is still on the grass. Although it was very cold up that sides in the morning and evening he still persist. Entering the lane, he would shout out "fish, fish," on his way back. He always have is order for both fish and crawfish, he sometimes had bread fruit or anything else he could find he sell and it was selling really fast. He approached a welder in the evening and telling the welder he wants a bigger spear, and he wants it well sharp and pointed, he then turned to the welder and showed him a big scale. It looked like ivory and shines like it's dazzling your eyes. The welder said its as big as a patch on a Soccer ball and shaped like a fifty-cent coin. The scale is a few inches in length and width, he told the welder that this one would make history if had caught it and brought it out the river. He said he shot this big fish and because the gun he was using was small, the spear couldn't stop it. It was too small and light so it couldn't penetrate the body of this big something he saw. He said he hadn't seen it properly, he had only seen the tail and fired on the tail so this scale is not even from the upper body of the thing he had seen. So, this giant fish he saw he swears he's going back for it tomorrow.

This is a prize fish he said so first thing in the morning he is going to kill this big thing and bring him out of the river. When he caught this one it's going to earn him a medal. He also stated he's going to needs help to lift it out of the water and put it on the banking because it's a giant. The welder told him yes, he would make him a big heavy spear with a sharp pointed tip. The welder did make the spear as the guy wishes and the guy himself made a new powerful spear gun that was bigger and better than the last one. He thinks this spear has the power to penetrate this big gigantic fish who lived somewhere in the river, on this stretch of the road from Dam Head going up towards Flat Bridge. This was better known to the public as the Gorge or as Bog Walked Gorge. After sharing this story with you, I will give you another story about the gorge road. People have always said something big was in the waters. It's really big and when it's moving it can be seen from far away, like it's parting the water especially when it's going up stream. From my personal experience and from the top of my head, I would say it's a crocodile but its clear crocodiles don't have scales. I'm just trying to thinking of anything big enough to fit the description of this thing. This Mysterious story has been going on for years and it's still going on today. I am thinking what the hell it could be; I have heard of mermaid and from what I know I have never seen anything to provide any prove that there is something called mermaid or river maid. Anyway this guy showed his new fish gun and gave it a test run to see if it was shooting straight and powerful, because tomorrow will be the day he's planning to make history. He was going to take out this big giant out of the water, before He went home. He told the welder he would see him in the morning or later in that evening after he finishes selling his catch. He heads off to cook his dinner have a shower and went to bed. The welder say he heard a knock outside of is place early in the morning and shouted who is it the welder say he could hear a voice in return saying it's me Kock. As I mentioned Kock was the fisherman, now he was coming to share a very strange dream he had with the welder about a fish he had encountered the day before. He told the welder that last night he had a dream about a big fish that talking to him and warned him not to come back into the water. He said the fish also told him that he uses something to hurt him and his children and that it's really upset. He described to the welder that this strange fish had big blood red eyes that looks as if they were bleeding. He said the fish was really enormous, and that the dream appeared so real. He said the fish also mentioned the scale he shoot off its tail and instruct him to throw it back in the water, the same place where he got it from. The strange thing about the dream was he never took nothing into consideration with what had happened the day before. He was so reluctant to believe what is going on or what is unfolding right in front of his eyes. This may sound weird but it's true. The welder said he look at him and said, "my friend don't go back in the river, leave the water alone". By this time, he was already saddling up to go and make is historic dive. He had in his position his new spear gun the scale from the fish and a piece of string tied around his waist, which he uses to carry the fishes he caught each day or each time he made a dive. Anyway the welder told him again not to go in the water and even told him to be careful, he said nothing can stop him from going in the river, he said he has to catch this fish and was going to make history today. He walked off toward the river and said I will see you later to the welder.

The welder say he watched him walked across the road straight towards the riverbank until he was out of sight. He said he is sure he saw him headed to the river as normal but never saw when he went in the water. He said all he could do was wait for him to return with whatever he caught in the evening as usual. This was done with him in high spirit and confidence. He always goes in the water from downstream and shooting upstream depending on how clear the water is showing and how the day fair off. Sometimes he makes a fortune for the day when the catch is good, he might rest the next day but early the next day he was on it. He goes down in the water as he went down, he shoots a few fishes real quick and then moving up stream. He was catching quite a few in just a short time. Up and down, he went, down and up again to tell the person on the bank he saw something. He went down again making a big dive from he made that last dive hasn't come up again. He was missing for minutes, minutes turned to hours until it turned into days. An alarm was raised and a search party was put together because it had days since he was last seen. Everyone got busy and started looking for him, they search the river bank starting from where he first entered the water. The first day pass and nothing, the second day same thing. Everyone was saying the spear gun and body would soon float up. On the third day they found the spear gun, but nobody was insight. They got divers and started searching all over the river, everyone saying he would ending up downstream because the current was strong, but the body didn't pop up. Now they start searching up stream they had already found the spear gun and some fishes. Everyone was thinking like how they found the spear gun the body wouldn't be too far. Listen this, when the spear gun was found it was broken into two pieces and appeared as if someone had broken it. This was getting serious and started attracting crowd, everyone who was living in and around Dam head and also the local communities Came out in bundle and groups chatting about the incident. The incident was spreading like wild fire, it spread so fast it was unbelievable. Anyway, back to the missing diver. They are still searching for him, still moving upstream, loads of divers came out to help both local and professional divers. I got to understand they were diving for hours that turned into days, but they still could not find him for almost a week. Somebody made a shout from what I was told, and everyone came running. This is the interesting part how they found him and the condition he was in. He was found way upstream from where the spear gun and fish were found, he look like he was in boxing a ring he didn't looking like a person who drowned. There was blood coming from his nose and his mouth looks like he was punched in the face several times. There were several bruises all over his body, he was in the water for several days, yet he was not water soaked like how a person would be when they drown. When checked it was discovered that he died hours ago and not by drowning, it looked like something, or someone broke his gun and threw it away and then gave him a fine beating. They said they were going to do an examination on his body at the Spanish town hospital. However it didn't happened, the coroner was always sick and machine was always malfunctioning for some reason, it was a mystery.

I never heard of him getting buried, the welder that made the spear gun said something strange is going on. He said he doesn't want to know what it is, or what is going on down there, he is satisfied with what little he knows. It might sound strange but it's true, he says nothing came of it, it was just mysterious and strange. Until this day no one still hasn't got a proper idea of what took place in that river. There're a few questions about this story that was always on my mind. First, if he was not Drowned what was the cause of his death. Secondly, what broke his gun, thirdly where did he get those burses from. The final question is what's really puzzling, how did he reach upstream, he was in the water for almost a week and he looks like he died only hours ago. The welder told me a story that made some sense and explain the spear gun he also saw him going down to the riverbank. He also mentioned the dream that Kock had, about something big being in the water, but he had never found out what it was. From the moment he had that dream after shooting off that scale from that big fish and seeing a fish with bleeding eyes in his dreams, she should have never gone bad the day after for no reason at all. The welder is well known around Dam head area so just in case you wanted to enquire further there is many more people around Dam head who will know this story.

This next story also took place in Dam head, in the same area where the river gorge road is and the same area where the Dam is. There is a Very popular club in the area which is known as the Drive, which I briefly mentioned before. It's about half an hour to forty minutes' drive out of the old capital Spanish town and about forty to fifty miles just guessing from the top of my head. It is on the right-hand side of the road coming from Spanish town and about twenty coming from Bog Walk end. It would be on the left-hand side of the road just after you past to the Dam. The club is immediately on the left, this club was owned by a prominent business man, who was also involved in a bit of politics and owned serval other businesses in and Around St Catherine. He goes by the name Mr Greene, in the early nineties, the club on a Friday Saturday and Sundays was the hit. This club house has go go dancers and several men looking for fun on the weekend and enjoyment would hand out there. They also had good food there too, like jerk chicken, jerk pork, roast and stem fish and festival. Women were there dancing literally naked, and you know men will always hangout there. We all know the saying ants Follow fat, well this place had fat galore. It was a nice little hangout spot, filled with fun and entertainment, many parties goers frequent this place. The regular attendees were police, soldier, security guard, politicians, top entertainers and loads of locals it's a spot for entertainment.

The Drive in is the perfect spot on the river coast, when you're going and coming from either direction. I mentioned earlier you can stop for refreshment and uses the bathroom for a quick leak male and females' boys and girls the owner is a very nice and polite person. From what I understood loads of delinquent boys would hang out there and would do somethings that was not good for the club reputation or themselves. There were two young men especially, they were well known to the community as area leaders and troublemakers. They convinced themselves that they were the Dons of Dam head. One was known as Taller and the other known as Bagg. They both walked together every day and night and often bullied the club girls and made the patrons inside the club uncomfortable. Most of the times they sold contrabands outside the club, from their respective homes and on the side of the road but never inside the club. One night Taller and Bagg attended the club, they were both drinking and partying just doing their thing. Both men were going around that night like they were looking for trouble, I think they had two much to drink in my opinion. The club got busy and other patrons and party goers started coming in, the night starts out like any other night. This guy and his girlfriend came in to have a drink, I don't know if the guy that just walked in new Taller or Bagg from before but an argument started between them. Within a few minutes the argument got heated and physical, loads of people starts running up and down. No one could stop them, very quickly the guy that came in with his girlfriend was on the ground holding his chest. He was stabbed by the two or one of the two and died. This started a man hunt for the two who were evolved in the stabbing, they were both arrested and charged with his murder. The mother of the deceased came to the club crying her eyes out and said they killed her bread winner. The police investigation brought a lot of heat on the club for a while. The mother of the deceased man said this was not going to end well, that she was not accepting his death this like. She vowed to do anything she could do to see his murders suffer. If it takes sleeping with a monkey or the devil, she will do whatever it takes to get the two culprits in and out of the law. She said she anything necessary even to call up on her god or even an obeah man she would stop at nothing until she got justice for her son. Listen this, they were both incarcerated for a while but not convicted for the crime and will soon be released back to the same community. After their release it was like a dream for the two, but the mother of the deceased man was not stopping at anything either and still craves the revenge due to her son.

They two were out for a while before they start giving more problems. Now this was what really interest me in this story. Bagg bought a car and started driving it around, I must make this clear, the decease mother comes back to the area and did some chants and other ritualistic things and then declared that she is giving him nine days to live. On one of the days Bagg was driving on the gorge road heading towards bog walked. His friend Taller was supposed to be in the car but for some reason he didn't make it to the car, for them to both travel to wherever they were going. Bagg drove for a bit, when he reaches at a particular spot on the stretch of road, out of nowhere came a bolder rolling out of the hills which even bigger than his car. It rolled and rolled until it just drops right on top of his car and smashed him and his car to pieces. The impacted squeezed the top of the car on him like a sandwich, it smashed him out like a presser and then the stone just rolled over in the river. He and the car were there for a while until they came and removed the vehicle. He was compress and crushed out completely they would have to cut the car open to get his remains to be buried. The occurrence leading up to his death was strange but true so that's the end of Bagg.

Taller was freaking out, he was going around and boiling and drinking all kinds of bushes, and going to his own obeah man to reverse whatever curse was put on him. I have seen him myself picking the bushes to do his magic. He was drinking harder than before he went to jail. He was talking a lot about the fatal night in question to his friends. Again, the mother of the deceased visited the area and did her thing once again. Everyone bore witness to this and was looking for what was coming next, looking for the unexpected. People began to warn Taller of the lady's present in the community. He pretends as if it didn't affect him, but you could see that it was wrecking him. One night he had a lot to drink and was sitting around the area drunk as a skunk, talking to himself. Every one carried on as normal, he had a few sisters that dances at the club. He was always hanging around early in the mornings as soon as you open your door you could see him standing outside, or heard his heavy voice roaring from far away. The following night he was doing the same drinking and carrying on as usual. The morning breaks the skies again but this times he was nowhere to be seen nobody takes it as notices until an alarm was made that he can't be found.

This may sound like a joke, but this man drank until he was so drunk, that he fell asleep on the train line. He laid right across the lines; you know what happens from there. Just imagine the site of that in your mind, the train cuts him in three clean pieces. His head was to one side, his torso and the legs were cut off and separated and dragged away by the train. A man said he saw him earlier and wake him up and sent him home, but it seems like he just moved further down and lay somewhere else on the train line. I heard that the deceased mother passed and look at him torn apart then disappeared. She never returned and no one ever saw her again. This was the end to Taller, everyone was saying the mother got her satisfaction and that justice was served. I mean well served too, other people from the area were saying, they wouldn't want to have a disagreement with that woman because they were convinced that this was some real obeah.

I was wondering why out of all the places he could have chosen to fall asleep, why did he fell asleep on the train line. It's not like this was the first time that he has drank too much and became intoxicated. This does not look too good; in my opinion something was wrong. I also think something was missing from this puzzle, I am sure. Some people were implying that someone had killed him and then put him on the train line, that it was just a decoy I don't know.

They also talked about a gold table that comes up in the Rio Cobre, everybody was saying that a golden table comes up every now and then in the river at a particular time of the year it comes up pulling down animals and humans in. It happens from time to time, it's rumoured that people have seen it when it comes up and that people have tried to hold onto it and trying to pull it out of the water. When this happens, the table starts receding, taking with it whatever is touching it under the water, and no one ever saw them again. People have said that the river needs blood sometimes, there are a lot of superstition associated with that river but I myself have never seen a golden table in my life. I've heard many of these stories over the years and it made me wonder if any of it was true. I am even wondering if the earth coming to an end is true.

Still on the Bog walk Gorge stories, one night I go to bed and awoke to heavy rain falls. In the morning all the Island new stations were broadcasting this change in weather. When I looked outside the lane was filled with water. Most of the boys in the area would come outside to play in the water. St Johns road had a lot of gutters that overflowed and caused cars and trucks to breakdown. This particular time the water was very high we all had to go back inside. A quick flick back on the news made me aware of a vehicle that had gone over flat bridge. It was filled with passengers; divers came to their rescue but it's too late. The currents were so strong it washed the vehicle away, it kept going down stream until it finally stopped further down the river. By this time everyone on board was dead. It was tragic and very sad they never stand a chance because of the strength of the water. When the rain subsided everybody in the community heads out there, trying to view the vehicle with all the dead bodies inside. It was a horrendous sight, all the bodies looked water soaked and were swollen, the worse of it all was the sight of a small boy lifeless and pale. Seeing all these things happening, I began to wonder if anything can be done to this bridge because this is something that repeat itself ever so often, year in year out or whenever there was heavy shower of rain. I am not an engineering but even I recognised that something needs to be done about flat bridge. The government of Jamaica needs to investigate what can be done to make this bridge safe for everyone. For the bridge to remain like that it's a disaster waiting to happen, that area was always prone to accidents and will always remain unpredictable if not changed.

Previously I have mentioned that I had three children and was doing all sort of jobs to support them. The easiest form of employment was working on a construction site, you only need to have a shovel and wake up early into the morning to walked around the newly built housing scheme in order to find work. Other were doing the same thing as myself, waking up early walking around looking for work too. As I've explained before I did every and anything on the site to make money because having three kids on board that's a lot of mouths to feed. I've also mention how the construction sites operates, sometimes the men on site will blatantly take your work from you and sometimes it can gets very violent and confrontational so anything can happens at any time.

I got some work to do on one of the sites and started doing it, the job is almost completed, and I was looking forwards to collecting my pay. I asked the man who hired me about my money, and it's started a heated argument. I was approached by this man who gave me the job and now he was saying he was not going to pay the amount of money we agreed upon. Now that the job was finished, he was saying that what we agreed on was over excessive. He'd already agreed to it in the first place before myself and the others even started the job, but now that the work was done and it was time for payment there was a massive argument instead. This situation shows that some people will agree with something if it means they get what they want, but once they get want they want they forget what they'd agreed to prior to getting it. I did mention before that this situation would become my reality.

My Time in The Dark Place

NOW THIS WAS IT COMING MY WAY, STARTING ME IN THE FACE AND WAS going to lead me in a dark place. This was what happened, I had an argument overpay bill (money). This was a regular thing that took place on the construction site, not only with me but with others who worked on construction site anywhere. We had a small misunderstanding, and this mishap will teach me some lifelong lessons, which I will never forget. I will also come face to face and meet and interact with some sick individuals. Some of the things that I found out are thing that I would only hear and read about or heard other people talking about. These stories were so gruesome, some of which I could never imagine or even dream of sometimes like that happening. These stories are not something I wanted to hear but because I was there and others were already talking about it, I had no choice but to listen. From what I can remember some of these stories were so disgusting it churned my stomach.

I will explain how I entered the dark place, what took place inside the darkness of this sad, sick and filthy place. It's filled with strange and sick looking people who were talking about things that made me so uncomfortable, sometimes it sicken me and even made me wanted to threw up. There was a darker side to the one I was about to enter, the darkness was so thick I could almost touch it. I Fell in this position it was a nightmare, it was easy to get in and hard as hell to get out. Your actions alone could grant you access to this place but it would be the decision of other if you are allowed out. Moreover it took a lot of money to get you out of the darkness, only those on the outside like family and friends can help you out or help you cope inside the darkness believe it or not. This place was so strange, it was filled with bright lights inside and outside throughout the year night or day, yet the darkness overshadowed the light. This place is also surrounded by high walls that had barb wire attached to them. The four corners of these walls were very tall you can only look up at the top of it. Inside the wall are another sets of walls which runs alongside them also very high which is similar to the ones I am currently describing. It was only a few feet shorter than the others but still higher than everyone beyond them. It was built so you could also walk between these two walls like a passage. The distance between them was about 15 to 20 feet and about another ten feet away from the second wall, where a third fence one made of metal wire fencing. It was also shorter than the second wall, this metal fencing was designed so that you could see through them. It had some square holes in it about two and a half to three inches wide, all three fences sported razor sharp barb wire at the top of them. The size of this place is about 40 or 50 times the size of a football field it could even be bigger in my opinion. There are also different building insides on the same compound which held some of the strangest names, which made me wonder why those types of names were given to a simple building. That was what I was thinking because I was a stranger to the dark place. Entering the dark place from what I remembered, I entered through the front door, with eyes wide open looking and observing my new surroundings. I recall hearing what sounded like loud crying, loud chatter and heavy banging, all kinds of sounds were coming from insides.

During my observation I noticed that there were dogs, massive ones, barking continuously. Some were sitting, some were laying down in chains, doing the same thing I was doing, which was observing everything and looking at everyone passing through and from inside these walls. I will later discovered that this place housed some dangerous and murderous individual, with some dark secret and sickening stories that will leave you needing counselling after hearing them. I will share a few stories that I heard while in this place. Upon entering this place, I realized that each of these walls and fences I told you about carry its own separate gates and all the building insides carries their own fencing and entrances. Also, the main gate I entered through still have two additional doors behind it. Entering this place with this level of security, I had to asked myself am I really awake or did I just enter a real life nightmare. The fact of the matter was it was no nightmare but my new reality. Everything began to set in motion, the minute I was behind the third door of the entrance, where I am going to be housed insides this man made hell. The room I will be staying in was known as the big room, and it held about sixteen of us all of which were men. I was looking around astonish and wondering how the hell I get inside here and trying my hardest to wake up out of a nightmare I was not having. This building had a lot of other rooms, it also had three landing first, second and third floor. The first thing I saw in the morning when look outside the cage I was in, were the spooky looking individuals around here. I am wondering when this was going to end, even though it's just started. Just imagine the horror of waking up and the first thing you saw in the morning, was a person you had to greeted with no eyes and no legs who ran around on the two small bit and uses is hands to swing around like an animal (monkey or chimp). I saw one legged person, several persons with one arm, there were others with no legs. I saw people that were blind in one or both eyes, persons who had large scars all over their bodies. I saw people with their teeth missing who had broken jaw. I also saw one man with a good portion of his nose cut off. There was another guy with a large hole in the top of his head like an indent, whenever he talks the flesh move up and down. I later learn that he was shot in the head by one of his rivals. People came to talk with me, asking questions trying to find out why I am there. They sometime congregate to talk with each other, and I could overhear their conversations.

There were many other buildings inside the dark place, with some peculiar names, such as green block, west block, south block, and Gibraltar. These names were there for a reason, but I can't tell you off the top of my head. My mind was on the verge of breaking down, but I am trying to be strong and maintain my sanity. My best bet is to try and leave this place in one piece, just as I came in, but while I am at it I'll need to grow balls of steel and stand my ground to be able to dealt with all who surrounds me here. I have never seen so many people lost their mind or go mad so easy in my whole life. As I transition from being free in the light, I started to venture all around the darkness. I spoke with a few guys, who told me they attended the same school I did. I have seen people insides the dark place, that I didn't even knew were still alive. In my head they were just missing from the picture, now I know where they were. I can see they are all wanting to go home, and anxious to leave this dark place just like me, or trying their hardest like myself, to wake up out of a dream they were not in. Sometimes when I looking at these walls and metal fencing and these insane individuals the darkness becomes even more dark. These are the days when I'm at my lowest, this whole mess up situation is trying its hardest to fuck with my sanity. However the further into the darkness I go, I realized that losing my mind is a possibility.

I entered a place call New Hall, in the building called Gibraltar, a friend I knew from a long time ago lived insides there and he invited me over. I would have to get permission from someone in charge, in order to leave my room and visit someone else's premises, inside the darkest part of the darkness which can still be found inside the dark place. I will get back to the darkest place shortly. Back in my room which is the big room, I'm still trying to familiarise myself with my new surroundings. While observing, I look up and saw a bit of newspaper stuck to the wall. I had nothing else to do, so to keep my mind occupied and relaxed I would read almost anything my eyes could see. I stood up straightaway and started to read the paper on the wall Which is known as the star.

I then heard a gruff voice out of nowhere shouted out something, which I did not hear clearly, however it drew my attention and I looked over in the direction immediately to where I thought the sound was coming from. After scanning across the room for a minute, I didn't hear the sound again, so I continued reading the star. What I was reading was really interesting, so I went closer to the wall, to see the words that made every sentences written in the star more clearly. My mood changed and I became so quiet, that the curiosity could be seen on my face clearly. The story l was reading about had both my eyes stuck on the paper like super glue. I was so captivated by the story that I decided to read it all off. From what I was reading, I became so focus on this piece of the news, that I didn't even realize that almost everyone in the room was staring at me. I felt a light touch from behind me, and then a hand resting on one of my shoulders. After Feeling this touch on my shoulder, I have no choice but to quickly look around, to see who it was that was touching me or find out what was going on behind my back. To how fast I spun around, it was obvious that I was being watched by everyone. They all burst out laughing at the same time, they found it was funny because they thought I was frightened. Bare in mind, I was in a place where my mind and body was not contented one bit, for the past how many days I've entered inside this place of darkness. The person who was touching my shoulder looked really familiar. We were both looking at each other, starting each other in the face and eyes. I am now wondering why the heck was this man touching me, but before I could ask the question, he beats me to it by asking, what was it that was so interesting that made me stand up and walked closer to the piece of paper on the wall. He then whispered in a low voice saying, he saw my face almost touching the paper glued to the wall. He also said that he'd observed me reading it, like I knew who and what the script in the star was talking about and that the way I was reading it, everyone took notice and began watching me.

Honestly, I knew of the story in the paper, but I didn't let on like I've heard of it before. I was being scrutinized for how intently I was reading, but to be honest if anyone else had seen the story I was reading trust me they would show the same interest as me. Anyone that came across this story "Cave man style rapist captured", would read and reread this story so that they don't miss a bit of information regarding this. This was what drew my attention to the paper on the wall and made me started reading it so attentively. Now, with this man standing before me, my mind reflect back on the conversations I had with a few people, who said they use to attend Friendships all age school. Suddenly recognition dawns, and we both realized that we were class mates from school. We started to have a conversation with each other straight away. We also talk briefly, about what's on the wall in the star. We continued to reminiscing until the conversation reaches back at school, from grade one straight back to grade six, where we both leave that school, and I moved on to the Spanish town secondary school.

Recognizing who each other were, we both smiled and greeted each other with a big hug. We shouted each other names at the same time. I said Onney, and he replied yes, and he asked is it really you Byron. I said yes and straight away we both started thumping off each other fist meaning (spud). Soon after we began to build back our friendship and trust. Everything was well with us, from that day he wouldn't leave my side one bit because I was new to the darkness. We both remembered the last time we saw each other, in the last year of school. This man turns out to be the strange behaving boy I describe earlier, that was in my class. He came to school with runny nose, he carried one book in his back pocket, he had loads of broken out sores in is head and he even brought a knife to school sometimes. I said to myself shit this was really Onney, I was picturing him from way back in school, the only thing that changed about him was his body. He was looking a bit tough and thick, but is face and head remain the same. His image remained the same he hadn't changed much at all trust me. The only difference about him was, his nose had stop running, there was hardly any sores, and his face was more mature and weathered like he'd experienced really hardship. They say old habits die hard, which was true in this case because he had a knife inside here, and a makeshift ice pick too. He even offered to give me one of the two weapons he had, said that I could chose the one I wanted, but straight away I refused it even though he tried to convince me of the benefit of having a weapon in the dark place.

I must admit I didn't like how he was pressuring me to take it, knowing the consequences if caught with a weapon. This place of darkness was not a nice place, I have seen it for myself. He started telling me how long he had been inside the dark place and how long he will have to stay there. He told me about things that can happen and began telling me of some really dreadful things he has seen since he started residing in the dark place. Listening to him was not a problem, what he had told me was true also, but getting caught with anything of the sort that he was offering me was a totally different story. I would be in real trouble with the dark angles, the ones who keeps and over sees the day to day running of the dark place. I would be or might end up in the hospital inside here, with somewhere on me badly damage, or some broken body parts broken, an arm or a leg. They will even knock your teeth out, that's how badly you will get beaten if caught. I have seen it happen more than once. They loved instilling fear by threatening you, promising these types of severe punishment. These Angeles who controls the darkness and makes the rules of the dark place were very wicked. They wore one specific costume, they even had different ranks. One person was in charge of the whole darkness every bit of it, he wore a different colour to the other angels. His costume was army green, whenever he walked around the darkness and visits its inhabitants, everybody got afraid including the Angeles that worked for him. His presence made everyone shook, like a child doing something bad and got caught by the parents. This person was the head of evil inside here, he didn't talk much he didn't walked fast either, his movements were like that of a sloth. Looking in his eyes was pure evil, every one cleared the way whenever he approached, myself and the others that resides here. The dark angel all walked with a piece of stick, which they won't hesitate to use and inflict wounds on you, which can even kill you depending on where the blow connects the individual on their bodies. Getting acquainted with this place was an eye opener. After settling down inside the dark place, the things I have seen, and the entire experience have change me completely. The place of darkness is governed by rules if you break them, you get a flogging, that will make you piss and shit yourself, most time you will ended up with somewhere broken or a few teeth knocked out of your mouth. The brutal way in which they beat you, when they were finished most of the time that person couldn't get up off the ground, and they'd also be covered in blood. This might sound gruesome that was how things were done, the way life was inside the dark place.

Having various conversations with Onney had enlighten me on everything. The depravity, and the way in which we lived inside here was just inhumane. There were no toilets in these rooms, you had to shit in a piece of cut off drum, that was used as a makeshift toilet. The piece of drum had to be emptied every morning. The Barford was another name for a toilet, was made right inside here, by some of the same residence who lived in the dark place. The Barford is also use as rubbish bin too. The Barford has two steel handles, which is weld onto it by someone who also resides here. The men who are going to be taking out the Barford wakes very early to do this each day. It's important that the Barford goes out early each morning to be cleaned and ready for use later. The men use this as a way to get out of the room and stay outside for a bit. Anyone who carries out the Barford got to stay outside the room and hang out side on the balcony for most of the day, looking over the walls onto the roads just outside a popular primary school and across from a popular church as well.

119

This part of the balcony is called the video you could see men sitting and waiting patiently to see someone they know, or a family member will come there just to talk with them. That was one of the reason everyone wanted to the task of taking out toilet in the morning. This task was no easy feat, the Barford was filled with rubbish and everybody's shit from late evening to early morning. Your stomach had to be iron clad to endure the stench of stale shit, it smells real horrible in the morning trust me, it does. The interesting thing when it came to bedtime was the sleeping arrangements. Men were sleeping in the ceiling in hammocks and the ground were covered with the other occupants. Just imagine fifteen or sixteen people in a ten-by-ten room with no bed or nothing to sleep on. The floor is share for bed spots, each person had a piece of cardboard or a piece of sponge to rest on. Now the interesting thing was how they came by the sponge and the cardboard or other contraband like knives, ice-pick, weed, cigarettes lighters amongst other things, were all sold to them by the same wicked Angeles. They are the ones who enforces the rules in the darkness, which made it even darker to me. The go as far as to supply the white stuff to the ones who uses it, once they can afford it, I was told.

This place is really dark and getting even darker to me. I am aware of what's going on, and to my understanding if you've been here for a period of time, you come to learn even more about even the Angeles inside here. This makes me even more nervous, it's just keep on coming and coming your mind is constantly in operations, no rest or relief from this turmoil. Some people live normal as if they loved it and behave Like they were born here, but not me. My mind was on the outside. Outside in the yard, off the building we were in, there was a bathroom about the same size as the room in which we lived. It had a few showers pipelined out on the wall, about five to six persons can line out and have a shower. Same as how the pipes are set out on the wall, there was also a place where you can stand and piss with a few toilet lined out the same as the shower on the wall. All of this, I described was not closed up. It was wide open so that the Angeles can stand and watch every person, when they are using the toilets, the showers, or the urinal area. I came to realize you can have a shower outside, take a shit and a piss but all this had to be done at a certain time of the day when you are outside of your room.

If you were in the shower and you had soaps on your body, and the Angeles said time is up, you had to come out of the shower and go back to your rooms with the soap on your skin. Even if you were doing a number two the meaning in bracket (doing a shit) and the Angeles said the time is up you had to stop shitting straight away, and move with that un finish shit inside your bottom. They don't care about you not one bit, they only wanted to know that when they make their count, everyone was in the building that's supposed to be there. If they had to shout out to anyone more than two or more times, to finish and for everyone to go inside their rooms, then this could cause you or someone to be nursing a broken bone or dressing a few swollen parts on your body, no jokes. Whenever you were speaking to any of the angels you must use (Mr or Mrs) to address the angel or else you'll share the same faith as others with, a slap with that stick they all walks with inside the dark place. This place is just filled with darkness, you just learn more and more each day. I saw men inside here with two to three hundred thousand dollars every day and even more than that sometimes. I just wanted to remind you that all these items they had inside here such as the (money, rizzlers, knives, ice-pick, weed and the white stuff) was all illegal for anyone to have in their possession.

Also be mindful that the occupants were selling this stuff for the angels. Some people can afford to get caught with them, because they were protected by the same angles, who said these very same items were illegal. Inside this place is really making me sick and I really can't wait to leave here, like right now. This shit is not for me, no way. My only way out of this dark place, was left in the hands of my older sister Remy. This will take a bit of time to process, because she is always busy working, and it is a sticky position I am in. It's like I'm sitting in limbo, the only thing I could do is let time takes it course. I should be out of here, hopefully, it just a matter of waiting.

After Onney tried again to convince me to carry a weapon, which I refused we started talking about a few other thing. We started talking about him. He began telling me about a guy who taught him how to rob and sexually assaults women. He never hesitates to start talking he found it funny. He also stated the guy who taught him this tactic, was a Rasta man from Mayfield Avenue in Kingston. I listen to him carefully, just to make sure if what he was saying makes sense, or if it is even true.

I asked him questions about what was on the wall in the star, he explained it briefly, saying he was trying to hold a girl, but for some reason he stop talking because someone had come in the room, and started staring at him. That made him stopped talking about that situation instantly. He then began telling me another story. He said he sometimes had sex with two or three women in one night. This was what he explained to me, how the man from Maxfield avenue showed him, how to go about it. He said they get a solid stone and put it in the foot of a pants and used a wire know on construction site as binding wire, which was used to ties steel together. He said they used the wire to wrap the stone in the pants foot, then twisted the pants foot and bind it properly with the wire. This was during the early nineties. A lot of crime was happening, especially rape during that time. Every weekend after a dance was finished, the stone man or Oily, as he was called would wait on the girls, who would said they were leaving the dance early because they were scared of the stone man. This guy was known as the stone man who knocks his victims with something hard over their heads, almost killing them. Sometimes if the women were walking with their partners, he takes pleasure in knocking the men in their heads and then goes after the females. He would wait on them, because he lived locally, and knew everyone and their route that they were going to took home. So, he waited patiently for them in the nearby bushes, naked as the day he was born.

He also said he uses something on is private part to make him hard and have a long-lasting erection. Which helps him not to ejaculates quickly. Hearing him telling me this made my damn stomach sick, but I just listen to him out. Trust me, I couldn't stand him one bit either, because I have two sisters that I love dearly, but as you know we were class mates from school. I kept it as normal to the best I can he was disgusting. He kept smiling when he was talking, but little does he know I was searching for evidence, because he had also attacked my son's god mother. She narrowly escaped him by wrestling him off and screaming out loudly which made him let her go and ran away. She was from old harbour road; she now resides overseas. I was now aware that this man, my classmate was the infamous stone man, but the other occupants of the dark place was still unaware of who he really was. He was only popular as Onney or Short man. He had confirmed something I knew about from before I entered the dark place. There was talks of a girl who bit him in his chest and also of another girl who stab him in the chest almost killing him. I asked him this question how he could even get an erection in a situation like that. I don't know how he doesn't read my body language and realized I'm disgusted by him.

The feeling from the information overload was giving me shortness of breath. He was killing me just by talking to him not to mention his breaths smells awful. I could tell that he enjoyed telling me this, I stayed silent trying to fight back the bile rising from my throat. I felt like I wanted to vomit. This guy, I was begging him to stop talking in my mind. Then he drops the bombshell on me, he told me he saw a girl talking to someone he knew. He said he joined them in the conversation, the woman was talking about how she wanted to head home early because she is scared of the stone man. He said he was like yeah; you are not going nowhere tonight. He said he was ready, that he had already stoned up his penis, so he could perform anywhere he gets a chance to grab a girl and fuck her off. I'm glad I did not take the knife or ice-pick from him because I might do the wrong thing. He told me that he once saw a girl who attended the St Catherine high school, he said he followed behind her, but she got away. He said he just wanted to fuck her so bad because she looked so good.

Continuing the conversation with Onney, I knew he was the one doing all those things. That piece of shit, when he mentioned the girl from St Catherine high school, my head felt like it was going to explode. My sister, the one that I mentioned earlier, she was the only hope I had to get out of this dark place, she was attending that school. So, when he mentioned that school girl, my sister flashed in front of my face. Onney was not a person I would want to see outside the darkness of the dark place. He goes on telling me how a girl bites him in his chest almost biting the nipple off his chest. He showed me the bite on the left side. I then saw a cut almost next to the bite looking like a hole, a burn or even a bullet entry wound just small dot. I asked him about it, he said that one night he held a hairdresser gal, his own word. He then explains how he grabbed her hands and was trying to get her to be quiet, by holding her mouth. He said she was not having it, he said she dipped in her handbag and came up with scissor, she then screamed out and gave him one stab in his chest.

He said, he grabbed the area, and he was going to fuck her up, but the wound was burning him badly and his chest was getting tight. He told me he had no choice but to let her go and run. He said he'd almost died, that he went to the hospital because he was not feeling good. He told me he took a taxi to the hospital, that the doctors remove is shirt by cutting it off him. He said he felt unconscious due to blood lost. He also said that the doctor told him when he woke up and regained consciousness, that he had internal bleeding, and that he was lucky that he came when he did or he would be finished. I am like yes dinner was served. He said as soon as he felt fit enough after a few days, he discharged himself from out the hospital and off the ward. He said he thought he might get arrested because the doctors were asking him questions, about how he came by this wound. He explained how close he came to death and how close the doctors saying it was to his Heart, and what they had to do to stop the internal bleeding. He said he felt some pains he can't describe. I was saying in my mind, that was what you are giving out to people now you taste a bit of what you are serving. In other words, he got a taste of his own medicine, good. I was definitely sure who he was now, so that was what led him to the dark place, at least that's what I thought. That dirty son of a bitch stone man, I hope he resides here for the rest of his life.

Onney also show me a room that was closed up properly, no one lived there anymore. I took a peek, inside there looked like a voicing room on a studio. I realized that one of our national heroes was also residing here for a short while in the dark place. That room was like a museum, no other tenant was allowed inside there anymore. That hero was a civil rights leader and was well known across the world as one of Jamaica's national heroes. His title was the right honourable Marcus Garvey. I don't know the reason why he was a tenant inside the dark place.

It didn't stop there, he asked me if I knew a guy called Thumper. I ask who and he started to describe who Thumper was. I told him yes, he said he resides here as well. I asked him where he said he would take me where he was. This will get even darker than it was. When I met up with Thumper who resides in the darkest part of the darkness, this place was called New Hall. Inside New Hall was pitch black, the darkness of this place was so dark it even smells of the death. This place that reeks of death was called also a Gibraltar. Anyone living in Gibraltar was a walking dead, if you know what I mean. When I entered Gibraltar, I paid attention to any and everything I saw. Just the looks on the residence faces inside New Hall and all the tenants faces of Gibraltar, Jesus Christ, it touch my heart. Listen, the occupants were another story. They all looked broken and hopeless, like they have no will to survive. I spoke with quite a few of the residents, I will share some of the discussion I had with the residents of Gibraltar, so listen up.

I was glad to hear from someone who was willing to talk. When I finally met up with Thumper, my eyes filled with waters because he was someone I knew from before, he was familiar. He was my eldest sister Sadie's good friend. Sadie was the eldest of the two sisters and the eldest of all my seven other siblings. There were eight of us two sisters and six brothers. Marlon Grant was his name, but he was better known to me as Thumper. He came across and greeted me, even the man I knew as the stone man was shocked because of the greetings I received by Thumper. God, I was in deep shit already as you know depending on my sister Remy get me out of this mess I was in. However, I was face to face with a man who was in even more shit than I was in. He was in a truck load of it so to speak. Emotions got the better of us, but Thumper had never discussed how he ended up insides the dark place. Thumper had introduced me to a few of his friend or neighbours, who resides here in the darkest part of the darkness. The darkest part of the darkness was where everyone insides there was to live out their last days or in other words they were there to died or be killed in due course. After we gladly hug each other, he shouted out you are Sadie's little brother. I said yes, however he also mixing me up with one of my younger brother Delving. Based on what he was saying I knew straight away that he recognised me. He started asking me for my two sisters. In my opinion, I realize he likes my eldest sister I could even go as far as to say he loved her off. I was in a place that I never dreamt I could walk a place like this in all my life. That I would even live to see and hear these types of things, I'm going to repeat especially from inside the place called Gibraltar. First, I will inform you of the last sighting of Thumper and where it had happened. This will not be a good story but listen carefully.

The last time before I met Thumper inside the dark place, was a few years before we were both in the dark place. It was the summer of nine teen eighty-nine, when all the school were on holiday. Both of my sisters were home, you already know they're both older than me. My eldest sister Sadie was a hairdresser and was well known for that. Every now and then she and my other sister Remi would put on a few bus trips to several different beaches across the Island. Everyone loved these trips and enjoyed those day out sometimes after work or during the school holidays. These were the days when everybody lived as one, no matter who they were and where they came from or the community in which they lived. Things like that was never an issue. Life and time have really changed, looking back on where we are all coming from and where we are now, you couldn't afford to trust people not even your neighbours. Looking back on how the adults in our community used to live back in comparison to today, it's evident that a lot as really changed. Even the youths of today, how they are, how they behave, willing to maul each other to death, it is a total mess. I would call it a real nightmare.

So my sisters had plans a beach trip to Hellshire beach in the summer of eighty nine. They couldn't get a bus this time, so they opted to use two taxis instead to make the trip, one of which Thumper would be driving. The other driver refuses to do the trip because of the price and went away. So Thumper called one of his friend who was also a taxi driver, to do trip with him and make to the runs to Hellshire. His friend that turned up was known as Sheela, he had a feminine name for a male, but anyway he turned up. We were all introduced to Sheela, who came to discuss the price with my sister and willingly took the charter, as it called. I didn't know how much they had bargained for, but I knew for sure all went well and everyone got to the beach. It was a good day, everyone had fun and returned home in good health, with the help of God. Just to make it clear that was the last time I had seen Sheela or Thumper. Soon after a shocking news started going around.

That a man by the very same name we had gone to the beach with, about a week ago had been killed or found dead, one of the two. He was also a taxi operator, I never put the effort in finding out, if it was the same person and which taxi it was.

Back to Thumper and insides the dark place known. Thumper resides in the darkest part of the darkness known as Gibraltar. We spent a lot of time together, myself, him, Onney and a few other friends. Thumper started asking about my sisters, just like I suspected, he let the puss out of the bag. He told me he liked my eldest sister, but she wouldn't give him the time of day, meaning no attention. Said she told him she didn't like him like that. Continuing insides, the dark place, by certain time of the evening each day, I had to go back to where I resides in the darkness. I was young and new to this lifestyle, so I was treated with that kind of respect luckily. I was called juvenile, youngster, little youth, youth man, youthy, all these names, because of my age. It showed in my face that I was young, I was only 23 year of age not very old, compared to my fellow house mates, who had years on me. I was an adult, but to them I was still a youth. Anyone over the age of eighteen is considered an adult according to the government. I was over the age of eighteen at the time but that was how older people regard young people in those days.

The three of us lived like brothers inside there. Every day as soon as morning lights, we got in touch with each other, looking out for each other. We shared whatever we had insides there. Onney and I reside in the same room, so we are mostly around each other in the darkness. I was a bit lucky I told myself, because Thumper cooked and offered me food every day. The food that he made was good. What the Angeles were giving us to eat was unbelievable. Thumper offered me curry chicken back and dumplings, with yellow yam and some soursop juice, which he makes insides here. There were no soursop trees inside that place, so I don't know how he got the soursop to make juice inside the dark place. The juice was really nice, it was well made. Before I inform you about who I met and who I was introduced to by Thumper, let me tell you about the food preparation, the sanitation, who prepared it for the angels and how it was prepared. Also, the type of food prepared insides the dark place. Callaloo was served very often with crushed

127

Bananas. First listen this, I must let you know there were loads of cats around the dark place, they breed and had plenty kittens.

The place was infested with cats and all these cats lived in the darkness, in the storeroom where they stored the Callaloo. The Callaloo was called puss bed inside here, because the cats slept on it. Not only did they sleep on the Callaloo, but they did everything you know cats do on top of the Callaloo, this include shitting and pissing and that was what we were eating insides the dark place. There was no difference with the bananas, it was also stored in a room, and they would use some of the occupants of the dark place to crushed them and got them ready to put in the copper to cook. Listen, the process in which this was done would churn your stomach. The men would put on these long water boots on their feet and jump up in the drum of bananas. Four or five of them would place the bananas in a bath, and then they all jumped on them to break them up. They were boiled in a thing called the Copper. This was used every day repeatedly. The tenants of the dark place that were there to die, all looked like zombies, a few of them looked normal. Some were skinny, their pants waist tied with a string to keep it from falling, their heads looked over sized and big, their eyes were sunken in holes, their cheeks hollow and their knees were bigger than their thighs. They all looked like they were mal nourish, trust me.

All those who were getting ready to died, had to wear full white suits, so they could be easily recognize anywhere they were in the yard. which was also known as the grass where everyone linked up most time to exercise and socializes with each other. Also, some take it as an opportunity to attack each other too believe it, they do. They harmed themselves with all types of weapons you name it and it was there insides the dark place. The Angeles had a special piece of tool or equipment, it was cleaned every week early in the morning. This was used to put them to death, any occupants when his time came, and they couldn't do or say anything. They had to die because that was what they were there for, nothing more nothing less. These occupants were like walking dead or zombies, they wouldn't hesitate to kill you either because they had nothing to lose, they already knew their fate.

Every week, this instrument or killing tool as I would call it, would be cleaned. You could hear it being tested and cleaned weekly without fail (blang blang blang). It was very loud, my heart bleeds for these guys, knowing what was to come. The Angeles treated these men very badly and reminded them constantly, that they were there for only one reason and that was to die. It was a sad story, because they had given up on life, the will to live and places to be. Gibraltar was no joke, if you ended up there, then you know it was only a matter of time before your life was no more. Even in death there was no escape, no freedom because when they were killed or died, they were buried right beside the kitchen in the dark place.

Bear in mind the occupants would have to bury the dead as well. The angels would just come for them when it was their time was to die. They would give them anything they requested or wanted to eat or drink. Any messages they wanted to send to family and friends. That was it is for them, when the clock strikes on their time, their necks will be broken (blang) with one slam on the tick of the clock. This I was told by a man who had seen several of his friends made that walk with the Angeles to never returned. He said he had also helped to bury a few of them, and that he knew some day he would meet the same fate, and someone will help bury him too. Just like that my belly moved, when he said that trust me. Personally, I have never seen it for myself. I was not in the dark place at that time, when a show like that was going on. Thanks to God, may all their souls rest in peace.

Back to some of Thumper friends he introduced me too and their respective stories. These individuals, I mean all the occupants of the dark place were from all over the island of Jamaica, all fourteen parishes. Some were there from abroad too, in the darkness for many reasons. The people or person who could take you out of the light and put you in the dark looks very much like people from plays or movies we saw on T.V. The men and women both wore glasses and long black gowns that reached their ankles and curly white Wigs, that was long and hangs down their shoulders and backs. They all used a little wooden hammer on their desks in front of them they would knocks it to get silence or to speak to the persons who brought you to them, in front of these weird dressing people. They all work together, one organisation working for one common goal.

Back to the occupant of Gibraltar. After going back and forth from Gibraltar every day, my friend would cook food and leave it for me. He was like a father. I started giving money towards the food for my dinner. It helped to purchase, yellow yam and chicken back, that was the thing in the dark place. These guys were able to cook in their room, let me explain to you how it was done. Zinc from the roof was used to make pots or they use milk or orange juice boxes. For the stove the would use the metal wires from the mosquito destroyer to connect to wires from a radio transformer as a conduit for electricity from the florescent light bulb in the ceiling to get current, which they connect to a makeshift hot plate, that they use to cook soup, fried chicken boiled dumplings, boiled eggs, orange skin tea and even toast. All the ingredients to make all these foods were sold from the canteen in the dark place. Also, the smoke and fumes from the destroyer would chase away the mosquitos. Despite all this, every time I tried to get comfortable in my new surroundings, mind flashes back in the light, to my life before. I can't stand it inside here, seeing this place and these guys, how they lived, really put things into protective giving you something real to think about in this dark place. I began wondering when am I going to leave this place, sometimes I think lord I don't want to wake up, but you can't sleep for ever that only happens one way, if you're dead and I am definitely a live and we'll thanks to God.

While in the dark place I began to see and meet some infamous killers I have heard about from when I was younger. I have heard about them on the news, and from people talking about them too. These killers that were residing in Gibraltar, I have spoken to a few of them on the grass, while going back and forth from their place to mine. Some of them address me as youth or just say hello. There was this one particular guy that approached me and asked how long I've known Thumper. I told him that I have known him for a long time. He said that he can see that Thumper checks for me and that He thought we were family because we resemble each other slightly.

We began speaking on a regular and he started telling me about his time in the dark place and that he's been here for a long time, that he was sent here to die. He said that he dreamt of leaving the dark place and that he has written to the ones who govern life and death part of the darkness, because that was his only chance of getting out. I personally was over this place and was just as eager to leave. My sister had sent me some good new, that I was longing to hear for a while. I was just killing time and waiting on that special day to come, for me to wake up out of this dream, or more accurately a nightmare. That day will be the day I'm free from this place. The only way out of the darkness was the same way you enter. You will have go back in front of the same organisation that put you there in the first place. You will have someone representing you, speaking on your behalf, this can take days, weeks or months before its decided if you leave or not. Meanwhile I wait I will continue telling you about my time there.

This man I mention earlier started giving me details of what goes down in Gibraltar and how the death procedure was carried out. I listen to him carefully because this information I didn't want to miss. He began by saying the angels are more strict in this part of the dark place. He said whenever someone was scheduled to die, they make arrangements and a time was booked for the next day. He said everything was done on time and not a minute over. For example if someone was scheduled to die at twelve, it had to be twelve o clock on the dot not a minute more or less, he also said the angels would tie both of their pants foot. The reason for this, what he told me made my stomach quiver. As I listen to this man speak, known to me and around the dark place as Blacks, only the angels will know his correct name or if he wishes to tell it to you. I on the other hand was not interested in his correct name, what I was interested in was what he had to say.

I continued listening to him, he told me that on the day scheduled for someone to die, about five or six angels would come for them. They will take the person either by will or force. I was told that if a person tried to resist, then they will grab them when they least expect it. They will suddenly start mistreating them, roughly punching them in their bellies several times. This I was told stop their breath causing them to gasp for air, and fold them self into a ball. They sometimes proceed to hitting them in their backs, like they were trying to kill them. He went on to say that when they were pleading for them to stop or even tried to talk, they will start to choke them with that stick that they walk with. They would use that stick to put pressure on their throats by the time they were finished with them, all their strength had left their bodies. They wouldn't have the energy to even walk by d. The a are angels

131

would just lift them up and carry them to where they meant to be. He said two Angeles would be to the left and two to the right side, one in front and one behind. He also informed me that, sometimes when the angels came for them, they could be heard from a far walking towards the room and speaking among themselves. Saying things they knew they could hear, telling them that they were going to die and that they should have died along time. He said that most of the guys would put up a fight, so by time they reached the place of death they were partially dead he said. As for the ones that followed willingly without a fight, they sometimes mess themselves at the realisation of what was about to happen before they reach that dark and sad place.

I can only imagine the dreaded fear that stunk to the pits of their stomach and that horrible feeling they felt knowing what's to come. When the machine of death start to operate making all that noise, the loud sound of metal on metal banging and banging, like a signal to say death is here. He told me that whoever the person was that was strung to the machine, you just knew he was dead from you hear that metal sound. He said once the neck was broken the man hanging from the machine would discharged or piss and shit himself at the same time repeatedly. All that mess ran down and settled in the foot of the pants, that why it was tied. The dead man would be taken away and buried behind the kitchen, or the body given to family members if it was claimed. This was something the Angeles would laugh and chats about for the next day, week or months to come. They would repeat what the man said and did before he died to his friends. Giving details of his last moment like a taunt, talking about it like they enjoyed it, like it gave them a buzz, without no empathy for the deceased.

My mind was in a mess by the time he finished talking. This was going to prevent me from sleeping, I would not wish this on anyone, not one bit. We ended the conversation because he said, he was going to have a shower before it gets too late. Blacks as he was called was from a Kingston address but now resides in Gibraltar in the darkest part of darkness. Bear in mind that anyone residing in Gibraltar was waiting to die, it was only a matter of when.

Walking back to my room from visiting Blacks, I heard someone shouted behind me "juvenile, juvenile". I looked around and saw a heavily bearded man shouting out to me, but I paid him no mind. I continued walking but decided to look around again. When I looked, I realized he standing almost next to me saying (waah gwaan). Meaning what's going on. I recognised him as someone who called to me before and we had exchange very few words. This man known to me only as John, asked if I smoked, I said no. Even after saying no, he still proceeds to begs me a cigarette. I am aware that I have been seen in the presence of persons who smoked, but he had never seen me actually smoking, of that, I am sure. I am puzzled, wondering what the hell he was saying, while I observed him closely.

On closer inspection I could now clearly identify who he was. Even though he was heavily bearded, I knew him. Those high cheek bones, his eyes that were sat in holes and his three front teeth that were missing, two from the bottom and one from the top was a dead giveaway. Not a sight that was easily forgotten. Most of the tenants in Gibraltar were missing teeth, they all dressed in white and looked the same as all the others. The hair on his head was spikey and thick, it also had a bit of length, but I know he was not a Rastafarian. I was curious to what he had to say, he saw me all the time going back and forth to see Thumper, he clearly wanted to talk so I listen to what he had to say. He asked me how old I was, where I am from and how I reach the dark place. I answered all his questions, he then asked about my family. I told him a bit about my family, he even asked about my sisters. A bit put off by his questioning, I answered him correctly even though I wasn't too keen to talk in that moment, but I still listened to him. He was not trusting anyone but himself, however he saw me listen to the others, may he think I'd listen to his life tales too. I told him I can't stay long with him; I made that clear. He started talking and my heart pains again because this man only puts me in the same position I have been with the other occupant of Gibraltar.

He began telling me about an accident that occurred while he was scolding his child. He said the child was crying and making loads of noise, and it woke him out of a deep sleep. He said he jumped up shouting at the child to be quiet, but she ran away and started making even more noise. He told me he got up and grabbed the child and started shaking her, bringing her back to bed. He said she started twisting and wriggling, trying to fight him off, because she wanted to do her own thing. He said he tried to calm her down but she continued to struggle against him and refused to listen to him. He said they were both in their feelings and were both getting angry. He told me after shaking her a few more times and putting her down, she started again crying for no reason again. Shocked by this, I asked him where was the mother, he replied by saying she was not home at the time. He said all through the night she carried on crying, even though he did everything he could to make her stop. He said by this point he was very tired and upset, so he grabbed her by the legs and swung her. With him holding her by the legs, she was hanging upside down, he said he heard a bang and then a slight sound like a grunt from the child. I immediately asked him, how old was this child, he answered by saying she about two years of age. I don't know if it was shock or disbelief that made me speechless. I could not believe what he was telling me, but it touch me in such a way that it made makes me cry. I don't know why I choose stop and listen, I should have just said hello and went my way. He said when he heard the grunt, it was then he had realised what had happened. He said the little girl head had smash into the solid concrete wall and split open like a water melon. He said there was so much blood running from her head, it was even coming from her nose and mouth. I was outrage by what he was telling me, wondering why the fuck he could even think to handle a child like that, let alone swinging her with such force for that to happen. I was just watching him, looking at him telling me he was so sorry. I was trying to figure out if this fucker had done it on purpose, or if it was a genuine accident. Even if It was, he deserve to rot in hell for how he handle the child. He carried on telling me the rest of the story, said that he called someone with a car to take her to the hospital, but when the driver showed up and saw the state of the child, he began vomiting. He said the driver cried out saying that she looked as if she died long time, because of the state she was in and that it looks like her body was starting to swell. He said he didn't know what to do. He said because of this accident he had lost everything, it had cost him is family and his friends, because he couldn't explain this to anyone. He told me this was not something that could be listened out by anyone, it was just too sad and gruesome. He goes on to say it wasn't something he likes to remember. He turned to face me and saw that tears were in my eyes and asked if I was ok. How could I be after listening to one of the worst things imaginable. However, I answered yes. Trust me you know this fucker had the nerves to look at me and asked if I can related. This dark place, have some sick fucks dwelling inside here.

I already told you, I cannot stomach some of these story from these individuals, but I am here, so I will just have to listen, while these fuckers tried to purge their guilt. I asked him what happened afterwards, he looks me straight in the eyes with a strange look on his face and didn't say another word to me. After a few minutes of silence, I just walked away and said see you around John. He was of a Spanish town and also a West Kingston addresses.

Now this story I am about to share, I heard it on the radio when I was younger. It was about a man who ate people. Yes, I meant real human beings, I even heard it in a song. Remember I told you about Gibraltar, well it had the most diverse and disturbing sets of individuals anyone could ever imagine crossing path with. I was about to encounter him for the first time, he too was also a permanent resident of Gibraltar and I was about to have my first chat with a real life cannibal. One day I went to meet my friend as usual on the grass. This man out of nowhere said to me "your friend is down there", I look in the direction he pointed but I never saw him where he pointed. I still look, I even walked down in that direction to see if he was there. After searching without finding him, I was told to check back shortly, which I did. I found him there, he said he'd been back for an hour. We met up like before, we chatted like normal I got some food and then went back to just chilling and sleep. The next morning I got up thinking about my sisters and family, it hit me how much I missed them. I am planning to go by Gibraltar, so after I brushed my teeth I walked out on the balcony.

There were loads of occupants outside looking over the walls, where a lot of females walked past each day. They called out to the women, saying all kinds of stuff, that makes them laugh. This occurs regularly almost every morning. Everyone gathered together to look over the wall, sometime your family members would pass by the area, or you could ask someone to pass and see you there, asked them for a lighter to light a cigarettes or a tobacco. I saw this man sitting on

135

the balcony, he looked a little distant to me just sitting by himself. He was an old enough man, and I was an open-minded youth insides the darkness, just going about until I can leave. I was not the same person as I was before I entered the dark place. I now knew how to navigate around the darkness by myself, and I can do a bit for myself. Which was good, because constantly walking with someone else or hanging around groups can posed as a treat on you in this place. The tenants of dark place have a way to just surprised you, it takes nothing for them to initiate a fight or any other violent attacks on each other's. Inside the dark place is also filled, with talented occupant as well as some infamous killers, rapist, robbers. All type of tenant are in this place, people from your early school days, people you knew from church, even doctor and lawyers, police and soldiers. I remember one lawyer especially he is a Rastafarian and he was also in the dark place for a while and just like any other tenants of the darkness they are treated the same way.

Now this man, the one that keeps his distance from everyone was called Wesman, because of the parish he was from. People had all kinds of name inside here, some of the names even sounds funny and I don't think they make sense. For instance, here are a few of the weirdest names I've ever heard someone being called. One man was called batty hole, one was pussy lip and the other shit house. I was curious and had to wonder what the person did to earn such a moniker, sound funny but it's true. Other names were there but those stood out the most and I just wanted to keep it brief. This Wesman, has a big machete looking weapon, that he carried around and didn't leave it at no time. I have seen him talking to himself sometimes, but after speaking with him a few times, I realized he was ok, but because others saw him speaking to himself, they thought he was mad myself included. I was asked by several persons inside of the darkness if I knew who he was, I said no because I really didn't know who he was either, or that's the god honest truth.

A quick conversation started with Wesman and I, we chatted for a few minutes before he leaves, saying he had to get back over to Gibraltar, because it was getting late and that he will link up with me tomorrow. It was strange but I was really looking forwards to seeing him again, because I was so curious because of what I've heard the tenants saying about him. I said to myself, I'm going bed, tomorrow is another day and I'm eager for it to come. Praying to God I make it alive and live to see tomorrow insides this wretched place, because tomorrow wasn't guaranteed, you might not live to see it either. I have seen it a few times, asking for someone that I haven't seen for a few days and was told they were dead, just like that. The next day Wesman came back to the very same spot and sat down waiting. He wore the same white suit, like everyone else from Gibraltar. I saw him and knew he was there waiting for me. I greeted him and let him know, I will come outside soon to talk with him. I knew he wanted to talk too, because he had turned up and also because no one else spoke to him like I did. Trust me, that can get lonely really quick insides and a lot of these tenants have been here for years, not trusting anyone enough to form a good comraderies to have conversations with other than just saying hellos.

Someone in my room was boiling some orange peel tea and I was waiting for some of it. The balcony was busy as usual with all kinds of tenant and occupants from all over the dark place. Your name will be shouted out by an angel if you were ever wanted by anyone of importance. After I was finished drinking my tea and ate a piece of my hard dough bread, I was ready for the day. I planned on asking Wesman some personal questions, which I already out lined in my head. I was eager to hear the answers from him myself. He was an older man and very popular around the dark place, he had been residing here for a while inside the darkest part of the darkness. I thought to myself that the occupants in Gibraltar needs better treatment but it was and is what it is. I knew they were there for a reason but nonetheless I was still sympathetic towards them because of how the Angeles treated them over there. I walked out on the balcony where Wesman was sitting down waiting on me patiently. We began our conversation and the first thing he asked me was where I'm from, and where my parents are from. I don't know if this was like a background check for them, but he was not the first tenant to ask about me and my parents origins. I answered him with no hesitation, the conversation gets on the way and I told him my mother and father is from Hanover, and that I have loads of family all over Savanna la mar in Westmoreland and also in Lucea in Hanover. The conversation gets even more interesting, when I began talking about some people in around Hanover, which he also knew as well, I said to myself shit, I have to be careful of what I say and how the argument goes, because he was familiar with most of the names I had mention. He was trying to attach himself to some of the names as even relatives. Realising this, I was even more cautious than before with the name calling especially with the surnames. I now realize he was like this, I was very sceptical of what I said to him, plus I didn't want to say anything that he might think was a disrespect. He was a lot older than I was and I dealt with all adults with respect no matter where I am, in the light or in the dark. He also knew lots of people all over Montego Bay, Westmoreland, and Lucea in Hanover. He knew some prominent people all over Lucea in Hanover as well. I looked Wesman straight in his face, I knew this very well, when it came to questioning someone, that eye to eye contact was very important to make a good summary, of a person, or even an animal. If you are trying to assess an individual just, try it and you'll see what I'm saying. I Kept staring in his eyes and answered all the questions he asked me. When it was my turn to asked him questions, questions that were already lined out in my head, I held his stare for any reaction. I just wanted to go through the questions with no back lashes like what I got from John, because I asked about what happened after the death of his daughter.

With this in mind, I had to do this wisely. I began by asking where in Westmoreland he was from. He said he was from Sav, which I knew and understand what he means straight away. I then asked him if what they were saying about him was true. He replied by asking who are they, I said the news, and told him I knew of his story from the radio, heard about it when I was small and now I was hearing others insides here with it too. Again, he asked, others like who. From what I gathered he was a bit protective and reserved with what he was saying. I said to myself ok, I have answered all your questions, and now it's your turn to answer mine and you're being weird. I said to him, it's either you answer or you don't, then I told him what I heard in the darkness and he paused. Staring each other straight in the face, eye to eye, he asked again what you heard. I put my back against the wall, just in case he was going to try to attack me. I knew he walked with a weapon all the time, and I remember the one I saw him with. The big machete looking object he carries in is waist.

My intention was to hear what I wanted to hear from him out of his own mouths, this shit is scary. I hear suddenly heard a sound (poop) and I jumped. It sounded like someone had farted. He saw the move I had made, and realize straight away that I didn't trust him. He had a small smile, just a smirk, before he was back in his position. He asked me again what I have heard. This time I told him straight away, in a soft tone of voice, I said "eat people". He said what? I said in an even softer tone, you could barely hear the eat, but you could hear people clearly. He mumbled something that was unclear, but then said he haven't eaten anyone in a long time. I tried hard to hid my astonishment at what he said but recovered by asking him how long has he been insides the dark place. He said about ten years, I ask him how long before coming in the darkness, had he consumed human flesh. He answered was the last time he had eaten a piece of human flesh, was about three years ago. Shocked at that because he said he's been inside for ten years, I repeated the question, just in case he had not heard me properly. But he said it again, that the last time he had a piece of human flesh, was about three years ago. I just shut off at that. I didn't want to know how he got that to eat, or where from, because of the length of time he stated that he was in the dark place. Also, that three years ago was the last time he said he had some human's meat. That didn't sounds good to me, and the logics I couldn't see because he was in the dark place. But he assured me that anything you wanted here in the darkness, you can get, which I already know.

I don't know if he was being sarcastic, so I just moved on to the next question. Before I could asked him anything else, he just started talking about everything, like he knew what I wanted to hear. He began telling me a barrage of things, things that will make anyone sick, things that will make anyone vomit. I on the other hand had to firm my stomach. I was not going to stop him from talking because I wanted desperately to hear it, in his own words, from his own mouth. He start telling me details on quite a few things, which was not sitting right with me. Then he began describing how he attacked, and how he hunted people, especially males. He stated that he didn't like eating women, and gave his reasons for that, but I will disclose that shortly. As I already stated I was not going to disturb him while he was speaking so

139

openly about things you would only come across in books. So, I spoke less and listened more, intent to just soaked up all he wished to share. He told me how he would walked with large sharp weapons, a knife or an ice-pick and a bit of rope. He also told me that he knew where to go hunting. Knows where to get little boys, and also where to find adults. I was listening to him and also watching his body language carefully. I also stared him straight in his eyes, so I could analyse if what he was saying made any sense, or if he was telling the truth or he was telling lies. So I watched his every move and listened intently to his spoken words, this all took place in the year 1993. He began by telling me how he would walked down a road that was not too busy, but it would have to be a road that people used to get to a certain community.

He told me that he was on a stake out, looking for a catch. He said he was looking up and down the road. From a far, he said that he saw someone coming towards him. He stated that the person was short from what he could see, and drew back in the bushes. Where he waited for the opportunity to presents itself, or until the person came even nearer. He said the person appeared to be a man strolling down the road while smoking. He said he waited on the person quietly, until he got within grabbing distance, but watched until the man walked past him a bit, before he made his move. Light on his feet and as quiet as possible he snuck up on the man. With one hard blow to the head from behind with a solid piece of wood, that he carved from a guava or the logwood tree. He said the young man just drop to the ground. He never went into any further details, other than to say he brought him back to the bushes where he does the cleaning up of his catch. He also stated that if the blow to the head didn't killed them, then as soon as he reaches the spot he immediately cut the throat of the person, for then to bleeds out all the battered blood from the body. He also told me how he would rest body on a sheet of zinc and use his razor-sharp knife to do the cutting when he was ready. I was surprised at how detailed and forthcoming with information he was. Telling me how he would first cut the clothing off the person's body. This had shivers racing up my body, making me feel like I wanted to smoke a joint or a cigarette and I don't even smoke. He goes onto say he had already dug a hole deeper in the bushes, where he buries the intestine because he don't used them.

Afterwards he would start to get his kill ready. He began by cutting both wrist off from the joints, then he cut both elbow in the joints, he then said he would severed both arms from the body then repeat the same procedure with the legs.

Almighty god I shouted; Jesus Christ this was a whole new crazy I did not anticipate. Take into consideration, all of this I was hearing, plus watching his movement and how compose he was, I began wondering if he was truly insane. Or if I was the insane one for being fascinated by a complete psychopath. Tuning back into his ramblings, I listened to him go on and on about separating the limbs from the body, joint by joint, limb by limb until only the torso and head remain. Which he states he would take off shortly. He described how he placed the head on a big piece of block, then goes for a big machete where he would make one chop. When he said the head flies off in one go, then he split it in two halves, I almost vomit, I had to swallow down the bile that was raging war inside my stomach. All these parts he said he would leave on the same piece of zinc to leak out all the blood. I watched him as he spoke of his past like he was in a trance. In details he told me how he cut the belly from under the navel up towards the neck. He said he chopped through the chest, with the same machete, which just burst through the ribs bone. Fucking hell, I was wondering if this sick fucker was a butcher. He carried on telling me how he opened the chest, and pulled out all the intestine and placed them in bags that he buried in the hole he mentioned earlier. He said when he finished sorting out the body parts, he proceeds to clean himself up in the river nearby, that was also surrounded by bushes. All this he said would be done before daylight. I seem to stir him back to the present by asking "so, you just left the pieces to drain". I don't know what he heard in my tone, but the look he gave me told me to tread cautiously. He looked at me until I became uncomfortable, before he answered my question.

He started by saying no, that he first chopped the torso and the other bits into smaller pieces. He said he splits the torso in two halves, then cut them across. After all the cutting, he then washed them and get them ready to be stored away. He said, he placed them into buckets, what we would call kegs. After placing the pieces in to the buckets, he would pour coarse salts, pimento seeds, loads of scotch Bonnet peppers,

141

onions, and scallions on to it, then closed the buckets properly. He then buried the buckets in the ground, on top of each other. To how descriptive and free flowing he was with his words, it seems to me like he wanted to unload this information or talk to someone about these things for a long time.

After all this was done, he would burn the clothing of the dead person, then clean up the place and have a shower in the nearby river. I was bursting to ask more questions, but I didn't want him to think I was being too inquisitive, and stop talking. So, I just listen to him, telling me about the events that took place in his life once upon a time.

Not only did he informed me of how he hunted, killed, cleaned and prepared his catch to be eaten, he also told he how he cooked and ate them, and why he prefers eating men's flesh to women. He told me how he had Hunted and catch women before. He said that he preferred when the women were not on their periods, because their flesh are easily spoiled and spring loads of water while cooking. Also, that he dislike the texture of women meat, it tasted a bit funny, gives a different taste from the men and was much softer. He said if he knocked out a woman and realize that she was on her monthly, he didn't even bother with her. I was a long way pass shock at this point, thinking this was not only insanity, but how descriptive the details were it spoke of a reality that was once his. My head was reeling from information overload and I just wanted him to go, but he was not ready to stop talking. So, I continued listen to him some more, even though I was getting frustrated with him. My mind started slipping and I was suddenly thinking what was going on with my family outside of the dark place.

Tuning back in I heard when he said one evening, he was at the same spot hunting. I don't know where that was, but he said he looked and saw a person coming from a far. He said the distance where he had allowed him to see them long before they reached where he was. He said he watched until the person was close enough, when he realised it was a woman, he said he waited until she passed by before he grabbed her from behind and hauled her into the bushes. He recounted this with such glee, especially when he said, she was so frightened he thought she would shit herself. He told me that after a quick check, he noticed she was on her period. He said he was disappointed and just played it out like an attempted rape turned robbery before he let her go. He said he had seen her around a few times after this had happened and smile to himself, thinking if only she knew how lucky she had been. He informed me that he would listen to chatter around, people around the area talking about the robberies and even the missing persons. Said that at one point he had almost grabbed one of his very own cousin on the same road he always used to snatch people. That shit he was recounting was very horrifying. I have been listening to him for a few hours, some of the other tenants turn up and started listening to what he was saying. A few had an alarming look on their faces, and I could see that the uninvited and unwelcome guests were making him uncomfortable. Being the type that kept to himself, I could also see the moment he decided that this shit show was over. With a pensive look on his face he turn his attention back to the yard looking at everything and nothing clearly a sign that he was done talking.

I was thankful for the unwelcome tenants that was a much needed break releasing me from his gripping life story, God knows he'd said enough. He had unknowingly given me home work, although I was not at home, but I have things to workout, things to think about. After the tenants leaves, no longer interested in sitting in silence, we were once again on our own. We started chatting but he change the subject and it was not so interesting listening to him talking that way. It was strained so we eased off the conversation a bit, just contented to sit in silence, even though I still wanted to hear more of what went down with his cousin. He had mention a friend that was also in the dark place and who also resides in Gibraltar. Again, you know what that means from he resides there. He must have done some serious shit to land a permanent place in Gibraltar. I am very curious about this friend, I would love to see him, wanted to know what he looked like and wondered if I have seen him around. But I won't ask him to introduce me to him. He was in a strange type of mood; his behaviour was a bit odd. I can see by just looking in his eyes, that he was very dangerous, his body language said it all. Though my mind was digging me wanting to ask him about this friend of his, I also wanted to learn more about his cousin's narrow escape, it was more of a priority to me. In addition to wanting to learn more about how he prepared this flesh meals and what he ate it with.

143

I clinched my toes together and tense my muscles as a form of mental preparation. I was already feeling sick, this was not going to make it better or worse, if I asked a simple question. I have been sitting and listening to him like a child would sit and listening to their parents. I can't see where I was doing anything wrong by asking another question. I don't think he should take this as a disrespect or even a violation either, in my humblest opinion.

After deciding whether or not to ask the question about his cousin. I said to myself it was now or never, so I asked my question. In a descent manner, if there was such a way to ask these things. Staring at him boldly, holding back the fear and shivers that coated my body. I asked God to not let him be upset and attack me. In a quiet voice I asked him, "suh a wah gwan wid yuh cousin? blood". Meaning (what happened with your cousin my friend). Looking at me in the same way I was looking at him and he said, I will soon tell you about him, the one Donovan he was lucky. I wanted him to lament more on the topic. It was by chance that I was just staring in his mouth, caught off guard by what the hell I saw in it. Seeing inside his mouth had nearly convince me, I was looking at a vampire. If you understand what I mean, he had teeth that looked like fangs. Two long teeth, similar to the ones that always shows in a vampire movie. The very same ones that elongates first before a vampire take a bite. How apt, this guy really fits what he his saying to me all day, those teeth gave me the creeps trust me on that. Time after time I kept asking myself was this real, I had doubts. But I realized the things he was saying were very serious and from the looks of his teeth, I conclude that he does indeed eat people. Why bother to try and dissuade myself, when he gives such compelling arguments. Exactly like how a mechanic would give details on how he took a part a car engine and rebuild it with confidence which speaks of experience.

With a faraway look on his face as if he was back in time where this occurred, he began telling me about his cousin Donovan. He started by saying he was on the same road he used for hunting, and looking form a far, just like he did with the others. He said he saw someone on a bicycle, riding towards him. He does the same as before going back into the bushes and waited, until the person gets close. My focus firmly fixed on him, I just stared at him and wondered where he was going with this. He said he position himself as the person was on a bicycle and not on foot. No sooner had the person rode pass, he allowed a few seconds before he made his move. One lick same as the others to the head. He said the rider dropped, because he was knocked out instantly. He said when he went over to give him another blow, he was like shit, this looks like Donovan. Upon closer inspection he said recognition dawns and he realize the boy was his cousin. He told me how he pulled him out of the road and left him on the side where he could be safe and not roll out in the road.

He was saying that he did not want to leave him in the road, for fear of a car or worse a truck might run over him. Who would have thought this harden man eater had any sympathy. He did say however, that he was happy to leave him on the side of the road because he didn't want Donovan to recognise him and he didn't really wants him to dead either. I was sick of him, thinking good. I said to myself I hope this taught him a lesson. I was thinking clearly he didn't want to put his family through the distress that come with the loss of losing a loved one. He didn't want his family to get hurt, but he was hurting other people and their families. I wanted to hear more about how he Cook the meat and eat it and the part he didn't like eating from the women.

A short while later his childhood friend came over to him. I have seen his friend before out on the grass. I knew this friend; I don't know his name but he was from Westmoreland as well. He said they grew up together from they were small, and that they did everything together. In my mind I was thinking, if he was doing all the things, he said he had done, then he couldn't have been alone. He alone could not have done so much, but I didn't want him to feel like I was prying too much in his business. My mind was just running at the moment his friend had overheard him telling me a few things. I could see that his friend don't approved of what he was doing or saying to me, just by a quick glimpse of his face. Wesman had just started talking about the cooking of the meats he stored and how he seasons them. His friend asked how long as he known me and where he knows me from. Casting a glance in his friend direction, he told him stop talking. He further went on to say that "you must be careful of whom you are talking to and be mindful of what you say", he warned him sternly. Not only could I tell that they were really close but that they were also good friends for a long time. It was kind of strange how they both ended up insides the dark place, in the darkest part as well and both resides in Gibraltar.

Things started to get on the way for me, my sister had gotten a date for me to leave the dark place and I was looking forward to that. My mind was in a much better place now that I have heard this good news from my sister. Westman friend was even more sceptical than before. He was behaving like he had something to hide. In my mind I already don't trust him, and I am staying in that frame of my mind. I think it was the right thing to do. I hate being around someone I have to be watching constantly, all day and all night. This was not a feeling I liked. One good thing was that I knew what they were about. Knew that they knew each other from a small age. They went to the same school, did the same kind of work together and even living somewhere, where they are going to die together. This was like a piece of puzzle I was determined to be working out. In front of me they both stood, I was looking at them and I wondered what was the matter with these guys. Wesman friend was so paranoid, I truly don't know how he survived insides the dark place. He was a strange character, very cautious with whom he spoke to. I could see he also had a weapon. I don't know what was going on in this man's head, but I could tell he just didn't trust me. There are people in the dark place I have not mentioned yet with some nasty stories too. I will share them shortly I saw some infamous faces insides and I was also shown some cold hearted tenants insides here, that were not residents of Gibraltar. But still lives in the dark place. Wesman's friend finally, convinced him to stop talking and walked away with him, but I have a weird feeling about his friend. I think they both hunted, snatched, killed and ate people together. That concludes the end of Wesman story. I did not personally know him from before my time in the dark place, I don't know his correct name. I only know 9 him from the news, and from meeting up with him inside the dark place, I only knew he was of Westmoreland addresses.

The Chiney man story

THE NEXT STORY IS ABOUT A MAN WHO HEATED A PIECE OF HALF INCH steel, about two feet in length and inserts it inside his baby mother's vagina. This too was broadcast on the news a long time ago; from I was small. I saw this old Chinese looking man inside the dark place, he too resides in Gibraltar. He looked frail, had short pretty hair that sat in a dirty mess on top of his head. He could barely move, I wondered what he was doing here, it was disheartening to see someone of his age and condition in a place like this. Having a bit of pity on him because of how he looked, I wondered what was going on with him out of curiosity. I asked around about him and everyone said daddy is a good man, nothing's wrong with that. I just wanted to know what the hell he did to be here, when he should be home with his grand kids and his family. He looked very ill but had the same wild look on his face, as the other occupants of Gibraltar. Both his eyes were sunk in a hole, his head looked extra big, his knees were bigger than his thighs. He too wore the same white suit, with a draw string that fastens at the trousers waist to keep it from falling.

This Chiney man was well respected insides the dark place. I think it's due to the fact that he's been here for a long time. His job was to keep the ground around Gibraltar clean and also the rest of the yard in the dark place. After asking about him some one started giving me details regarding why he was here. I learned that sometime around the nineteen eighties, the Chineyman went home and wanted sex from his baby mother. He said rumour has it that she refused him, and that he tries a few more times and was still unsuccessful. He said he heard that this carried on for a while and still nothing happened for him. Annoyed by her refusals, he started getting upset with her easily. I thought to myself that this does not sound good not one bit. Rumour has it that he starts to speculate that she has another man, and that she is taking him for a fool. Convinced of his own theory, he started to become angry and angrier because he was not getting what he wanted from her. He thought he had to find out what was going on, and wanted to know if she was having an affair with someone else. He needed to know if that was her reason why she was not paying him any attention or giving him any form of comfort meaning sex. He was known for violent outbursts I was told, they lived together so no one really knew what went down behind closed doors. Throughout all this his woman wasn't doing a thing like what he was thinking. Moreover, she recently had a baby, that she was looking after and didn't have the time to do what he thought.

It was confirmed that he beats her a lot, and I even heard that he beats her very badly too when he drinks and gets drunk . She has make a lot of complaints to the authorities, her neighbours and relatives about the regular beating from him but receives no help from anyone. The situation was really bad, it was a shame she was forced to endure something so cruel from someone who was supposed to love her. After repeated attempts to get help, but sadly non was given she continued to live in that hell. On top of all that I was told that he smokes hard drugs and was often drunk more than he was sober from what I got to understand about this man. Her cries fell on deaf ears even though every one noticed her black eyes, busted lips and the swollen lumps in her forehead. Her neighbours heard her crying out for help in the nights on numerous occasions while he battered her. They overheard him swearing and shouting at her, berating her, yet no one thought to intervene on her behalf. The evidence of her torment was there for all to see whenever she had to venture outside in her community.

This situation was a disaster waiting to happen and it didn't sound too promising for her either. I knew it was not going to end well for her. I was told he went home one night after he had had a few drinks. Fuelled by the alcohol that convinced him that she had a man, he began brooding preparing to enact what he had planned. Not saying much, he decided to make a big fire in the back of the yard. He started out collecting rubbish from around the yard which he threw into the fire. Pretending all was well, he swept the yard back to front. When all this was done, he went and demanded what he wanted. I was told that he told her that by any means necessary, he will not stop until he gets some sex and that he wanted it now. He started to touch her all over her body, even on her private parts. She tries to remove his hands and that caused an even bigger problem. While trying to removed his hands from her body, he slaps her in the face, as usual going for her eyes. She tried to fight back by scratching and biting but she was not match for him and his brute strength. Her lack of submission plus her fighting him made him more violent. He began punching her in the face like it was a punching bag. He kicks away both her feet, causing her to lose her balance straight away and fell to the ground. While she was on the floor, he kicked her in the face several times, and then stamped on her tummy repeatedly. Laying on the ground crying, while the son they had together was there watching and crying for his mummy. Meanwhile his dad beats the living shit out of his mother.

He kicked her again in the head knocking her out. After which he went outside for a few minutes in which he places the two feet steel in the fire. Then went back inside to check she wasn't moving. All this time he had the fire burning and the steel heating. He began stripping her of her clothing. The move roused her, he was trying to have sex with her, in her battered state. She helplessly begged him to stop but he would not listen. After he had sex with her, he knocked her out again for a second time. Then he went back outside to retrieve the iron that was in the fire. When he came back from outside the yard this time, he came back was with a total different intention from before.

I was told that the red hot steel that he came back insides the house with, the one that was getting hotter and hotter while her carried out his vicious act. He placed it beside her unconscious body, then her opened her legs and inserts the hot steel inside her vagina. The steel was about two feet long and he pushes it all the way through her vaginal canal and through her belly. Burning everything in its way, damaging her cervix and uterus, as he forces the steel all the way inside until it bottom's out. To make matters worse the bit of the steel that was first inserted had jagged edges, so the damages were catastrophic as it ripped apart her insides. She screamed in anguish as she tried her best to get him to stop but with her body bruised and batter, she had little to no energy left. The pain was so severe that she passed out from it, without him having to knock her out for a third time. The steel he left inside her to cool down, there was blood mixing with piss all around her. With the intensity of her screams the neighbours finally decided to intervene, but it was a little too late, the horrific and tragic ordeal had already taken place. The scene that they were faced with will be one that they will never forget. Her unconscious body was found in the most horrible condition imaginable. She had multiple contusion all over her naked body, her eyes were swollen, lips busted she ever appeared to have what looked like bite marks. But that was not the worse of her injuries, fully exposed they could see the tail end of the steel inside her vagina. The neighbours quickly got her into a car where they took her to the hospital. It was at the hospital that the severity and depth of the injuries were revealed. At first glance the doctors they thought she was sexually assaulted, but further examination would reveal the tragedy that has befallen this poor woman. When all the examination was done, it revealed, a facture eye socket, head wounds, on top of the battered body, the damage to her inside, she also have a facture pelvis. Her unconsciousness was a concussion caused by the multiple blows to the head. Even though the doctors and nurses worked really hard and did everything the cold, she succumbed to her injuries and died. I was told that it was a heart breaking moment in the hospital, I heard that all the staff that worked on her, were left in tears. By this time news had reached her family of what had transpired and they were there at the hospital waiting along with the neighbours for the doctors to brief them on how she was doing. However it wasn't good new that would be delivered. I was told that the red rimmed eyes and the look of utter despair on t doctor's face, caused every to start bawling before they even heard the news. It was a moments of complete devastation, her family and the neighbours, everyone was just in shock.

As the reality of the situation hits, the ones she had previously complained to, the feeling of guilt and shame caused them to break down like they were experiencing physical pain. Standing in the corridor of the hospital as the doctors explain the gruesome details of the injuries she suffer and what happened up to the moment she took her last breath. That was the moment the real grief hits, not only were they grieving her death, but they were grieving how much they let her down. How they ignored her cries for help, they grieved for the loss of life that they could have saved but did nothing and now it was beyond late. Cry as they might, the outcome was still the same and they will be left with that despair that the grief would leave its wake. She died feeling afraid, heartbroken and dismayed, that she wouldn't get the chance to be a mother to her son. A son that witness the brutality of what his father done to his mother, the only consolation about this shitty situation was he was very young, and time will allow him to forget his mother's tragic death. What his future will be like, I have no idea. With a dead mother and an absent father, who was on the run, I hope that all her family who hadn't stepped up to help her would do so now. It wouldn't change anything, but will allow them to be there for him and help him which they didn't do for the mum.

Upon enquiring I was told that the Chineyman had gone missing since this had happened. No one knew of his were about. I had heard the story when I was much younger but not the full extent surrounding her death, like I knew it now, now that I was living in the same place as him. I saw him in the dark place, years later. It was beyond sad, listening to the story made me feel an overwhelming sense of loss and hurt. It was such a strange feeling because I didn't know these people but still felt sick to my stomach about what happened. Now that I was here and seeing the state that he was in, knowing what it was only a matter of time before he too, will be walking the aisles of Gibraltar towards the death toll gave me peace of mind. He didn't even looked like he have the strength to walk around and do his job properly and that was to clean up the yard around the dark place. But this was the path his life took him because of jealousy. His life was what it is. He just had to endure each day; I have no idea if he felt any remorse for what he had done, but here he was suffering. He'll live with the consequences of his actions and learn as he awaits his death. Chiney man was also known to be from a Spanish town address I was told.

Being inside the dark place, I starting to get accustomed to the way of life here. My family was at the fore front of my mind, always thinking about what was happening with them my and worrying about their wellbeing. I knew the ropes inside here, I learned to do things for myself insides the dark place, like making my own food, Like fried chicken back, dumplings, yellow yam, and green banana. This I did on the makeshift hotplate we had in our room which was made from the mosquito destroyer, the shine metal bit that was stuck on the mat on. I even learned to cook in orange juice boxes using it as a pot or sometimes using a milk box. I was wondering how this was even possible. I was also boiling porridge in an empty plastic water bottle on a fire, that was not burning the bottle or melting the plastic. This was how I was living insides the dark place, normal everyday things that people took for granted, was a luxury to all the tenants of the dark place. For example you couldn't even take a shit in private or fart freely or too often it would be seen a violation. But this was the way it is.

Going about my day as usual, I saw a man across the grass talking to a friend of mine. He was watching me like he knew me from somewhere. I decided to acknowledge him by saying "yow", he responded by saying "yes youth". This man looked quite calm; he didn't even speak loudly. I took a good look at him from across the grass and when my friend came back beside me, I asked him who was that man he was talking to. He said you seriously don't know, he didn't even give me the chance to say anything, he said that's the guy who killed the famous singer from a group in trench town. He began saying that the man was a very popular musician and singer in Jamaica and around the world, and that he was not just in a group. This man I was asking about [6]also resides in Gibraltar, so you know what that means. After I finish conversing with my friend, I decided to return my room. While walking towards my room, I was approached by two guys, who just randomly came to asking me where I was from. Though I found it strange I still told them Johns Road. They said they knew a lot of people from Johns Road and I said ok. They told me they were from Frazer's content, better known as Red Pond. They also told me their names, and I knew who they were straight away I recognised both names. I can even recall their stories, it too happened long ago, now they were both living in Gibraltar. Nothing was different, their appearance was the same as all the other occupants of Gibraltar. With the signature looks, eyes sunken in a hole, very big head, and protruding knees, it was like they were starved to all have that emaciated look, before it was their time to die. I think, one of the reason they looked the way they did was because of the stress. The pressure of knowing they were as good as dead, was not only taking a toll on their mental health but wreaking havoc on their physical appearance.

I knew what was up with them, and I got it. To have to live and settled in a place, to have a routine in the very same place, whereby design was made to take away your life, would fuck anyone up. No letting up, no two ways about it either, they were here to die, and that only happens with the occupants who resides in Gibraltar. The dark place was not occupied only by the guys of Gibraltar, but also occupied by other tenants, which was not there to die but to spend time. They won't meet the same faith, as the guys of Gibraltar. As For me, I had to find a way to occupied myself. I just listened to all these conversation from all the tenants especially the one from Gibraltar. It had me thinking a lot, about what I was going to do after leaving. I learned a lot by being here my mind set is different. I am solid as a rock. I can say I've gained tactics from being here, life training tool and skills which would make me moved and think like a robot or a trained military man, fighting for survival. Trust me, when I listen to most of these terrible conversation, I used to feeling sick and disgusted, nothing bothers me anymore. I was now a changed man, physically and mentally I have now learned to condition my mind to what was going on inside here. I started going to shop by myself and buying my groceries and cook my food myself. Learning all the tricks and trades that will enable me to live while here. I even learn some cool things too, like how to make one stick of match lights twice. I learn how to make the pots from zinc myself, learned to make the hot plates, I have also learned how to make my tooth brush a very sharp and deadly weapon, just by rubbing it on the wall. I was now standing shoulders to shoulders with everyone inside here, but I still manage not to get involved and keep myself out of trouble inside. I start moving around the dark place by myself putting all my fears aside and man up. I have access to all kinds of weapons too like knives ice-pick machete and other weapons around me. I have learned to believe in myself more than before. I was only young; I still have a future in front of me. I was hoping to leave this place shortly and have made up my mind to do so in one piece, like how I came here. I've seen people gets chopped up and stab every other day, so it wasn't guaranteed that you would be the same when it was time to leave. I once saw a tenant used a toothbrush to stab out another tenant eyes. I have also seen knives used to cut other tenants in their faces and all over their bodies, time and time again. I have even seen hot water mixed with sugar, cornmeal, flour, a bit of soap and bleach all mixed together and thrown in other tenant's face and eyes, it was not a pretty sight. Seeing all those things happening, I was well aware of the danger that could befall me and was determined not to fall prey to those attacks by any means necessary.

The Donkey meat and Dog soup Story

I WAS PLAYING CARDS ONE DAY ON THE BALCONY WITH SOME GUYS, I didn't know them all, but everyone wanted to keep their minds free by playing a game or just wanted to play for fun. I overheard someone saying something but couldn't quite hear what it was but every one began laughing out loudly. Someone was asking another tenant "how much a pound you sell it for again". I had no clue what he was selling in the dark place, as I was not fully focused on their conversation but on my game with my eyes staring down on the cards in my hands. The same thing was said for the second time "how much a pound". Wanting to know was happening around me, I turned around to get a look at who they were talking about with this "how much a pound thing". This was what made me laugh a bit. The guy shouted again "Meat, meat cheap cheap, dog and puss dog and puss". He repeated it again shouting even louder. "Meat meat cheap cheap dog and puss dog and puss". I was wondering what he meant and what he was saying because this sounded like the verse of a song. But everyone was looking in the other man's direction and dying with laughter. In front of me stood a man I heard about a few years back. This was the man who was going around selling donkey meat for beef. I heard he sold cat and dog meat too. I looked at him, just taking a quick glance from the corner of my eyes. These other tenants were making a joke of him, but I could clearly see that he didn't think or find it funny. I could no longer pay any attention to the card game anymore; this made me feel like I was going to laugh to death. Even my chest was getting tight with how much I laughed, I had tears running from my eyes and down my face like I was crying with how much they were taking the piss out of him.

I said to myself shit, this is him. It even got more funnier when they started to point out his friend, who was at Half way tree at a popular spot where dances and parties were kept. They both sold soup night and day, I was told the soup was the lick in those days. He sometimes sold it in Port More too and he had a lot of customers all over halfway tree, Port More and the surrounding areas. This was going on for a while roughly around the late eighties to the early nineties. I was informed that his clientele was varied. He supplied the people from the hardware store, banks, bars, pharmacies, doctors, hairdressers and barbers in and around halfway tree and Cross Road. He sold to security guards police and soldiers, nurses, DJ, singers, sound systems operators, taxis and bus operators. No one was out of bound, it was like having their very own private chef on speed dial. He catered to the mass. I was told by him one day while we were having a conversation, that ladies would bring their own bowls and cups from their homes to get their soups in. They would leave their containers with him, to be shared out and ready to be collected at lunch time. I don't know if he was trying to be funny, but he told me that he obtained several girlfriend because of his heavy handed sharing, of this meaty, rich, thick and steaming hot soup. He told me that he prepared this soup with chocho, carrots, pumpkin, potatoes, green bananas, okra and dumplings. He also said he made sure it was loaded with meat, he said whenever he shared for the ladies, he made sure it was filled with meat. He laughed when she said "you know how the ladies love plenty meat". This I know to be true.

He moved on and began telling me how people found out about what he was selling. He said one evening, he and his woman were having an argument out at the popular party spot. The argument started over jealousy, as usual I won't say nothing to that because I am a man also and it's only natural if you love the person, you were with it can happen either way. The argument got heated because some man was making moves on his girlfriend. He said he then threaten to slap her and she made it clear that if he slapped her, it was not going to end well tonight.

While they argued there was a long line of customers waiting to be served. They were lining up to get the soup with corn that was also filled with forbidden animal meat which he boils in the soup and was selling. He also said that you could get a good smoke from him too, meaning a spliff. He was there to make some money, so he sold everything people usually buy when they were out having a good time. Things like cigarettes, rizla paper, lighters, tobacco, Guinness, dragon, red stripe beer, Heineken, biscuits, sweets, jerk chicken, roast fish and jerk pork. He had everything on his stall selling and his woman was there to help him. The argument didn't stop despite the fact that they were surrounded by people waiting to be served. He was persistent in telling her that he was going to slap her if she carried on. Not put off by his threat, she reassured him that there would be consequences if he did and that it would not end well. This she repeats again even louder than before. By this time everybody started collecting their soup and began drinking, others were standing waiting on jerk chicken and pork amongst other stuff. Realising that people were starting to take notice of their argument, he got upset and gave her one slap in her face, the one he had promised and all hell broke loose. It was like she couldn't wait to get this off her chest. She screamed out like she had an amplifier in her throat, repeating "Stop selling the people dem, dog meat and dogs soup, a long time you have been doing it, it's time for you to stop it". "You selling puss, dog and donkey for meat, you too fucking wicked", she cries out in a loud voice. She even went as far as to tell the people where he had the animal heads and skin, hiding around the back of his yard, in buckets. Everyone started to scream, throwing away what little was left in their cups. Some literally started to vomit. While others were furious and began shouting obscenities, saying that was why he was giving them so much meat one man shouted. Another man shouted out that he and his baby daughter just drank all the soup and didn't leaven any for his baby mother, that was why he was there to buy more. He proclaimed how much they love the soup, to now realising what the fuck they were eating for years. These people were his customers and had been supporting him for years. He sold there night and day almost every day. People started dropping their cups along with everything else they had purchased from him. It was like a chain reaction, now they were wondering if this jerk pork and jerk chicken, were in fact pork and chicken they have been eating from him for years. Deciding they needed retribution for what he had done to them, they all tried to apprehend him. He was too swift for them, he jetted off like a rocket no one could hold him to how fast he dashes off, running away leaving everything on the stall behind.

This revelation made every one sick to their stomach, the utter mortification causing them to vomit like hell. Others were shocked but didn't care, they didn't even mind either. One man even stated that they've been consuming his food for a while so why stop now. He even went as far as to comment on how delicious and moreish it was. From what I heard he made a lot of money from selling his dog soup. The matter was reported and the police along with all his customers went to his house. It was pure disaster, a completely different story when they arrived. Dog heads, skin and other parts belong to dogs were there in buckets the evidence plenty for everyone to see. The guy who was troubling him in the dark place, calling him meat man, is called little Blacks. According to Blacks, he knew him from outside of the dark place, Blacks gave only jokes nothing else. Some said he's an idiot, but I had nothing against him. Anybody that made me laugh inside here; I enjoyed being around. In such a dreary place, a cheerful laugh was always needed.

The times was coming up for me to go back in front of these people. The ones who wore strange clothing, clear eye glasses and long gowns that reached their ankles and sits at a desk with a wooden hammer which they would use after they spoke or when they wanted silence. I began praying like hell nonstop, wanting to leave the dark place. I was sick of the darkness. I met a tenant by the name of Norman, he became a good friend of mine inside, until I was ready to leave. The dark place can make you or break you, either for better or for worse. I have listened to all occupants around the dark place and it's funny to know what some people thinks about life itself. Others I have spoken to including Christian who strongly believe in God and Rastafarian who tells me there is no god, who solely believes in Selassie. But almost all the residence of Gibraltar that I have spoken to, strongly believes there is no such thing as a god. As for me and my beliefs, I am not a person who likes to discuss religion, people believe, or even one's sexualities male or female. I am always neutral when it comes to these things, because they are very serious, these topics can result in loss of life. This is happening in and around the world we live in toady. It's very clear to see worldwide, that religion cause divisions and tension. In my opinion, no matter what kind of regions, anywhere these things are active there is always war.

The courthouse chapter: After the dark place

TODAY IS THURSDAY AND TOMORROW WILL BE FRIDAY. IT'S THE DAY I'LL be back in front this organisation, with these people who wore strange outfits. Tonight, will be the longest night I have endured inside here, trust me. I am holding onto faith; I have a Bible and a special suit of clothing to wear tomorrow. I have also prayed a special prayer before I went to sleep. I was only waiting on time now. Ten o clock was my time, I am hoping all goes well too, because things don't always go your way. However, my sister is confident in this friend she has, who will be supporting us both. Time is important and I contemplating what's next. I was a bit worried, but I will have to do it. All the tenants in my room wished me the best of luck and told me I was heading home. They were all supportive and I thank them all for their encouragement. I was up almost all night; I could hardly wait for day to break. I was looking through the windows every minute in and out. I was so anxious, I just wanted to leave this place. So, I prayed and I prayed, knowing God will answer my prayers Tomorrow.

Just as I was beginning to doze off, I heard the doors knocking. It was one of the angels telling me time to have a shower and get ready for the day out. Little did he know I was already ready for this day out, long time. Standing up looking at the Angeles outside the door, he was staring at me saying you're home today. He shouted my full name from a piece of white paper in his hands. I was ready for this, funny enough I had my clothes put out and waiting. I saw others who will be going out the same day as me. Everybody was getting busy; you could hear loads of talking outside from all over. I was going to have a cup of tea, the same oranges peel tea a usual. I am making it on the makeshift hot plate inside the room. I didn't want to wake or disturb the other guys who were still sleeping, so I did my best to be quiet while I moved around the room as it was still early. Having done all I needed to do, it was time for the angles to take us back to a special place in the yard, to count how much of us were going out. They gave us our belongings, all packed in a clear see through plastic bags with your name is written on it. All of us stood in a line, the line was linked together by each of us holding on to each other by our wrist. The right of mine was joined to the left wrist of the other person. Our two hands was held together by a platinum bracelet, opened and closed not by you but the angels or the person who took you out of the yard. These bracelets were specially made for these kinds of occasions. It was not meant to be worn to dance and parties, neither is it the ones you put on to look elegant or lavish when attending a ball room or a function. This bracelet is placed on you by someone else and they are responsible for taking it off too. Once counted and secure, to prevent any form of attempt escape, we are all loaded into a special built vehicle. This particular vehicle was designed to transport cargo like us. Ready for loading, we all climbed into this custom-made truck, packed together like animals. One of the angels would always be there to stand guard, ensuring we were never left alone.

The driver was dress in full blue jump suit like he was doing construction. He had a gun with him that was in a leather holster around his waist, similar to what you'd see in a western movie. It has the ability to reach you from a far distance and has these little copper things inside that can cause damage to people or even death. Even if it's pointed on its owner, this piece of object respect no one. Once it fired it's going for the intended target. Unless it hit something making it go astray, then anything in its way and I mean anything man, woman girl or boy even babies, the moment it's fired you have no control over it anymore. The larva like gold liquid that it spits out, will shower down like rain on anyone in its path, putting them to the ground and under it too. The angels use it on the vehicle for protection. The truck moved fast towards this studio like building. Everyone was there to welcome us. It's getting closer to the time I was given, and I was beyond nervous and shaking. I talked to my sister's friend who was supporting us. He gave me some good words of advice and encouragement. The place was so busy, you could hear names being called out loud, gavel knocking regularly, you could hear it from anywhere you were inside the building. The harsh sounds of raised voices and angry curse words being shouted, to hush whispers. Anything from people jingling their keys, the clicks and clanks of doors, to the sounds of farts that echoed through the empty rooms. Not to mention the pungent smell of piss and shit that was all over the place, emanating from the filthy toilets. It was like all the sounds were amplified. All the comings and goings were overhead, people talking about what they were going to do when they leave. Some were planning on fighting with their baby mothers and wives, while others were just ecstatic to be going home. One man was so pleased with the outcome of his case that he shouted out that he was going home to gives is wife pussy a good tongue fucking. He was smiling saying that he can smell pussy in the air. I just laughed to myself thinking, he probably smelling the pissy toilet and thinking its pussy. After being coup up together in one room with so many men, smelling all manner of evil, everything will be smelling like pussy to him. Unfortunately, not everyone will be celebrating at the end of the day some will be returning to the dark place.

My name was called out and I heard them coming towards the room I was in. I see everything and everyone waiting for me were all smiling. They asked me to stand which I did. I was still shaking, even after the lady in the wig and gown asked me to take a seat which I did. My supporter stood up to advocate on my behalf, singing my praises to everyone listening. Commenting on my good behaviour and how much of a hard worker I was. That it was my first mishap and that I have learned and grow from this experience. By the time he was finished everyone was agreeance because l told that I could go back into the light. My prayers were finally answered. I took a moment to thanks God, my sister and her friend, for pulling it off, pure smile.

After what felt like forever, I was heading home. I was hungry instant and wanted something decent to eat. I also wanted to shake off my defender's hand and thank him once again. My sister and I are planning to head home together, this are a good Friday for me and it's not even Easter. I got a hot Guinness to drink. My sister and her baby father bought it for me. Things got a bit tough with my sister because she was not happy with the predicament, I was in. So we are going to start talking about some serious things now, the future it's called. I was thinking about my kids and how they haven't seen me in a long while. My sister's intention was to get me off the island and that was not a bad thing.

Heading to our house in Willowdene, my sister rented a house which she shares with another couple. They are okay. I am good even though I feel like I'm in a bit of a daze. Seeing the light of day and having the ability to move around freely, with no angel watching my every move or using makeshift hotplate. No more shitting in drums, no more sleeping on the ground. I had no body telling me when to wake up or when to go to bed. I had to take a moment to process that there was no more darkness. Inside my head I thought about a few of the guys I left behind in the dark place. Guys like Onney, Thumpa, little Blacks, and Norman. My heart goes out to these tenants. It was sad, I never knew people was living like this. If I had not experience this for myself then I would never believe that people actually survived living like that. If someone had told me these things, I would clearly say it's a lie. Times is the master of all things as my mother would say. More than once I have heard that saying, that time will reveal all things. Things not even you or I would expect but that's life itself, it will always have it's up and down. Thinking back in time way back, I have seen the passing of many rich and high-profile official. Presidents, singers, movie stars, footballers, cricketers and the list goes on. We all have a standard to live up to and the fact of life is very simple. Just work hard, do the right thing, do good and good will follow you. Be fair to other and treat them as you would yourself. In other words what you don't like for yourself don't do it too other. Also, the Moses law is expected eye for an eye, a tooth for a tooth. I have learned these policies and I respect them. I don't like stealing and I don't like to associate myself with these types of people. I see myself as an honest man always working for what I want. I also have class and principles about myself. I don't want people around me that will do things which will drop me in trouble. I respect myself for these reasons. I will never associate myself with underage girls. I don't want them to even hang or harbouring around me or my property either with or without their parents knowing, same for boys. Also stolen goods, I don't want it around me either. I will never force myself on a woman at any point, wife or baby mother. Even if they're laying besides me naked as day they were born in my bed.

These things I have practice and all this I have mentioned, I live up to. I have confidence in myself with women, anywhere I go women are drawn to me for some reason. I have nice ways about me. I carry myself well, dresses decent and always smelling fresh, wearing a nice after shave or some cologne. My hair is always cut or neatly cornrowed when I was growing it. I have a neat gap between my front teeth, my teeth are clean and white. I am of brown complexion, brown eyes, black hair. I am nearly six feet in height and medium built. I am kind to women and there are others sides of me which ladies like in private. Another thing I don't like is violence against women. Thing likes these can lower your standards or even make you lose respect from people all around you, like your friends and family. These things I mention are behaviours which are common in the community I lived. It's happening around other places, that it seems like it's becoming the norm. Life is even more complicated and dangerous today in that aspect, because they are not only raping the youngsters today, they are killing them also and that's a fact.

My sister and I are making our way from Old Harbour, where the studio like building is located. It will take us approximately twenty minutes to half an hour or less depending on the traffic. Going in from that Direction the car is cruising and I was looking through the windows, I could see everything clear in front of me. My sister was happy for me to be home, I too was over the moon. I began telling her about my time away and about some of the guys I met in the dark place. A few months away isn't very long but living the way I did, made it seems like forever. I was feeling tired, my eyes burn, and I wanted to sleep but I won't sleep until we get home. Just a few minutes left for us to get there. We passed Featherbed Lane and Liba Garden then turn on to Willowdene. They were a Jerk spot at the top of the road, so we stopped at the big tree and bought jerk chicken. We got our order quickly and drove off again. We are home now and as I walked up to the gate I was greeted by skinny brown dog. He was looking at me like he was trying to figure out who I was or what I was doing here. I walked toward the grill and my sister's partner shouted he has the keys to the front door. I walked around the place checking things out. My sister headed to the kitchen, had something to eat, then she went and took a shower. She went straight into her bed. As soon as she was in bed she started snoring, I know she was a goner to how quickly she fell asleep.

I will wake her up, but in the morning. I am staying in the house tonight; I don't plan on leaving the house at all. Day is approaching, the night runs fast. I'm in one frame of mine now and it's to get some breakfast. It's a Saturday morning, so breakfast was ackee and salt fish with fried dumplings. This was good not even good but great. I was feeling great and wonderful, like I'm on top of the world. Nothing is sweeter than life and freedom. Thinking back to the dark place, I don't know how the rest of the guys were doing but I know they are still in the darkness doing what they have to do to survive. You can't afford to be afraid of anything in that place, you know how it goes these days. After the experience I just had, I was now change and fully focus on getting my life together. Content to put everything in the past behind. I was now like an eagle soaring to higher heights.

I wanted the chance to change to prove to myself, to my sister and everyone in my family to my friends, that I am a better person. After helping my sister to make breakfast, we all sat and ate together. I decided to pay a visit to my kids and their mother. To say that they were all surprised to see me was an understatement. I was greeted with big hugs and warm affection. It was emotional to be reunited with my kids. Seeing their little faces and knowing I have three mouths to feed; I can't sit down and rely on my sister all the time. I Have to find food for my kids, so I took few days in the house by myself, to think about what I was going to do. No one cares where you have been or where you are coming from or how hard things are for you at the moment. They want what their kids need. My duty was to provide for them, so it was back on the road again, looking for work. The quickest place to get a job at that time was on the site and that was where I was heading. You know man look food in desolate places as the saying goes and its true, speaking from experience. After leaving the dark place with dark experiences, I am in the light where I can gain more experiences, this time out in the clear and free world. Some of these experiences are very emotional, physically and mentally and they all have to do with children facing abused of all sorts from family member. Their mothers crying for help and advice from me, but we will get back to that shortly first let me share something with you about that occurred in my sister's house it's funny.

I kept on hearing these weird sounds coming from the next sides of the house that my sister rented. I don't know what was making that noise, but that side of the house was occupied by the couple I had mentioned earlier. I don't know them, and I don't have a problem with them either. They were a nice and a quiet couple. I would use the word couple to describe them, as it sounds more appropriate to me, than saying a man and his woman. They were a bit older than I was, so you know I'm talking about adults. I was hearing this sounds for quite a while, a few times as soon as my sister left for work and when her baby father's not home either. He was out working too, after recently losing his job as a police officer. Now he was a taxi operator running from Spanish town to Red Pond. After hearing these sounds for more than a week, it appears to be getting even louder. I was curious so I began timing the sounds, I even listen to how loud it gets and how often I heard it. Sometimes the sound is so tiny, it sounds like a kitten's cry. It was the sound that drew my attention, so I was wondering if there were any young kittens inside the house, but I was not convinced. I was thinking maybe I should take a peek or just leave it for a while and see if it dies by itself, but nothing changes. I had made more than one attempt to tell my sister or her partner, but I forgot. I even thought about telling the lady about sounds that I heard coming from her house sometime and asked her if she had any pets which had babies around the yard. But on second thought, I waited a little before saying anything to her. I have seen her more than once in the yard, I have said hello but I'm not much of a talker, so we didn't chat much with each other. Same for her partner as well. I heard the same sounds again but this time it sounds more like the animals were talking. This piqued my interest even more because I have never heard of talking cats or dog either, so this made my curiosity goes even wilder. I made up my mind up, I had to take a peek the next time I hear the sound again. No jokes at one point I was wondering if they had left the television on inside the house and what I was hearing was in fact characters from a television programme. This happens quite often so I knew I would hear it soon I'm sure, I'm confidence it will happen after everything goes quiet for a while. As soon as I started dozing off, I was startled by a sound, and it woke me from my sleep. This time it sounded like something dropped and broke and that's what actually woke me. Remaining still on my bed, face on the pillow, I could hear whispers. I thought to myself this doesn't sound like a dog or a cat. I have to figure out what's making this sound today. The noise sounded as if it was coming from near me, I had to wonder if I was dreaming it or if it was in my head. Either way I had to look to clear my head of this taught that it's a dream.

I thought what the hell was going on. I got off the bed, put my feet in my shoes because I didn't want to walk on the cold ground, because it would make me cough, catch a draft or start sneezing. From what I could piece together, I was positive I heard someone telling someone else to pray if they wanted piece. It was about ten o clock when I first heard the sound so I lay back and kept listening if I would hear it again. Not long after I heard the saying again. "If you want some you have to pray first before you get it". Immediately after that I heard a struggle and a bit of laughing so now, I was making a move to go and have a look. I was saying to myself, I must be crazy if I thought this was cats and dogs laughing and sounding like humans. I need to see a doctor or seek medical help, I was thinking it must be my time in the dark place that's fucking with head. But first I must take a look before I come to this conclusion. I still haven't figured out what's happening, and it was almost lunch time. So, I wondered if that was why she was telling him to say please before he gets lunch or a piece of whatever it was to eat. I moved silently to the window and got as close to the wall before pressing myself flat out against the window. Peeking from one corner of the window with my eyes focus and my ears sharp.

I was now able to see inside the house. I was overly cautious; I didn't want them seeing me and thought I was up to something totally different. My view was unobstructed, and I could clearly see what was happening. Not only that but the sounds were now clearer than they've ever been. What I saw was no joke, what I saw the couple next door idea of worship. The lady was laying down on her back, with her two legs raised in the air wide opened. She used her hands to spread her labia, holding her vagina open wide displaying her centre by holding apart both sides. Teasing her other half saying if he wanted it, he must say please and kneel down and pray to it before he gets it. Now that was some next level shit, no word of a lie. He dropped to his knees and began praying like his life depended on this one prayer. What I saw made my eyes bulged about two inches from its sockets. He was naked as the day he was born, with his dick erect in front of him. He was holding onto it and stroking it like a baton eager for action. The way she positioned herself on the bed, her pussy was right in line with the spot I was peeping from. So, you know I could see straight in the middle of her vagina. I saw her clit; I don't know if her dark skin colour had anything to do with it, but it made inside her pussy red like fire. It was like a beacon to lost souls. I quickly pulled myself away and from the window and began praying too. I thought to myself, I could do with some of that. If her hearing was as good as mine or if she was listening, then I'm sure she could hear me praying out in the background. Being in the dark place, with no form of female contact, after leaving I could really do with some of that. Every time I saw her, I wanted to pray. My baby mother had given birth a few weeks ago, so she was definitely not ready for that as yet. He prayed and his prayers were answered. He started doing his thing, so I went outside and started sweeping the yard. Leaving them alone to do what they're doing. I had heard and seen enough. I didn't want to hear them again trust me. After I had a moment to process what I've heard and seen, I couldn't stop laughing, especially when I remembered how she was holding open her vagina. To be honest I was a bit shocked, I now know the games women loves to play with men and use their pussy to make grown men acted stupid. The image of him bowing down, praying to the pussy will not be something I forget easily. What I thought were cats or dogs only to find out that was actually going on inside the house was hilarious. I could never look at either of them again without grinning. Now I'm wondering if other ladies make their men pray to their pussy.

My friend son

I HAD A FRIEND THAT I HAVEN'T SEEN OR HEARD FROM IN A LONG TIME. I have known her from when I attended secondary school. She lived in Port More St Catherine her name is Clarence. She was always quiet and soft spoken, she has three lovely kids, two girls and a boy. The boy was the youngest of the three. She did well raise them, like her they are soft spoken and well mannered. I was working around her house for a while. I use to work next door to her house when she was living in Willowdene Spanish town, before she relocate to live in Port More St Catherine in a place called Water Forth. it's still in St Catherine but a little closer to Spanish town itself. Clarence was always working, I use to asked her for a cold drink or some ice, because the sun was always so hot on the site. Depending on the time of the year, the heat was so scalding, it usually cause people to faint a few times on the site. It was so hot sometimes that we tied our heads with cement bags or towels and wet them every now and then to keep our heads and body cool. Clearance would call me at night sometimes to have a little chit chat, not long just a quick little friendly conversation. We talked about a lot of things, about the work site and Willowdene. She even told me that she was not with her husband anymore. I don't know how to take that, or why she was telling me that. Anyway, while I was working near her in Spanish town she would take the kids with her everywhere she was going, until they got a bit older. Seeing her with the kids all the time was fun. I would play games with them sometimes. We would play Ludo and snake and ladder and any other games that they knew. After playing these games we sometimes have lunch together. The two girls look more like twins Marie and Mari were their names. The boy was called Mykal. Mykal was more of an introvert, always quiet and would play games all day mostly by himself. He sometimes played with his sisters and his sister's friends just the same, but he was more interested in playing the games girls played. Nothing's wrong with the games he played but his behaviour was kind of strange to me. A few times I have been with them and the things he'd done were concerning. I would get him check out properly by medical personnel, just to be on the safe side. His movements were also kind of odd to me, I'm not certain how to describe it, other than to think he could be a special need child. I was not certain though, so I did not say anything. People can be very sensitive about their kids. Plus, I didn't want to say anything that would hurt my friend feeling or makes her upset. I didn't want to put her in an uncomfortable position, that may impact our friendship because I've unknowingly insulted her. He grew up around me for a while, so I only wanted the best for him, but it was not my place to pry. I sometimes follow his mum when she drops him off at school after she comes home from work.

I kept in touch with her after the sites work came to an end. We still keep in touch to this day. She would call me sometimes and say hello and I would do the same every now and again. She would fill me in on how the kids are doing. She was a stay-at-home kind of person, always in her house if she was not working. She can ask any one of her three kids to pay a bill online or do anything on the computer. She would do anything for these three kids, her whole life was centred on these children. I know for sure that she works hard to give them everything they need. She bought them tablets and laptops to do schoolwork and play games. Mykal was always on his laptop typing and doing homework, he was also doing well in school. One day I was in Spanish town and ran into her she was with him as usual. She asked him if he remembers me from down the road, he said yes. I said hello to him, and he did the same. He replied in a soft voice saying hello with is eyes blinking his eyes lashes at a rapid pace at me. He had long and thick eye lashes that women would envy. The look he was giving me was kind of disturbing, but I didn't anything about it. Just a quick look at him I think I saw something his mother did not see.

I notice he has a distinctive walk, and he wore some unusual looking tops and jeans. How he styled his hair was different. But just like before I said nothing. I talked to his mother for a few minutes, while I was talking to his mother, by the time we were finished talking, I saw some younger guys came around talking to him. The guys dressed the same way he did. I wondered who they were and if they attended the same school. Not paying much attention, to whatever he and the other boys were up to, I was just glad to see them. Continuing the conversation I asked his mother about his sisters, she said they were with their friends having a sleep over for the weekend. We chatted for a bit before we said our goodbyes.

It wasn't long after that, that I heard He left school and was pursuing a career in engineering, which is so good. His ways hasn't changed one bit, he still goes on his computer as always but now he swapped the girlie games for the dance hall scene. He goes clubbing and parties all over one regularly. By then he was an adult, so he went where he wanted unbothered. His mother loved him blindly, so didn't mind him hanging out with loads of girls and doing the same things girls do. This has been happening since he was a boy.

Early one morning before daybreak, I heard my phone ringing. A quick glance at the time revealed that it was three am. Thinking that this must be urgent, somebody must be dead or dying for anyone to be calling me at this hour, I answered the phone. It was Clarence, she said she was sorry to be calling at this time, but she really wanted someone to talk to. She asked if it was ok to talk and I said yes. Knowing the time, she called and the sound of her voice, I know something was wrong. Her tone didn't have that nice and calming effect like it usually does. Instead, she sounded as if she was crying, utter despair radiated from her end of the line. For a while she didn't say anything, just stayed on the line sounding as though she was trying to catch a breath. With a sigh she asked if she could call back because someone had just turned up. I thought how odd but I didn't push to talked just asked if her kids were okay. She hesitated before answering yes. I told her to feel free to call back anytime, because I could tell something wasn't right. I waited for her to call back, and a few minutes later she called back, then cancel the call. I waited giving her time to composed herself, if that's what she needed. Again, the same thing happened. I found this behaviour very strange, because she never used to behave like this at all. She would normally get to the point whenever she called. This cancelling and redialling was starting to piss me off because it was way too early to be dealing with this shit. The phone rang again, but I had already decided that this was it, if she hanged up again. I picked the phone up and kept quiet giving her the opportunity to speak. Finally, she began to speak, she sounds a bit tired and asked if I wanted to play a game of cards. How fucking odd, of all things. I said yes, just to see where she was going with this, because at the moment I was nowhere near her for us to be playing card games. She made more than three attempts to talk about why she really called but cuts the conversation short. I was thinking something is wrong with her. She was a strong woman which I knew very well, and she raised her children by herself. I know this for a fact that she didn't get any help from the kid's dad. So, for her to be beating around the bush like this has awaken my curiosity.

I would say time has a way of sorting things out. But as I sat listening to Clarence rambling on and not getting to the real reason she had called, I'm beginning to questioning that statement. In my gut I knew it has something to do with one of her kids. I can be a patient man so I waited for her to tell me what's going on. Sometimes you think you know your children well. Even when you are as devoted to them as Clarence was to hers, and pays special attention to them, they still find ways to keep things hidden. I don't rush her, I was curious about the calls, although she was cutting them too regular and fast. I was wondering what was going on with her. I hadn't even realised that so many hours has been wasted, it was now morning. My phone rang again this time it was my son calling. I took the call and listen when he spoke excitedly, he was about a game he wanted for Christmas. That was not a problem, I was back on the road doing odd jobs here and there for money. I knew I'd get this game for him somehow. I have learnt a new skill lately; I was like a listener now. I can listen and have a conversation with anyone and they can have confidence in me and I have a lot of confidence in myself. Being able to speak on varied types of conversation with men or women. I like to make peace in all situations that must come first. Not straying off topic but there are certain things I like in a woman. I like a woman who can stand up for herself in certain circumstances also, whether good or bad. I like a woman who carries herself like a lady, dresses like a lady, put her out fit together with exposing herself. Hair nicely done. I like maturity in a woman, especially when she acts, he age and not her shoe size. I like a home maker, a woman who knows how to prepare a decent meal and how to maintain her household. A woman who respects herself and her age.

I prefer eating from an elderly woman than a young girl, no disrespect to young girls but that one of my rules. I have things about me that ladies always like especially my cooking They like when I cook stew peas and white rice or curry goat, even chicken and rice and peas. I like a clean kitchen and toilets in a house, I will help do the washing up if the woman was busy. I will wash any clothing for them too, they love me for that. I like wearing blue and white, they are my favourite colours. I like my fitted cap matching my trainers or my t-shirt. I like everything matching a blue jean with a white t-shirt and a blue peak hat. I like trainers which is fully white or mixed coloured, black and white a bit of blue or purple on a trainer. I like a nice big face watch with brown leather band or silver band, one ring on each hand and a nice chain. My chain has a big B pendant encrusted with diamond shaping like the pendant itself. These things about me woman love. I like to sing and write nice love song; I will also sing for the ladies depending on to the mood.

Back to Mykal story. Mykal was invited to a party to which he was very early. Mykal dressed real nice, every one that came into the party took a look at him but he has never change his ways, not one bit. He was always standoffish or on his phone with someone nobody knows. It was getting a bit more noticeable to everyone; people were seeing him around hot spots and red light district. The spot where he hung out were not safe, his mother started getting complains about sighting of him in serious and strange places. He was warned more than once by his mother and ask questions about his where about, he told her something she wanted to hear, just to shuts her up, it happens over and over. He started to move really really strange. Shouting at his mother, telling her he was an adult. Telling her that whatever she heard is true. He asked her for his passport and his other personal documents. He told her that he don't wanted her washing his cloths anymore, he don't want any one going in his room either or anyone going on his laptop. His mother was glad to grant him his wishes just to make him happy and comfortable. She did as he wanted, she stopped washing his clothes like he asked. She told his sisters not to troubles his stuff, don't touch his laptop or enter his room for peace's sake. But after she stopped washing them, she found out he was not washing them either. They were thrown in a dirty basket and were piling up. They started giving the room a funky smell she don't like, nor did she like how he kept him room. She decided she was going in to give it a good clean. She began sorting out his clothes to put them in the washing machine. After picking up several t shirt and jeans, socks and towels she found two condoms in his pockets. she placed it on the side of his laptop, she saw about a dozen underpants in a draw which were dirty. She starts picking them up too, but some things caught her attention. There was what appeared to be dried bloods in all the under pants she saw. she takes a good look and starts crying, the first thing came to her mind was if he had haemorrhoids or cancer. She immediately calls him and asked him if he his ok, holding back tears. With the worst case scenario running through her mind, convinced that it must be cancer, she told him she was taking him to the doctors. But he was not interested. She asked a few friends that she had in the medical profession, what it could be, all saying it was best if he was seen. They didn't want to make any assumptions solely on what she was saying. One even told her that blood coming from the rectum could be a sign of cancer, but that alone isn't enough to indicate that it is, so he need to have a thorough check by his doctor. She cried her heart and eyes out, with him standing in front of her, begging him her take him to the doctors. She assured him she loves him, which he already knows and understood. She began pleading with him. With tears running down her face and her nose running, she started beating her head like she was going insane. She begged him, Mykal what's going on. He hugged her tightly and started crying. His two sisters joined them and start crying too. That was the bond of their family. If one was hurting, all would feel it. She told him she was going to book an appointment for him right now, with the phone in her hands by she started dialling the doctor's number, his sisters had already done it with another phones in the house. Just trying to do what she could to help her brother. He cried out and said to his mother, "where did you see blood?" She told him. He asked her how she came to see that, when he asked her not to wash his clothes anymore or go in his room. She told him she won't do it again, that she only wanted to clean is room for him when she discovered his bloody underwear and now she is worried. He looks at his sisters, hugged them tightly and told them he loves them. He told his mother he wants to speak to everyone, but he needs a drink first, which everyone quickly ran to make him a hot and a cold drink, when he refused. Stating that he needs something strong, he needs alcohol.

She told him what alcohol she had, and he accepted it. He said thank and immediately began drinking it like it was water. Still holding on to his little sisters, he screams out aloud and asked her if he told her what's wrong with him if she would still love him. She said yes, he looked at his sisters too and they all gave him the assurance that he needed, that they would still loves him no matter what. He held his head down while biting his lips, fingers tightly clench. His mother looking at him clearly seeing his distress, starts worrying even more, bracing herself for whatever medical condition he has. With tears running like a river down his face, he whispered, what caused the bleeding. Mum, he said, my virginity has been taken, that's why the blood is there in my underwear. I had sex the other day, for the first time and it hurts like hell, and it won't stop bleeding mum. With sobs wracking his body, he confessed to his mum and sisters, that he was gay. His mother and sisters burst out in tears. Quietly he told them that will move out. His mum cried for him but for a different reason. In Jamaica homosexuality was frown upon, especially back then. Men were murdered for being gay. So, she was terrified that the same thing would happen to her son.

She almost pops an artery trying to call me until she got through. After everything was discussed, a further check of his laptops revealed lots of nude pictures of men on his laptop. His mum pleaded with him to go to the doctor just to be on the safe side, because he told her that he can't stopped the bleeding. When I spoke to her, she cried asking me for advice. All I could say to her was continuing to love and support, him he is yours. She cried for days upon days but nothing changes, he was determined to leave. She begged him not to leave but he did leave anyway. When I saw her next, she showed me a few photos of his boyfriend and asked me if I have ever come across any situation like this before. I said no which was the honest truth. It like it was a popular thing, like it was in other countries. People kept things like that a secret because they feared for their lives. I was trying to keep her calm, I told her not to pressure him, let him relax his mind. The greatest thing is that she knows what's going on, and it not cancer. There was just too much crying, she cried as if she lost him, as if he had died. It was hard even talking to her. I myself felt it like I was one of the parents trust me. I told her to still take him to the doctor and get him checked out. She replied she will if her allowed her. I also told her to ask him if they protected themselves. Which she said she did, but he didn't answer. I don't know what's going on, but for me the silence speaks more than anything else you know how it goes or what I mean. She showed me a few photos and I was in shock. My head was gone again. The boy she showed me was another of my friend's son, living further in the housing scheme closer [0]to a place called Libya Gardens. I knew this little boy from he was born. Both his parents and I are also good friends. They still lived in Libya. Shit, I said to myself this is really a small world and it's proven to me more than once. A few months after I saw her, she called me one day and told me, that Mykal had moved back in with her. She said he brought the boyfriend home to meet her and his sisters. She told me, she accepted him back as I had instructed her, and he goes and comes with him all the time. She said she wish she had never found out the way she did, but the greatest thing is that she knows. In this life you have to try and move forward, each day you lived and you learned. Nothing surprises me these day for example father killing son, sisters killing sisters, and grandchildren killing their grandparents. Sometimes the very children we make and raise, we have been careful of them too. Sometimes they will help towards your demise and even your downfall. They will take your life if they can too, especially over wealth. Any assets you make have, money and property. These things will make the youths of today really go wild.

The boy that rapes his brother chapter

BACK IN NINETEEN NINETY-FOUR ONE OF MY COUSINS USE TO MAKE hand bags in her house and sells them from the back of her yard in Spanish Town. She was a trying girl, determined and works really hard. She sometimes does hair dressing at home to make a little extra money. She has two sisters that are not related to me. We talk quite often but as you know everyone has their own things to take care of, their life to live and business to tend to. My cousin has a sister who was much older than her. She has two sons and lived in Kingston. Her baby father lived in Old Harbour St Catherine. The eldest brother would take the younger one to school, while his mother goes to working. A separation between the mother and father causes the kids to split. It was decided that the mother would keep the older brother and the younger one was sent to live with his dad in Old Harbour. The younger boy had to leave the school he used to attend in Kingston and start attending a school much closer to his dad's home in Old Harbour. The brothers kept in touch with each other from time to time but they didn't get the chance to see each other often anymore. The parents remain friends. They talked to each other, but they have both moved on with their lives with different partner. My cousin's name is Margaret, and her two sisters are Keisha and Primrose.

Primrose was the eldest of the sisters and the two boys we are talking about are her sons. Their names are Damion and Devon. Damion was the eldest of the two for some reason, he has been acting distant and hasn't been to see his brother for a while. Thinking that the brothers had a falling out, Primrose started asking why Devon, the younger brother hasn't come to see her. She asked the dad, but he says that he's busy and the Devon doesn't like it in Kingston anymore. His mother tries everything to make him visit them in Kingston but finally, he told her that he's not coming back there. When she asked him why, he said he doesn't want to talk about it either and that he just wants to stay away from Kingston. He told his mother to say hello to his brother, and that he will think about visiting them someday, but not at the moment. He also told her that he was tied up with work and his girlfriend. She told him he could bring her over, that she would like to meet her. She went as far as to tell him, she just longing to see her baby, that even though he is grown he will always be her baby. She even asked him if it was his father that told something that made him not want to visit them. He told her no. He had a good relationship with his father, so he thought nothing about telling his father about the conversation with his mother. His father was upset at what Primrose was insinuating. That he had said something to deter Devon from wanting to visit his mother. He called Primrose and ask her about the conversation that she had with the their son and asked her how she could even think such a thing about him.

The conversation almost caused a quarrel with both parents, because the father didn't like what he heard. Anyway, it was sorted out between them. The father also explained that he had started a new job and that he has no free time, and he won't be able to take time off work unless it an emergency. She apologised to him and told him, that she was just missing her son because she hasn't seen him in a while. The father promised that any chance he gets they will both drives over to Kingston for a bit. She told him she would appreciate it, and that she can't wait because it's years since she last saw him. Commenting how much he must have grown. The father's say yes to her, that he fully grown and not her baby anymore. He is twenty going approaching twenty one, and Damion his going onto thirty years of age. The parents kept in touch but the two brothers hardly communicate with each other. Everyone noticed the discord between them, even their aunts talks about it. However, no one made an effort to find out what happening between. Everybody has their own thing doing on, no time to waste on other people's dramas, family or not. They are grown men, having girlfriends, having to work and earn a living. They both have their lives to live, having little to no time at all for socialising. That I could understand, they were no longer children with parent to support them, they had to do that for themselves.

Primrose was forty nine years of age going onto fifty, so she decided to throw herself a massive party to celebrate her fiftieth birthday. She started making plans for the party although her birthday was still a few months away. She was excited about this party and kept telling everyone about it, so they could start making preparations. She wanted her fiftieth to be a grand event and didn't want the people she loved missing out. Everyone loved her, plus she was a well-known woman around the community. Even people outside her community knew her, because she did hairdressing and sold things from the back of her yard. Hence the popularity. She knew lots of people anything happening on the road she heard about it quickly, nothing goes on without her knowing. She was like a mother to many in her community, she had this lovable, welcoming personality, you couldn't resist wanting to be around her. She wanted to shared her craft with others so she taught people how to make the bags. She was quite busy, so having the extra set of hands might come in handy. She loves a good party, so every now and then she will go to one, but mostly she just stays at home selling the hand bags she made and doing hair. Primrose had a lot of customers who supports her business both ways. Her handbag business and the hairdressing. Some suggest that she expands and start selling cloths or even start selling food and open a mini bar. She told them she will gladly consider their suggestions, but she don't think she has the space in her yard to do all that. However, the idea of having a mini bar in her yard sounded good, because she knew a lot of people already and the bar will bring more customers especially male who loves women in bars.

After thinking about having a bar at her house, she told her sisters about it. They both thought it was a good idea and gladly accept the offer to help put the plan in action straight away. Primrose began clearing out a part of her house and started building on it, to convert it into a bar. Long before she even finished the bar, costumers started coming to make their orders and asking for drinks. This was not strange for them because they already knew things like this would happen.

Primrose continued to sell her hand bags and other stuff, she was able to get the bar finish and fully stocked for her birthday. So not only will she be having her fiftieth birthday, she will also be having a bar opening. She worked hard and spent a lot of money, so maybe she will make some if not all of it back. The men she had working on the bar, worked really hard and fast for it to be done in time.

Inside the bar, she installed a big television that descended from the ceiling and a small pool table. Spot lights decorated dimly lit area and music played from speakers all around. She had some really nice chair and small table for her customers to sit and have their drink. A few little touches and it was completely ready for business. For a small in-home bar, it was nice and cosy. The neighbours thought the bar will do good for the community; the area needed something like this. Her sisters were there assisting and giving their full support. The sister was really close to each other, always supporting and look out for one another. The week before the party, they met up with each other to just chill and discuss the upcoming party. They asked her if Devon will be attending, she answered yes. With the party only a few days away, she worked night and day tirelessly to get everything done. Insides the bar was looking really good, she had helium balloons in number fifty, birthday banners hanging around and tea light decorated the tables. She knew the look she was going for and had previously got her dress and shoes to match. The only thing left was her hair and because she was a hairdresser, that was no problem at all. She had organised for a deejay and a MC to host her party. For her fiftieth she went all out. Primrose takes pride in her appearance and kept in shape. She ate well and kept active. Looking at her you could never tell she was fifty. People often commented on how good she looks.

It was the night of the party, and everything was in full swing. Primrose stepped out looking hot and sexy as hell. Her sisters were not letting her get away with all the attention because they came dress to impress or dress to sell off the bar. These sisters were beautiful, each had nice clear complexion, without a blemish in sight. Not to mention there they were curvy as hell. So, men will definitely be flocking to the bar. Men skin caught fire in these women presence, whether they are married or single. They were that sexy and good looking, plus they had likable personalities. They knew this, so the used what they had to their advantage, hence the busy bar. Primrose herself had an ass you could sit on and not fall off, and she is always smiling like there's no trouble in the world. The party was off to a great start, the bar was that busy.

Even though it was Primrose fiftieth, the sisters were more excited to see Devon, because they haven't seen him ages. From time to time Primrose would call her son Devon and let him speak to his aunties. They too miss him a lot and just can't wait to see, and hold him close.

Devon misses his mother too, but for some reason he hates Kingston. I was thinking it was the violence in Kingston that was the problem and he was scared. Or he just didn't want to leave his girlfriend side. At this point I was thinking maybe he was pussy whipped and could bare to be away from the kitty.

One day after speaking with his mother, Devon went straight into the bathroom and remain in there for a while. His girlfriend couldn't hear the shower running, toilet flushing or any movement for that matter and began wondering what he was doing. Thinking that he might be using his phone, she gave him another minute before calling out his name. Devon, she said but there was no reply. She repeat his name again, then push the door to the bathroom open, only to find him crying in silence. He was staring at his reflection in the mirror, like he was losing head. He looked at himself as if he was unclean. She asked him what happened, he said nothing as he tries to stop the flow of his tears. She knew something has obviously upset him and wanted to know what the problem was. He kept repeating that nothing was wrong. She told him it had to be something. Nothing wouldn't cause you to be crying like this, or staring at yourself like he was staring at shit.

She assumed something must be wrong with his mom and he was not saying anything to her. She continued to asked questions but got no answers. She asked him if his big brother was ok, he said yes in a gruff tone of voice. The way he responded made her suspect that something was clearly wrong. She could see that his whole demeanour had changed, by her asking about his brother. He stopped crying, he then washed his face and step outside the bathroom. She didn't like that he was not telling her what had caused the tears and this sudden stone behaviour. She started monitoring him closely. He was not a violent person, nor was he emotional either. So, for him to go from one extreme to another, she knew something was definitely wrong. He began talking to himself, which she found strange. She tried everything for him to opened up to her about what was bothering him and still he said nothing. She was worried about his behaviour and decided the minute she found herself alone, she will be calling his mother. To find out if she knew what had caused this change in her son. She didn't like it and found it way off. She had this feeling in her chest, that something horrible had happened. She started obsessing over what in the world it could be, to have cause such a switch in his behaviour. For him to have been speaking to his mum, then locking himself in the bathroom, to his weird behaviour, she knew it was something to do with his family. She even considered the possibility that he was sick and hiding it from her. She loved him a lot, and since she found him that day like that, she has been sick with worry. She was trying hard to do whatever she could to make him feel better and improved his mood. She just wanted them to be happy like there were before that call.

She was starting to become unwell. She was vomiting and couldn't keep anything she ate down. At first she was thinking maybe it was the stress from worrying about him that was making her sick. Eventually she decided to visit the doctor and Devon went with her. Once inside the doctor's office, he asked her how she was doing, she began explaining what's been happening and how she's been feeling. He asked her if she had eaten anything before coming in and asked her if she was feeling any pain or discomfort. She told him she wasn't in any pain, she just can't keep anything down. The doctors told her he will run some test go be certain, but he thinks that she might be pregnant. The doctor went ahead and checked her Blood pressure and pulse, her temperature and her blood sugar. When he was satisfied all was okay, he gave her a little test tube and asked her if he could have a urine sample. He directed her to the toilet and told her to come back when she's finished. When she returned with the sample, he did a pregnancy test and also checked her urine for infection. The test confirmed that she didn't have an infection, but she was definitely pregnant. He asked her about her last cycle and told her that she was about six to seven weeks pregnant. He told her to book another appointment in a few weeks for a scan, that will tell her exactly how far she is and her due date. The doctor advised her to try and keep her stress levels to a minimum and not get too worked up because it's not good during pregnancy. With a prescription in hand for prenatal vitamins and anti-sickness med they got ready to leave the doctor's office.

Devon was happy, this was good news for him. He said to himself, I am a going to be a father, a man with real responsibilities, I need to start thinking towards the future. There and then he started planning his future, one that includes his partner and his unborn child. Right at that very moment his head, his mind set changed. Straight away his intention becomes clear, he wanted that baby more than anything. Before they could leave the doctors told them to call or book an appointment if they have and problems or concerns. Devon put his arms around her and then thanked the doctor for his help. Walking out on to the Street with his girl's hand in his, he told he wanted to take her to his mother in Kingston. He told her that he knows the been a bit off lately but promised her he was going to change a lot of things. He told her he will be more opened and that he will try to spend more time with her, he wants them to be more committed to each other and that this is the perfect time for her to meet his mother.

He told her about the party that his mother was having. That she was celebrating her fiftieth birthday and bar opening and asked her if she would like to go with him. He was rather excited to introduce her to his mother and share the new about the baby with his mother. Also, he couldn't wait to gives his father the news and had asked him not to tell his mother before he had a chance, he wanted to surprise her on the night of the party. When they got home, they were both discussing the party, each talking about what they wanted to wear. They both decided on matching outfit, same colours, same everything. They wanted to look good for the occasion.

The party and bar opening is well on schedule, everything was organised and ready for the big day. Everyone has got their best dress ready, looking clean and sharp for this event. Primrose had spoken to her son and his father, and they both confirm that they will be attending. Devon told his girlfriend he wanted her to look nice, so she should get herself a dress because times was running fast. It was only a few days before the party. The weekend was just around the corner, days away. As I said before everyone was ready and couldn't wait for this party. The day of the party was finally here. Primrose and her two sisters were dressed and looking up to scratch. Devon, his baby mother Lisa, and his dad drives out from early, heading to Kingston. They stop for a bit to put some air in a flat tyre, they got on the way. He changed the tyre and continued on their journey. When they arrived at their destination the party was in full swing. The place was packed with people and buzzing with excitement. The house could hardly contain the crowd that showed up for this party, everywhere was packed to its capacity. The ladies were looking fabulous. Everyone was dancing, there were plenty of food, more than enough to drink, people were just enjoying themselves and having fun.

They parked for a bit watching the crowd. Primrose came outside and asked everyone to gather around the table so they could sing happy birthday to her. Everyone went inside and gathered around the table, everyone was squashed together due to limited space, music stopped and everyone gets quiet for the birthday song to start. After it was finished, the crowd went back to doing what they were doing. My cousin was curious about the standoff between the bothers and wanted to watch out for the greeting between the two of them. She decided not to say anything to her sisters, she just wanted to observe their interaction. After a while she called Primrose over. When Primrose reaches her sister's side and saw Devon, she screamed aloud and ran to embrace him. She held Devon and squeezed him tightly in her arms. Anyone watching could tell that she misses him badly. She then greeted his father like wise. Devon introduces his girlfriend to his mother, telling her she was going to be a grandma. Primrose was excited, she hugged Lisa and began running her hands all over Lisa's belly. You could tell that she fond of her. Some of the guests were outside partying, so they made their way inside the house, to where the rests of the family were. All this time Damion was inside his room, he came out soon after Devon and his girlfriend went inside. Devon was sitting with Lisa on his lap, he was sitting across the room, when Damion walked out the room with a smile on his face. He began greeting every one of his mother's friends before he looked over at his brother and his girlfriend. I don't know if it was the eye to eye contact from the two brothers that cause the place to erupt immediately.

Devon stood up so suddenly that his baby mother fell from his lap and crash to the floor. He rushed his brother in a fit of rage, smashing a battle on his brother's head. Blood splattered all over the room, the bottle broke on impact, causing glass shards flying everywhere. His mother and sister grabbed him to pull him and his brother apart. The crowd got busy, everyone was shocked and tried to move away from the fight. My cousin said she heard him whispered something, but couldn't make out what he was saying, because he was crying. At that point everyone vacated the house, leaving only the family behind. His mother was furious with his behaviour and asked him what happened. She shouted at him saying, "we haven't seen you in such a long time and look what you have done to your brother's head". Both of them began crying, even the aunts were crying about the situation. His mom told him that he needs to apologise for what he's done. But Devon kept shaking his head, he looked at his mother then his aunts and shouted he raped me. His mother could hardly believe what she heard and asked, "what did you say". In a much clearer voice he answered, he raped me. He repeated himself again saying he raped me aunty, he rapes me every day before he took me to school. Everyone was floored by his declaration, but it was his mum that was utterly devastated by this revelation. She cried and kept asking him if he was telling the truth.

He repeated himself and grabbed at his brother again. They were both crying. Devon cried for the hurt and the abuse done to him by his brother. Damion cried for the shame he felt, knowing his family knew what he had done. The mother asked Damion, if what Devon said was the truth but he didn't answer. He was just crying like a little boy. Devon told his family that he raped him when he was showering for school. Told them that he held him from behind and would cover his mouth, then he'd pushed him so that his belly would touch the wall. He told them that Damion would then take him from behind, while using his hands to play with his dick. He told his mother and aunts that one time he bled for almost a week, that he had to wear a tampon. He told them how Damion told him not to say anything, and that he pushed his finger in his bottom and asked him if he knows what that smells like. The things Devon was saying, not only were they disgusting but his family found it hard to believe that Damion could do such horrific thing to his brother.

My cousin was the one who told me about this, she also showed me her nephew Damion picture. I realized then and there, that he was the same young man in the photos on Mykal laptop, he was Mykal's boyfriend. The same Mykal who lives in Waterford Portmore. She told me that when she found out, she couldn't stop crying her eyes out and that she begged for this to be a family matter and family secret. I asked her what the father's reaction was, she said he grabbed Devon and pushed him into his car and sped off. I also asked what happened to Damion. She told me that he confessed to being gay and that he had always found boys attractive. He apologised to his mother and told her that he'd only done it once. I found that hard to believe but who am I to judge. Back to reality, a lot of families has dark secrets and if you heard them, it would make you wonder whether situation like these really happen.

As I stated before many families have dark secrets like these hidden, that they can't explain or talk. Unsurprisingly these things are more common than it should be. I will tell you about a man who impregnated his sister three times. You will hear about brothers who goes with their sisters. I knew a man that caught his son sleeping with his woman, this happened in St Johns Road. The father was also a police officer, when he found out he killed his woman immediately and then shot himself in the head, he died instantly. Some family members fight and kill one another over land and property. Plenty fathers molest with their daughters, and it's buried in secrets. Many times parents struggle so that they can provide a better life for their children. In some of these instances the children grow up and become disrespectful and ungrateful, with no regards to the sacrifices the parents made for them. I have observed and listen to these stories over time and have learned that no matter how much you invest in your kids, there will always be one to disappoint. Some of these kids today have no manners at all, trust me. There is too much story to tell, if I continued to talk about ungrateful kids. I have seen Damion a few times going and coming from supermarket. His mother had tried her best to rectify the situation between him and Devon. However, despite her best efforts there was too much hurt and heart ache for Devon to reconcile with his brother. Devon girlfriend had a girl baby that he loved and adored. He doesn't mind his daughter seeing his mother but refuses to let Damion be around her at any point. Damion remains the same his mother and father argue about it sometimes, they don't like that he is gay. They will have to accept the situation and move forward, which they all did even if the family remains broken beyond repair.

The family secrets chapters

As family members we are expected to move and pull together but as you know this does not happen. Life have its ways how it reveals and deals with its course. Settling matters and showing us things, we sometimes don't even want to know. Things that when reveal makes us unhappy, but that is life. I have witness from time to time, in all my fifty years that life always shows us somethings that are unexpected. I will relay a few things that other people might be able to relate to, situation that many have encountered. In all honesty in these situations, somethings are best Left alone because what you don't know won't hurt you.

Many times, in a family, you'll come girls with children and no fathers. It's best most of the time not to asked who the fathers are for peace's sake. The answers might be shocking or in some cases even embarrassing. Talking from my experience, I have seen it. I wouldn't say I have if it weren't true, by chance I have seen a few or I could say a lot. The reason why I said this was because I spoke to a girl, I knew a long time ago. I asked her about her sons dad and her reply was to asked me why that question. I told her nothing specific, just that my son said he knew the boy's dad and that I knew him too. My son didn't remember his name, that was why I asked, to find out if I really knew him. My son was always talking to me about his friend at school, telling that his friend father wasn't dead or living aboard. That he was the one that picked up his friend from school sometimes. I knew the boy the spoke of, I was friends with the family. Rumour in the family was that he had died, another was that he was in the states. Perplexed by this, I wondered why they would say he was dead or aboard if he wasn't.

I am talking about years upon years' worth of talks of him being dead. I myself don't know the truth but because it was put to me out of nothing, I just asked the question. She asked if I really wanted to know, I told her yes, but only if you wish to talk. I have Heard about the baby daddy being dead conversation before. She asked if I've heard something, I told her I might have. She looked me straight in the eyes and said, if I wanted to hear what she had to say, then I must first let her know what I've heard. I told her what I've heard, and she immediately say, no and stopped the conversation. After a while it appeared that she was going to telling me her side of the story, but as we started, I knew something was off. I don't know if it was a trust issue or what she was thinking but the conversation changed, and we started talking about other people and their own family matters.

She asked me if I was still working with the same firm I was working, I said yes. At the time I was working as a security guard in West End Negril. It was a job that I have always loved and enjoyed. We continue speaking and she again asked, if I really wanted to know. I said that it was up to her if she wanted to share that information with me. But at the same time, I don't want you to feel pressured in telling anything that you're not comfortable with. I was playing fool to catch the wise because I really was curious to know who her baby daddy was and why it was such a mystery. We continue to talk, then she said something that really had me puzzled. She said, "it your friend". I was completely lost for words. Very little surprises me but trust me when I say I was beyond surprised.

I have quite a few friends but I have never heard any of them with that story or any of them saying they had a child with her. In my head I was trying to work out which friend it could be. I said Melisa I can't guest who it is, you will have to be more specific. Before we could get into that, I saw her father coming and said look your father. I pointed at him coming from down the road. She looked and me and said, "oh case closed, that's your friend, my father". She continued to stare at me saying, is he not your friend. I was like what fuck. I was totally gobsmacked, she said ask me no question I tell you no lie. I could not believe what she was saying but she said it again. Even told me she has lost a child for him too. She made it very clear that he was her baby's father. Her father was my friend for real, never in a million years when she said your friend, would I have guessed it was him. I said fucking hell, no wonder they were saying he was dead. If I were her, I'd want him dead too. She said she was scared then walked away. He was someone I knew for a long time, and it was hard to imagine he could do something so heinous to his own daughter. I lost all respect for him, I could no longer trust him, especially around my kids. After a while we drifted apart, I wanted no part of his friendship.

The abortion story chapter

I HAVE COME ACROSS MANY ATROCITIES, IN MY LIFE MANY OF WHICH ARE by association. I've seen a lot of things people only read about. The next story I will disclose, is about the family that used to live beside my yard. I might refer to them as stories, but they are not. They are real events involving real people. Life was rough with these people, just like it was with mine or worse. Different families experience hardship in different form, but still make the most out of a bad situation. One day my neighbour asked me if I could get a taxi for her to go somewhere. I told her I will, but honestly, I never called my friend that owns a taxi, I had completely forgotten. I heard her calling out my name, asking me if I called the taxi yet. I said oh... I forgot. I could hear her cursing me out. I told her I'll do right away, she was literally pleading when she said please. What I couldn't understand was, her father runs a taxi and the car was park outside. I said to her, your father car is there, why don't you ask him. She said if she did want him to take her where she was going, she wouldn't have asked me to call someone else. She said to me, when the taxi arrives, I should let it come by my gate and she will come around. She asked me to call her over when it's done. I did, then she said she wanted me to follow her to where she was going.

I told her I was busy, but she begged me please. I saw her picking some tea bush, you know here in the country we just picked tea bush from anywhere brew it to drink. Cerassie, medina or even fever grass, these things grow wild on the sides of the road. When the taxi arrived, I did as she wishes, I called her over my yard. Back then we didn't have any fence so we would each walked through each other's yard. She puts the tea bush in a bag and started getting into the car. We drove to a place called Pointl Hill. When we got there, she when into this lady yard and told me and the taxi driver to wait on her. She was the one paying him, so I said no problem. I was outside with the driver chatting while we waited for her. It might have been about an hour, but I couldn't hear or see her coming. I decided to walk around to the back of the yard, towards something looking like a makeshift tent. I saw a few others sitting down, wanting to know what was going on inside I did a peep. To my surprise I saw my neighbour lying down on a small table with the lady's hand almost halfway up her vagina. I was so fucking frightened; I nearly drop dead. There was so much blood, I knew then and there I was not supposed to see this this shit. Quietly I run back to the car and said nothing.

A short while later, I heard her calling me. I walked around to the tent and saw her walking towards me. She could barely walk, she was moving so slow and looked as if she was going to collapse. Quickly I moved to her side to steady her, pretending not to know, I asked her what happened and if she was ok. She didn't even have the energy to answer me. The woman from before was a complete contrast to the one leaning on me for support. She was strong and lively, the woman who cursed me out for suggesting that she used her dad's taxi was a shell of herself. This was rather strange; I knew what I saw but I rather not say anything. The taxi drops us back at my gateway, she came out the car still barely able to move. She paid the driver who was observing her movement but said nothing. I helped her towards the veranda, where she slowly sat down on a chair. I sat beside her waiting to see if will would say anything. She showed me a bottle with something looking like dirty water in it, saying it's a roots drink and that it was good for her. I asked her good for what. She began telling me, she went to see that lady because she was pregnant and couldn't allow her father to find out. She is staring crying, saying she just had an abortion. That the drink in the bottle was a mixture herbs and the bushes she picked. That the lady brew it for her to drink because it would help to terminate the pregnancy. I taught it was tea bush that she had picked and asked her if she knew the name of it. She said it's called dog blood. In my mind, I said why would anyone drink something called dog blood. But that was neither my business nor was it my place to judge. After what I saw, I had to shake my head, my mind couldn't process what I'd seen. This woman was holding something that looked a like a clothes hanger, or something form of hook, that she was inserting inside her vagina. That was a big risk she had just taken. She could have been killed, trust me and all because she was hiding the fact she was pregnant from her dad. Things like these are happening in families all around the world.

Younger girls going to shady back door clinics, to get rid of unwanted pregnancy and risking their health and safety because they don't feel like they have a choice. I have seen many things in my life that I wish I hadn't, trust me. She could have died, but God was good. When she sat down you could see dark coloured blood running down her legs and messing you, her clothes. She looks sick to me like she was barely hanging on. I felt like crap because I followed her without knowing where she was going or what she was going to do.

Bad times with my family chapter

DURING MY LIFE I HAVE BEEN THROUGH A LOT, HOWEVER I HAVE LEARNED to master my problems and overcome them. On countless occasions, I have had bad days where my family and I argued over senseless or minor things. These things do happen from time to time, plenty other families lived like this. Remember life is what you make of it. Speaking from experience, it's very hard knowing who to trust. I've seen a lot these days and sometimes you dare not trust your own, but such is life. You can love someone and they don't love you in return, like wise you can raised a child from he or she was born and that very child grow up and turns against you. They will hurt you with reason or even says damaging things about you, especially if that child can't get their own way. They have this mentality that because they are getting older, they don't need to listen. Sometimes it the fact that they are getting support from other family members. Family members that knows that what the child is doing is wrong, but still condone this behaviour. Without speaking to the child, letting him or her know that, that its unacceptable. This can cause a rift in any family structure, where people feels like they are pitted against each other. I have come across situation like these myself. Speaking on this topic, there are a lots of bias behaviours going on, where it clear to see that it's just preference or favouritism going on, and it's common in my family. So, I'm assuming it's like that for other families as well. But life still goes on, you have family who will hurt you or say things that will hurt you from time to time. They say things even though they know it will cause a problem, even have the audacity to want to have a say over the things you work hard to achieve. Furthermore, if you don't know what you're doing, they will try and hold onto it like it's theirs. Even that's not enough, sometimes they will do and say things about you that will even hurt you and your children or other family members. Sometimes you just have to do you and not be bothered with family. I am not saying this to cause any problem just speaking my truth, my life is filled with ups and downs, with family being a part of it.

I am wearing these scars right now, the hurt of it all makes me feels like a black sheep sometimes. I'm treated like I am stupid, often times I don't feel loved and that's my honest opinion. If the truth should come out, that's exactly how I feel.

I have lost a lot with families in the past, even with my own children. I have been hurt several times physically, mentally and emotionally. I have had very bad things said about me and the lies talked about me. I would rather they slap me in the face than listen to those damaging and degrading things that they say about me, but such is life. I have given love, and for my love I receive hate in return, plenty of it too or in some instances very poor treatment. But time is the master nothing last for ever, only the loves of God my mind-set is completely different now.

I know they are fully aware of what there are doing, but we all know that if you ask silly questions, you get ridiculous answers. if you play silly games, you will get stupid results, so I just leave it alone and move on. Coming from a place of darkness going through a lot of rugged and disrespectful situation, talking to people, I realise that when I speak, they turned around everything I say into something totally different from what I said and mean. These people are all adults, so they know fully what they are saying and doing. You can see clearly what some people have in-store for you. I am in a good state of mind, I am kind hearted and I love helping others. But in spite of all this, I was never treated kindly or got help when I needed it. I had to beg and plead and that was not my policy. I rather do without than asked people because I always got a lot of empty promises, so I don't like asking for anything. I learn to work for what I wanted and make do with the little I had. No work was too hard for me to do, I never stop trying.

I love staying where there is peace and quiet. My moto is love and be loved. I am a respectable person, always saying thanks whenever I received anything from anyone. I expect the same when I give anything to anyone family or friends. I greet everyone with love and a warm smile, it doesn't matter who the person is, whether it's family, friends or children. I expect the same in return. I played a major role with helping to raise my niece and nephew and other family members. I love my nieces and nephews, whenever I see them I always greet them with utmost respect. I expect no less of them and the same goes for their parents, my brothers and sisters. I know very well that sometimes us adults have to be careful with what we do because sometimes kids will make us adults falls or quarrel over trivial matters. I am not only saying this for myself but once you have kids it's a possibility.

The patty lady and her church sister story

MISS LATHON WAS A LADY THAT BAKES REALLY NICE PATTIES. SHE IS A God-fearing Christian lady that loves her church with a passion. Guessing from the top of my head I would estimate her age to be between fifty-five to sixty. She always speak kindly to anyone, man, woman, boy or girls after she sold them her delicious patties. I was working as a security guard at the time at a property next door to this lady house. As a security I would always stay up throughout the night and I would see people going and coming. I put myself in a position at night where I am not easily seen. I did this for my own protection because this area that I'm talking about was known for violence, so I had to secure myself. I myself bought patties there also like everyone else. At lunchtime Miss Lathon patties would have a crowd gather outside her house to get these Delicious patties every day.

I noticed that she always has one of her church sisters there with her in the yard. She not a person who keep a lot of friends either from what I can remember. I am not certain if she has children of her own because I've never really takes any personal notice but I am sure I've seen kids around. Her church sister's role was to help her bake, serve and washing up dishes, cleaning the kitchen and the yard at the end of the day. Also, she would assist in the weekly prayer meetings, held by Miss Lathon. Miss Lathon patty business starts to grow, the crowd grew bigger and bigger, I was more vigilant than before because the site was in full operation. The construction site was near so there plenty of activities going on. My duties were to watch over the site, the equipment and it's material, but I gave a lending eye on miss Lathon business and her premises. I would say she was grateful, having a security presence to watch over her business. She was an older woman, with a thriving business in an area prone to violence, plus it was just her and her church sister, so having a male presence was appreciated.

I don't know her church sister's age, she might be the same age as Miss Lathon or younger but you can never tell because people's body show signs of aging differently. It's all down to how you treat your body, whether you eat healthy and exercise, drink, smoke or have health related issues. It all plays apart in a person's appearance, making you look younger than you are or older. I gave this woman the same respect I would Miss Lathon, it was ingrained in me to respect my elders from a young age. This lady was a hard worker, she was ok from what I would see. Any minor problem she had she would call me to assist her. Anything from people not wanting to pay or behaving badly I would gladly assist. My job anyway was to protect one's property and one's safety. Even though she was not on the site and I was not getting paid to secure her or her business, she was right in front of me I had little choice but to give an eye, even if she didn't asked me to. Her church sister was helping out also in that aspect but sometimes woman prefer the assistance of a man in certain situation. Not that they are incapable of dealing with a certain situation but considering their age and the area I would say it was best to help them. Plus, they remind me of my mother and sisters, scared of even a spider.

Keeping an eye on Miss Lathon was my own decision and I didn't have to do it, but I tried to give an eye just to make sure she was okay. Sometimes I would sit on her veranda and watch over the site, no one knew where I was located on the site and that was just perfect for me. I was very vigilant because I have seen a lot happened time after time. Since I began this job, I noticed that Miss Lathon started to bake bread, bulla's and buns by order. She would make and package them neatly and put them away for customers to collect. Since it was doing so well, she decided to add buns for Easter, cakes for Christmas, parties, weddings and funerals. It didn't matter, whatever the occasion, she would do it and did it really well. Anything to do with baking, you could see that it was her passion she did it like a professional would. As time went by Miss Lathon taught her church sister a lot of things, she thought her how to bake and even started helping her with her kids. They were doing well together as friends and church sisters.

Miss Lathon was such a good woman and friend to this lady, that she suggested that she made and sell her own patties, for extra money to look after her children. So, the church sister began her own baking business. She was baking patties, pastries and other things, she sold them to even Miss Lathon customers too. Things were going fine with the two Christian ladies working together, they both said that they are sisters in the lord.

The business grew even bigger, and they both began thriving more and more. As usual my job was watching the site, ensuring everything was in order. I would have my lunch there every now and then, the patties were always good, so I had no problem eating them. Whether it was chicken, beef, Callaloo, cabbages and salt fish patties, it made no difference they were all delicious and were also selling fast. The customers were coming from near and far, she made sure everyone got served quickly, to minimise the crowd gathering in the yard. Miss Lathon started leaving her church sister to hold her business down whenever she had to go away for a while. They were both doing good together, she was confident that her church sister would look after her business in her absence. The church was on board and supported the business. Miss Lathon was the type of person that allowed very little to bother her, she was really easy going, people respected her, she worked hard that's why her business was thriving the way it did.

One night I was on site and heard some sounds, the dogs were barking a little extra. I decided to look around to make sure all was ok, but I didn't see anything unusual. I thought it was strange for the dogs to behaving like that, something must be happening. Everyone on site woke up, looking around the place for anything amiss but nothing was out of order. After a while the place got back quiet again so they all went back to bed. The site had work men that worked late, some travelled from other parts of the Island that was far away. They stay sometimes for the week and go home over the weekends, or sometimes stay the weekend and even fortnightly. They will be on-site in early in the morning.

One morning Miss Lathon calls me over, I went over quietly to asked her what's up. From the look on Miss Lathon face, I knew straight away that something was wrong. She told me she found something in her yard and asked if I could check was it was. She led me outside right behind her door, I could tell she was a bit scared to even look to see what it was. At first glance I could see that it was a big black bag with something inside of it. When I checked it, I saw blood coming from the bottom of the bag. I had no idea what I was going to find but that didn't stopped me from opening the bag a little faster, only to realise it was the head of a dog inside the bag. Miss Lathon lets out a scream, so loud I was certain it would wake the entire neighbourhood. I told her to be quiet, while I look around properly to make sure no one was still one her property. After confirming it was safe, I went back on the site, got a fork and a pickaxe and dug a hole. I tied the bag properly and threw the bag in the hole and buried it in the ground, with just only me and her knowing about it. I could tell that she was in shock but to say I was surprise about this discovery was an understatement, I would have never guess it was something of this magnitude when she called me over. We began thinking what the hell was going on here. She was distraught, she was crying and saying look where they chose to throw this thing. She looked at me with tears streaming down her face and asked why someone would do such a thing, knowing this was her place of business. I tried to console her the best I could, I felt it for her, she was a good woman who didn't deserve this. After she was calm enough, I left her to go back to my duties. I didn't say anything to anyone at all. I was thinking that, if somebody wilfully found the time to do this, then I need to be more vigilant. I was busting my brain trying to work out who could have done something like this. It was a cruel and wicked act, trust me. I decided to take a personal interest in Miss Lathon house, while I am up in the night. I watched over her yard carefully, but I can't see anything at all. I don't know who would want to do this to Miss Lathon I was shocked.

Miss Lathon cried night and day; the situation had her stressed. One day during the lunch crowd she got extremely busy and the line stretched way behind her house, it was that long. Only to overheard someone says, that they saw a big black bag out back. Again, I was called to check out the contents in the bag. When we looked inside the bag, we saw the same thing like what we found the last time. A dead dog's heads inside and the body of the dog was missing. Straight away you know what was going on here and the impression it leaves. Someone was trying to sabotage her business. I was really upset with this turn of event; this was not something we could hide anymore. Everyone who knew about it was sympathetic toward Miss Lathon and her business. She didn't deserve this, I can't see the reason for this but bad mind and jealousy, it was clear. We had no idea how this would affect her business; people can be sceptical when it comes to food. Both her and her church sister was devastated by this and wondered who would do such a thing. Some costumers began talking about it, while others just bought what they want and leave. Some made very bad comments and suggestions, but that didn't stop Miss Lathon from baking and doing her thing, even though she was distracted and stressed over what was happening. She needed the business to pay her bills, maintain her family plus she had other things to take care of. At one point she considered stopping her business but I supported and encouraging her not to stop doing what she was doing because that was her lively hood.

What was really happening I pondered to myself, this was very serious, I tried everything to find out what was going on and who was behind this. I tried to play it cool and not to show any linked between me and her, just to see if I can find out anything or catch those responsible red handed. Because anybody doing this, I would really like to ask them one question and that's why. Why would you do such a horrible thing to this kind and caring woman. I'm convinced it was just jealously nothing else, trust me. I can't see any other reason for this kind of action, people began asking how something like this occurred and what's with the dog's head, and who could put such a thing there. They were asking the very same questions we were, something was wrong they know it, we knew it, because it was clear.

I was sitting on the site one night when I heard a sound. It appears as though someone was trying to break in, on the site. As quietly as I could, I bent down and started looking around. I could hardly see anything in the night, I tried to look as far as I could see in the dark, only to see what looked like a man coming towards the house. I bent down as low as possible and watched the man approached near where I was. He looked left, then right and then over Miss Lathon's house. He went closer towards the house and looked directly over the walls. After looking thoroughly over the walls, he then went back to direction he came from and returned with a box. With brisk steps, he approached for a second time, and quickly dump the contents of the box over the wall. Finally catching the culprit in the act, I crept up behind him as he turned to walked away and stopped him in his track. I said to the person "don't move", the person was so frightened he jumped. Not expecting anyone to be there because of how thoroughly he thought he looked. Using my flash light, I shone the light onto the person's face, only to realise it was no fucking man but the very same church sister who helped Miss Lathon with the baking. Disguised as a man in a big hat, black jeans and an oversize hoodie, she looked the part. Using the coverage of night to do her wrong doings. I thought my eyes were deceiving me, I couldn't believe it was the same person who wept with Miss Lathon when she found the dog's head. I asked her why she do something so heinous after everything that Miss Lathon had done for her. She stared at me for a moment then began crying. I warned her in a firm voice does not do it again. She begged me not to talk, she was crying, shaking and pleading so much that I agreed not to. She swore never to do it again and because I didn't want anyone finding me in this situation, I took the box and put the bag that she threw over the wall inside. When I checked the bag, it was a whole dead dog this time. I dug a hole and buried it, while thinking to myself a Christian woman did this, then again the devil was an angel so there you have it. I decided not to tell Miss Lathon because she was already having a break down and I knew this would utterly devastate her. Plus, I didn't want to send her blood pressure soaring. She truly loved her church sister like family, you could see from her actions. But these are the things people will get a head, maybe she thought by doing this it will deter people for buy from Miss Lathon and she could probably take over. I can't say for sure because I don't know her mind set but I know for certain she was not a good woman; she was bad minded. It was hard for me to see her day after day pretending to care, running Miss Lathon's business alongside her like nothing happened. However, they continued working together, kept weekly prayer meetings and went to church together.

The story of Andrea and her police brother

I WAS WORKING ANOTHER SECURITY JOB IN NEGRIL WHEN I COMES across a girl named Andrea who I knew and recognised from Hanover. Andrea kept on coming to buy cakes and other pastries from a bakery near to where I worked in Negril, she has been doing this for some time. She grew up doing this until she leaves primary school and moved on to high school, where she met other friends and started bringing them with her to the bakery. You could tell that they loved the pastries from that bakery, they were there nearly every day. Negril is well known for tourism and other businesses like, motor bike rentals, car rentals, various night clubs, and night spots, hotel and other things people would enjoy participating in day and night. Negril also had numerous beaches that attracts many tourists because of the availabilities of sea bikes, glass bottom boats, horse riding, snorkelling and many more enticing things. I was working at a popular hotel in Negril at the time, Andrea had went away and I haven't seen or heard anything from her for a long time. I mean nothing at all about her for a decade or so. Now I'm seeing her for the first time in a long while and she has grown. She was in her teens when I last saw her but I knew her from when she was a child and her brother Dave would always take her to school and back home every day.

I knew her parents and siblings very well. Her father was a police officer, her older brother Dave was a police officer and also one of her older sisters. So, there were three acting police in her family, she was the youngest of them all, so everyone took care of her, dropping her off to school before going to work. But Dave was the one who mostly took her to and from school. I used to go by their house, and I would sit down and talk with all of them when I visit but their father was a busy man so I would hardly see him in the yard. I knew Dave and Christine very well, before they all became police officers. The other sister was a nurse and worked in the Spanish town hospital, they were all nice people. Every now and then they would keep parties and invite me over which I attend a few, not all of them. Their mother Mrs Daisey was a very lovely woman, she was hard working from what I can remember.

I was speaking to her one day and she told me about some pain she was feeling in her legs and her knees, she said the knees were hurting her really bad and she thinks it's arthritis, she was convinced. I told her I was off to work and that we will talked a next time because I am running late and in a hurry. She said that's fine, run along but she still wanted to talk to me when I can find the time, she insists.

Mrs Daisey and I would talk every now and then when we saw each other, whether in the streets, around the area in the shops and any other places we might meets. Mrs Daisey always washes clothes around the back of her yard, I would stand by the fence and talked to her while she was washing or hanging the clothes on the lines, she enjoyed talking to me. At that time Dave was home more regular than everyone else, until he went and sat the police test at the academy where he passed, completed his training and graduated and began working as police officer, in Green Island police station, in Hanover. His sister was working in Lucea police station, that's also in Hanover and his father worked in Grange hill police station that's just a little out of Hanover. Back then we were we are all good with each other.

Andrea and I started talking about school in Hanover we reminisced about old times. She expressed how much she loves the police work and intended to join them after leaving high school. She told me she was interested in the security guard work I was doing and asked how she could join the company. I could also see that she liked talking to me as well and was interested in my job. She asked me if the pay was good, and I told her yes. I even told her that if she was really interesting in the job, I would try to find out if there was any vacancy and let her know as soon as possible. She said she was definitely interested and grateful that I would enquire about the job on her behalf and that she would wait until I get back to her with an answer. I sent a message to my supervisor asking about vacancies, he received the message, and I was waiting for an answer from him, which he said he'd give me before the weekend. He had told me previously that he was interested in hiring two females' security staff, so hopefully by me referring Andrea she'll get the Job. He said he would enquire if any of the other supervisors had employed any additional staff and check the books first, because it's company regulation and employment rules. Everything had to be done above board and by the books, when hiring new staff, the, procedures had to be followed correctly. A check of the books revealed that no one has been employed. Andrea now had a chance for an interview and a shot at the job. But first she had to sit the entry test, which she had passed with flying colours and was waiting on an interview, which will be held on the weekend. She was so excited; she could hardly wait for the weekend to come to get the interview out the way.

The weekend came very quickly, and she went and did the interview and got the job as entry level security. She did the induction and will start in a couple of days. She asked to be put on the night shift because she prefers to work at nights. I totally understand her and where she is coming from. It's less hassle and she'll have more free time trust me. I used to do nights myself, the night shift is always more quiet but just remember the night is always more serious and riskier. Most of the guards said the same thing about it being more dangerous but the job has to be done anyway, so someone has to do it. A job is a job, people have to work to survive and that is life.

As time passes, I could see that her confidence in me has grown and she began confiding in me. We talked about every and anything, form way back when she was younger and attending school. We also talked about the present and things she hoped to do in the future. She told me how much she enjoys and loves parties, that she even got an invite to one that her and her friends will be attending that weekend. She asked me if I was interested in going but I told her I would be working that weekend straight through. I told her that I had asked for the extra hours because I needed the extra money. Whenever we ran into each other, we would chat for a bit, especially if we were on the same shift. We would chat at lunchtime time or when we were leaving work together and taking the bus. People would call me all sorts of names because of my job. I was sometimes called names like gaurdie, security or even watchy, but Andrea would call me by my given name, Byron. I think it's because she knew me very well. She would often say that every day was different, or every other day was different doing this job. There were lots of interesting and exciting part to this job, but it all depends on where you were posted, and it fun sometimes too. Again, it depends on where you are based. If you were stationed in Negril, then it was always fun especially in the West End. That area had many luxury hotels, big name ones that were well known all over on that stretch of road. They featured seven miles of white sand beaches, that attracts tourists for all over. The hotels were very good and were always busy too, so the chance of you being bored was rear. Working in the hotels in Negril came with a lot of risks you had to be very vigilant and aware of your surroundings. I had a lot of experience from working as a security guard in a chain of hotels. One thing you need be cautious about it that people will lie, if you are not careful. They will even see you with your own things and accused you of stealing it from out of their belongings from their rooms. I was told by my supervisor not to wear anything expensive or anything Which was not relevant to the job while at work. He warned specifically about jewellery, not just me but all of us working as security. He said we were allowed to wear our wedding bands and a simple watch, and that we must always have a safe place to keeps all of our belongings, that if we chose to wear expensive jewellery make sure we have proof of purchase. It has happened before were visitors and tourists have accused security guards of stealing, or they'd say things against them. Unfortunately, in these situations, the costumers always get the benefit of a doubt, on any compound from it was reported. If that happens, you'd be reprimanded and told you should have known better, especially if you are a security guard with more than 3 years of experience under your belt. I personally have never been in these situations or experienced anything of the sort, in this specific job. But I can tell you this for nothing I have seen and been through a lot especially on construction sites all over the island.

Anyway, as Andrea settled into a routine, I observed how uneasy she was around strangers and how afraid she was around certain types of men. It was like she was categories them in her head for some reason. She watched their size and built of their bodies, plus she always wanted us to travel together. She always wanted me to accompany her if she went clubbing and parties. She would ask me some weird questions about men from time to time, like if they are strong. She would see a man and automatically be judging his strength for some reason, I don't know. I answered the questions to the best of my ability but for some reason she was scared of something and not saying it, but it was clear. I asked her if she had a boyfriend just out of curiosity and she answered in a low tone of voice that she doesn't want to talk too much about men. I could see that her body language change and became tense when I asked that. She was reluctant to carry on with the conversation since I mentioned her having a boyfriend. She was less forthcoming, and I could tell she was holding back something. One day I asked her about her parents, she said they were all ok, then she whispered something that I could hardly hear. I asked her to repeat what she just said, but she carried on as if I hadn't spoken. Then she looked at me and said I shouldn't ask her about her siblings. I found her entire behaviour at the mention of her family a bit strange. I asked her what the problem was, she said there was none she just prefers not to talk about them.

I know it was not my business but I thought it was odd, that she didn't want to talk about her sisters and brothers. I thought to myself, that maybe they were having a family dispute, because families sometimes fight with each other. However she is adamant that everything was good, but I still didn't believe her, her attitude when talking about them was too strange. I Knew something wasn't right, but it is what it is. Anyway, we carried on talking avoiding subjects' family related. I got a call on my mobile phone, I looked at it to see that it was my son calling, I answered the phone and chatted with him for a bit, letting him know I'll be home in the morning. I made him a promise that I will take home something nice for him. Back then, if you told a child that you were bringing a gift home for them, better believe that they will be waiting up for you to come home. I always tried my best to keep my promises to my kids, so I will definitely be taking something home for him. I decline the offer, telling her that's it was my only day off in a long while and I wanted to spend the day with my kids. She said she understood, but I must promise to go with her next time. I just tell her we'll see. A few hours later somebody rang me, I think it was one of Andrea's friends, saying Andrea wanted to talk to me. I asked if she was ok, but I got no answer. If she wanted to talk, I was ok listening. She asked if I could come to where she was. I had no intention nor was I prepared to leave where I was, plus it was not a good time. She made a comment which I found strange, that she was scared and didn't want to leave without me being there. She was crying that's why her friends were calling me, they thought we were family or involved in some way. They thought I might be able to pick her up, like I was the one who she was going home with, but they got it wrong. Andrea was just someone I knew for a long time; from she was very young. I can't understand why she only wanted me though, when she went to this party with her girlfriends, and it was about six of them traveling together. Yet she was still scared. I thought to myself that something was going on, what could be the problem, when she was travelling with so many other people and still felt scared. I was honestly curious and wanted to find out what frighten her and caused her to be so petrified.

I got dress and left my house. I made it to the party in good time. I scoped out the crowd trying to identify her from the many faces present. Eventually her friends spotted me and came over, telling me she was over there and pointing in the direction where she was. When I found her, I approached her and asked if she was ok, she replied yes. Anyway, I asked her what's up with her, she said she was not feeling so good, and she wants to talk. In my mind I was like, this better be important. I said to her, I'm here listening, feel free to talk when you're ready. She waited until her friends all left. Then she began crying again. I looked to the heavens for strength because I didn't know what to do, or what was even wrong with her. After a few minutes of crying, she began telling me that she needed to talk to me about something personal. She said it was very important and everything she is about to tell me is private. Then she said something I was not expecting. She said she knew why she couldn't keep a boyfriend and if she eventually found herself with one, he would do the same as the others. He would leave soon after they slept together. I asked her why is that and why she thought that was the reason for them leaving. She burst out in tears, sniffling her nose you could see the tears running down her face. She said she don't like men. She said it aloud, repeatedly. (mi nuh like men, mi nuh like men). I reminded her that I am a man, she apologised, said she was not talking about me. That what she meant to say, was that she didn't like her brother Dave, who was an active police officer.

Immediately I ask her why, she started explaining the reasons why she hated her brother. When I heard the reasons, it was a good thing I was sitting down, or I would have fallen on my ass. Thank god I was sitting down from when I was trying desperately to calm her down and stop her from crying. This seems as if she needs counselling. I am good at listen but Jesus Christ, this one blows my mind, this one just messed me up big time. I thinking about Dave, whom I have known for a long time, I knew the family. All this she was telling me was hard for me to process trust me. At first when she started, I thought she was going to say something like, he stole her money or whatever. I seriously was not expecting what she was telling me. This needs more than just me, I needed something strong to drink to process what I was hearing. What I was hearing sounded really mess up and disgusting. All the while, my mind was picturing Dave and the rest of the family, from when we were younger. I definitely needed a drink but on the other hand I needed to listen to this sober. I have heard plenty of fucked up things in my life but this was up high on the worst thing ever. I don't know if it was because I knew the people involve, why I thought it was so horrific, but it sounded terrible. Andrea looked like she would burst if she didn't get what she wanted to say off her chest. She pleaded with me, to let her tell me everything that happened to her when she was small. I felt it for her very much, this was what she told me out of her mouth in her very own words.

She said Dave was always bathing her from she was small, when she was about five or six and probably even younger, from what she can remember and taking her to basic school. She paused and that part and started to vomit. She told me that he always stuck his tongue in her vagina form even smaller than five and inserting his finger inside. She said he was doing this for years until she was about seven, he would insert his middle finger part way inside her vagina, telling her he was opening it for his tongue to fit in properly. She said she never understood what he was saying or doing to her. That at first when it just happened, when he was just bathing her, she taught it was ok for her older brother to be doing this. But as things progress and he started using his fingers and tongue, she knew it was wrong. That big brothers are not supposed to do things like this, she lamented. Sitting down and listening to this made me really cautious with all my kids, especially my daughters. This puts something different inside my head and made me sceptical about trusting people with my children. There and then

I was wondering what my daughters were doing and who they were with at the moment. I even felt an urge to call them to check they were safe. The things she was telling me he did to her was disgusting. This man was a police officer, his duties were to serve and protect, yet he violated his baby sister in the worst way imaginable. I was just listening before saying anything, I didn't want to disturb her, not one bit. I was thinking Dave was a real mother fucker. He was only pretending to be an upstanding individual, but he was the worst and he was going to get what was coming to him. She continued talking, she said sometimes he would kiss her, sticking his tongue in her mouth and also in her ears too, all the while his finger was in her vagina. She said one day he just pull her head down on his lap and put his penis in her mouth, she said to how far he put it she started to gag. She said after that he would make her suck it every day before going to school, even when it choked her. She said she got so use to it; she didn't gag anymore. Listening to this made me feel like insects were crawling all over my body. She began crying even more, when she said this next bit. She said he was the one to take her virginity. She said one day he just pulled her down on him and inserted his penis. She said the pain is so intense, it burns and felt like she was being ripped to shreds. She said she tried to push him off, but the more she resisted the harder her pushed. Plus, she was no match for a huge grown man, who was very strong. She said she remembers feeling like she was about to pass out. She said she can recall the size of his dick, from the times he put it in her mouth, and it was not small. She said she was so scared, that she remembered his strength and how he held her down on the ground. She said she still remembers how much he sweat and how he held his hand over her mouth, to stop her screams from coming out. She said all the while her body kept trembling nonstop, she couldn't stop shaking, she remember this vividly like it was yesterday. She said she can recall how her belly bottom cramped and how sick she felt. She said even though she begged him to stop, he never listen, he pretended as if she hadn't spoken. She told me that he stopped and pulled out of her, that when she caught a glimpse of his penis it had blood all over it. That all he did was, rinse it off and put it in her mouth for her to suck. She said she preferred it in her mouth because she could hardly manage the pain. She recounted all this in tears, my heart broke for her. She continued recounting the horrific ordeal of her past, and all I could do was listen and console her the best way I could. She said after his was finished with her, she was in so much pain she could barely move and that she had blood running down on the inside of her legs, she bled nonstop.

The next day when she was at school, her tummy was so cramped and she was so sore. She told me that he watched her. He watched her every move and didn't want anyone in the yard to find out. She said on the second day after he did what he did, she was still in pain but that didn't matter to him. He just held her down and she was forced to endure the same brutality. That the force he used to enter her, ripped open any damages he left behind and chiggers the bleeding again. She said she couldn't help it, she peed herself and that the urine burnt like hell. She kept repeating that he was very very strong. That's when I realized, all those times when she'd asked about strong men, she probably was associating them with her attacks. That was the reason why she was scared of them also. Looking at her, I could see that she was clearly traumatised by these incidents, she could not hold back the tears. At that point she had been crying for so long that she was shaking. She told me that one day he was about to rape her again, and her father just opened the door and saw her half naked. She said her father asked her what was going and why she was she half dressed. She told him nothing was wrong but that her father suspected something and asked her again but she said it was ok and that nothing was going on. She said she could still remember the look on her father's face, he looked like he was going to kill Dave. That he looked at Dave and asked him what he was doing. She told me that her father threatened Dave, he told him he better pray and hope, he wasn't doing what he thought he was about to do. That he pointed his service pistol at Dave with his finger on the trigger and told him, he would shoot him dead if he was thinking of hurting her. She told me she began crying, pleading with her father, telling him that nothing was happening and that Dave wasn't doing anything. She said she felt sorry for Dave and even though he deserved to be shot for what he did. She didn't want to be the reason a father killed his son. She told me that Dave was also crying and telling their father that nothing was happening, he swore it. I wasn't doing anything daddy. Her father said make sure and walked away but came back giving Dave one last look. She said the way her father stared at Dave and behaved, she knew for sure he would have kill him, no doubt about it. She said shortly after that her father left for work, when he came back he watched Dave and her. She knew that her father suspected that Dave had done something to her or was about to do something. She said she could see that her father just wanted to kill him.

She placed her hands in mine and asked me what I think she should do. She is convinced the whole experience has impacted her so much, that she has issues trusting not only men but people in certain position. Also, she thinks that the other reason why she can't keep a man is because he stretched her out down there. She was crying, I too was crying. she was leaning on me, I felt really badly for her but at the same time I didn't want her leaning on me or me embracing her. She was in a fragile state and I didn't wanted her thinking this friendship was more than it was. But I can't tell her that, I just comforted her and tried to show her the support she needed. I personally think she needs professional help, some counselling, to help her deal with all the pent-up emotions she was experiencing. Something was wrong she is crying harder and harder she needs help.

I asked her if she'd told anyone other than me about it. She said she told her mother and sisters about what happened but didn't like their reaction towards it. They were all telling it should be kept in the family as a family matter, because they didn't want anyone knowing about it. She said it's all a big hush hush, that they were more concerned about what people would think if they found out about it. The disgrace it would bring to the family as well. She said they were even trying to say it was all lies and kept asking her questions about it repeatedly, even though she had already told them what happened. She said she hated talking about it, and on few occasions, she has ran into women who had experience abuse by family members. She said she feels sympathy for them and wishes she could do something to help because she too is like them. She asked me what I think she should do that she wanted my advice. But I don't think she was ready for the advice I would give, I believe her family should all go prison. Half of her siblings and her father worked as law enforcement, so for that level of abuse to take place there was some form of negligence was involved. I talked to her as I would a close friend or family. She was a small child when this happened, never fully understanding or knowing what was going on. Now as an adult she fully understood realised what was done to her. She said she feels nasty and is disgusted with herself, and often considered suicide multiple times. She said she even wishes her brother dead too. That she feels worthless and would do anything for this feeling of despair to go. I told her the only way she can get any justice from this was to report it to the police and let the law handle it or even tell her father, but I now learned from her that her father has passed away a few years earlier. Before he died, she told her mother and sisters that she was going to let her father know about it. They said no and they begged her not to tell him because they knew very well he would have killed Dave, that it didn't matter how long ago it happened.

She said intimacy was a major issue for her, that certain things triggers her and caused her to have panic attacks. This was serious, she genuinely believed that by him forcing himself into her, has damaged her physically and now she was left with an extra size passage. He has ruined her not only physically but emotionally also. Every time she tries to get intimate with a man it ends with her shaking and in tears. She feels like she will never get back to normal at no point. She said she attempted suicide, but she was spotted and stop from doing so by a family member. She cried like she was going to die. I tried my best to calm her down, but she wouldn't stop crying. She insists there was huge hole beneath her. I told her that's just in her mind. She told me if I didn't believe her, she could show it to me. Very quickly, I replied no, it's ok, I believe you I don't need to see it. She was very serious that her best part of her has been taken by her brother. She said she knows it's irrational but she hates every one called Dave and can't stand the sight of them either. She cried for the entire night. I don't know what happened prior to her friends calling me or what triggers this emotional over load, but she was hurting real bad. This is why parents need to be very vigilant with their children today. I kept asking myself where the mother was when all of this was happening.

These days this is what's happening to plenty kids at home. These behaviours are common everywhere. We need to look out for the signs and insist to know what is going on with our children. Sometimes the people you suspect or expect to do something bad, it won't be them. It is usually the person you least expect and likely trust that will be the culprit in these situations. It is heart breaking to know that, as parents you have to question your children safety with even family members. That you really can't let them out of your sight. I am a parent, and I am addressing any parents that read this book, be cautious of who you let around your kids. I don't care who the person is to you, be vigilant. Don't turn a blind eye to certain things, because they are family or close friends and you love them. Don't be afraid to watch their behaviour around your children even if they lavish you gifts and cash regularly. Don't be afraid to question why your child is uncomfortable around this uncle or don't like that cousin. Often time it's a reason. Talk to your children about inappropriate behaviour from family and adults in general. Love is blind, and it will miss leads you. Parents please don't leave your children boys or girls with these so call family you love. These predators' men or women because they might be giving you large sum of cash or might even give you a flashy car to drive and paying your bills or whatever to keep you quiet. Don't leave your kids to lose their innocence, don't leave them to suffer knowingly. Don't ignore the sign or telling them they are lying when they complain to you, as was the case with Andrea. Don't ignore the sign or your gut instincts, Like Andrea's father did. Parents, please look out for the unexpected. Dave can be anywhere or anyone around you or Andrea can also be in your household today and too afraid to come forward because she is scared her own family might not believe. Remember monsters and predators or out there and they don't only prey on little girls, they prey on little boys too. It can be a person who is around you in your circle of friends or popular in your community. I am begging you parents or guardians if you see anything suspicious or just suspect something is happening but not certain, please check it out, ask questions. And in worst case scenarios please talk to somebody about it as quick as possible. Andrea, please remember you can save other persons, not just here where you are but anywhere around the world. If you know of a Dave out there, there are numbers to call and report him. To the Andreas out there, don't keep this as a secret and suffer in silence. Leave a note at school with your teacher on their desk, write a note stating that you need help. Speak to someone, and do remember this Andrea, you are loved and will get help and support.

So, I am reminding you Andrea we are all in this together as parents. Don't be ashamed to talk. Now to all the Andreas and Andres around the world, who have been hurt in this way. I am pleading with you to come forward and talk to someone so you can get help and support you need. You don't have to deal with this on your own, it's not your fault. You did nothing wrong. Please don't be a shame to talk. Say something please. Remember to suffer in silence is potentially doing yourself more harm than good. There will be support for you. To all the little boys and girls around the world living with these types of scars and suffering inside please say something come forward and let us all break this cycle of child abuse. And to all the child abusers out there and around the world, the message is clear just remember that your crimes won't go unpunished forever, you are being watched. And lastly, to all the abused children out their just remember you are not alone.

The story of a man who was dying and told his son to take his wife

My cousin Marvin and I was standing talking about fixing his old car that was giving him problems. He was thinking it was the crankshaft causing the problem. The car was an old one, a Nissan Sunny to be exact. It was starting and shutting off, he was considering putting it in a garage, but is a bit apprehensive because he thinks he can fix it himself because he knows about car engines. I asked him how old the car was, because it broke down more often than it drove. I told him to sell it, but then again nobody will want that to buy either, so he had a problem on his hand. The car couldn't start up at all. For the few seconds that you turn the key in the ignition, the amount of smoke it produces, you know it's only a matter of time before it started to blaze. This was not good for him because he couldn't move when he wanted to. Although he bought loads of different parts for the car, the same thing happens. He was planning to take out the old engine by himself and wanted me to assist him with the lifting of the engine. This engine was really heavy, and one person won't be able to lift it alone trust me on that. It won't work, it needed at least four men to lift an engine out of a car.

I started helping him with fixing the car, it was old, so it took a lot of work. One minute you think you are getting somewhere with it, but the second you started the car it shuts off again. We both knew the car had done its time, but for some reason he can't seem to let it go. Back before the car reach this state of can't start, it was just problem after problem. It wasn't good either because you can find him sometimes on every side street or sometimes in the main road in the hours of night trying to fix the car because it has broken down. I personally think it's not safe for him, that he should try and get rid of it. I tried talking to him but apparently, he chooses not to listen. This car was hard work if it drives one week it breaks down for two months. He was convenience that he can make it work. Marvin had a thing for old cars and believed he had extensive knowledge when it's pertain to car engines. One day

213

he went out and came back with one of the very same car same year, model everything.

I ask him what's up with this purchase. He said he bought it for parts, that he needed to fix the other car. I said to him smart move, but I didn't think it was, I just didn't want to be negative. But it will be the same thing, problem. There's a saying that says you can't keep doing the same thing and expect different result. In his case, he was using a broken care to fix a broken car, expecting a decent car. I don't understand that logic. Plus, it was another load of work to change over these parts from one car to the other and twice the time. Marvin has a lot of faith, trust me. Many times my friend Reds and I talked about his earnestness in fixing his car, and that if we had the money we would buy him a good car and scrap the old ones. Not even to bother selling them, just rid of them completely. It wasn't good for him or the environment, because whenever the engine starts it gives off this horrid smell like oil burning and plumes of smoke. Even though he was fixing it, it wasn't getting any better, if anything it got worse. But nothing would change his mind, he was obsessed with fixing this wreckage.

Marvin has two other brothers and a sister and lives with his mother. He has another brother that lives abroad and another one who lives in the area, but not with them in the same yard. His father also lives in close proximity to Spanish Town in a place called Bog Walk. Marvin's father fixed refrigerators, freezers and washing machine for a living, his name was Mr Greene. Mr Greene loved Marvin dearly and would do anything for him. He would also help Marvin to fix these old cars, he himself used to have an old car as well just a different make. They were big fans of old things needing repair. His father's car was even more older than his car, it's so old Ford don't make that model anymore. The only positive thing I can say is that he himself was very old too and had to stop driving because of his age and his sight was deteriorating. He was way into his eighties and already couldn't see out of one eye and now the other one was becoming problematic. Marvin being the good son he was to his father began taking over his dad's job of fixing refrigerators, microwaves, and washers etc. Helping him out because of his ailing health. Marvin was a man with many trades, he was a fisherman and often went fishing, sometimes at sea or in the rivers around the area, when he was free and not doing anything .

I enjoyed watching him fixing his net lines, rods and pots for fishing, he was good at doing this. He also had a boat engine in his house, whenever he was going fishing, he would use the boat engine to put on a boat and do what he called trawling or deep see fishing. He likes going crab hunting and enjoys hunting other things too. Marvin was the kind of man that did any job for a buck, he runs taxis, and even sold the fishes he caught after coming back from sea or river. On a few occasions he asked me to go with him, but I refused, because I don't want to be in any vehicle car or boat operated by the engines he fixed. My faith in him is not that strong. Moreover, he talked about several encounters with sharks in the sea while fishing and crocodiles in the bushes while hunting crab and other things. He is very brave, when I listen to him talking about the size of the sharks and crocodiles he encountered out there while fishing or hunting, I have to decline, my bravery has limits, my life is only one. These adventures were a definite no-no for me, I would never put myself up for grabs with any wild life or play bait for anything either. I don't believe it's safe, but it was his choice whether or not to put himself in danger. That's a situation he'll have to face alone.

In spite of his recklessness, Marvin was a very honest man. He and his father were very, very close and they did lots of things together regularly. He would take his father to all is hospital appointments, his father was sickly he was an elderly man at the age of eighty-five. He has a few health issues, but Marvin was always supportive to him, helping with every move or whatever was happening. Of all his children, he loved Marvin fiercely and confided in Marvin a lot. There was nothing he wouldn't give or do for his son. He trusted him with everything and anything. They are always seen together in Marvin's car, or they can be seen in other vehicles together. Marvin's father discussed everything with him, nothing was considered too personal for his son to know, he was privy to information no one else knew. Like the fact that he was the only one that knew his father has a lot of money in the bank. He own acres upon acres of land, owned multiple houses, had a bar and a few shops amongst other things. He even raised livestock, he had a some pigs, goats, cows and have even a few donkeys. From what I could see they both loved animals. Mr Greene wife had a lot of respect for Marvin, she like that he looked after his father and supported him. Marvin was not the wife's child, he had a mother that he shared with his other siblings, but she too loved him like he was her own. Marvin would cook daily and bring food for them both all the time. He also loved Mrs Greene like a mother, he wouldn't do anything in this world to disappoint her. Whenever she prepared a meal, she would share Marvin's dinner like she did for her husband.

If you saw them in the street, you couldn't tell they were stepmother and stepson, they were really close, they treated each other like mother and son. Marvin had decided to invested in livestock like his father, he had purchase a few goats, pigs, chickens, turkeys and was even planning to purchase some cows and sheep, once he had the turnovers from the other livestock. The thing about Marvin was, he didn't mind manual labour, he was always involve in something or the other. He loved cooking, his father's favourite meal to eat was curry, so Marvin was always preparing curry goat or curry chicken, anything to make his dad happy. He saw his father more than his other siblings did, he visited him literally every day. His father's health was deteriorating rapid, so he used the time he had to help take care of him. His father was reliant on him too, if he needed anything Marvin was the first person he would called, because of his poor health, he visited the doctors and went hospital regularly. He was in constant pain and taking a vast amount of medicine. Inside his house was like a mini pharmacy, due to the amount of medication he has stored inside the cabinets. Anywhere he went, he always took his medication, his situation was dire and the prognosis wasn't much better.

This was not looking good for Mr Greene, but he was still holding on. The money he had in the bank, he told Marvin about the account and even where the account details were. He also told him about who owed him money and other important things. Mr Greene was a businessman and he had a lot of commitments and unfinished businesses that he needed to take care of, which he was trying to sort out because his health was deteriorating fast. He was very weak and could hardly manage to stand up on his own. Lately he had trouble keeping his food down and often vomited when he ate or drank anything. His weight decreased significantly in a short period of time, it was noticeable by the hollowness of his eyes and gauntness of his cheeks. He had a raspy quality to his voice, and he began speaking slowly. I recall Marvin telling me that his father had fallen down a few times in the house and banged his head. He was in constant pain and complained that his back and stomach hurt badly. Mr Greene needed assistant with continence care, because he was doubly incontinent and needed to wear adult pads. His body shivered constantly and needed blankets to keep him warm.

One day Marvin and I went to visit his father, they were talking and I saw Mr Greene whispering with Marvin and laughing. I couldn't hear what he was saying, but from the expression on Marvin's face I assumed it didn't sit well with him. This was the first time I have ever seen Marvin and his father having a disagreement. Marvin looked outraged and annoyed. I could see his father was trying to convince him to do something he was uncomfortable with and didn't want to do. I wondered what the issue was, but because they were not talking to me, I kept my cool. I was never invited in the conversation by either of them, so I played it like I didn't hear anything. Mrs green was standing there, she wasn't taking notice of what was going on even though it was kind of noticeable. She wasn't paying much attention to the situation, she just carried on talking to her husband at the same time, and doing what she was doing. I continued to watch Mr Greene and Marvin across the way, still having that tense conversation by themselves. I couldn't hear the conversation, but I saw clearly it wasn't a pleasant one, nor was it going well. I was wondering what was going on, it was unusual for Marvin to disagree with his father. I wasn't going to be nosey, but I knew something was definitely going on between them. After a while the situation became less tensed, and they started talking about random things like catching and cooking fish. Marvin was good at catching and preparing fish as I have mention before and everyone loved when he cooks.

Marvin could ride a bicycle or his motorcycle if his car wasn't working. He sometimes performed a lot of stunts on the bike. Marvin was skilled in a lot of things; he was also good in climbing trees. At nights he always walked with a light on his forehead, even in the daytime he goes around with the light, because he was always fixing something. Whether it's a car, refrigerators, washing machine, microwaves or any others thing. He was very much like his father, when it came to fixing appliances. Marvin was always teasing his father, that he liked fishing and going to the sea but and he really couldn't swim. Mr Greene would just laugh, he did it for enjoyment. He enjoyed going out on the sea on boats or on the sea side, he also like throwing fishing lines. I thought his father was very brave to go be going out on boats, in very deep waters and couldn't swim, but he was an old man and doing that brought him joy. These are the things he can no longer enjoy due to his health issues.

One day Marvin got a message to call is stepmother. He was at sea fishing, when he checked his phone and got the message. He immediately called his father wife to find out if he was doing ok or if she was ok. She told him, his father wanted to talk to him urgently. Mr Greene's Health had started to improve a bit and he was a lot more conscious. He started talking more strongly. His intension was to sort out a few documents and other things because he knew his time was limited and where he was heading. Time was closing in on him fast. With the help of his lawyers, he wrote his will and signed it properly. With the will sealed off, in an envelope his instructions were for his son to do what he asked. He wanted his son to do something he didn't want to do. The same thing that caused the misunderstanding between them earlier. It was the same conversation that was brought up again, the one where they couldn't agree. I was there listening and still couldn't make sense or understand what was happening between the two of them. I was on the uncertain side, so I did what I always do and minded my own business, even though I was still curious and wanted to know. I stayed quiet and listen to see if I could figure out what was being said. I finally realized what was going on and what the argument was about. Believe me, I have found myself in a position to see and hear thing, but this wasn't something I could have predict ever hearing.

I could not believe what Mr Greene was telling his son. He was telling his son, that he wanted him to take his wife after he dies. He told his son that he wanted him to take over for him. At first I was confused and wondered what he meant. But then I heard him say, that he want Marvin to have her, that he would rather Marvin having her, than another man. He continued to plead his case, like he was trying to convince his son. Telling his son that he knows he was the best person to take her because he would look after her, like he would. The strangest thing was, he meant every word and believed what he was saying. He wanted his son to comply and honour his wishes. He even went as far as to say, that he knows his son didn't have any woman so it shouldn't be a problem for him. Marvin just stood there shaking his head, telling his father that he could never or will ever honour that wish because it was absurd. He said I can't do that. Now remember, Marvin was in his early thirties and his father's wife was in about eighty five years old. I had to wonder if Mr Greene was losing his mind, or if it was a prank, but it wasn't. Mr Greene was as serious as a judge. This didn't sound good at all. I just stood there taking it all in, trust me I was trying really hard not to laugh. I knew Marvin must have been embarrassed because I was there, listening and hearing everything. I'm sure he would have preferred to not have this conversation. I knew for sure that Marvin wasn't going to do anything like that. People was like this; they will try to force there will on you. He knew the reason he was doing it and was trying to make his son accept what he was saying. It also seems as if the wife was aware of her husband request and was ok with it. Marvin was completely against the idea and found it gross and disgusting. But Mr Greene didn't care, he thinks his son was the perfect one for his wife and no other man.

The sad story of visiting another country

MY SISTER REMI DECIDED TO MIGRATE TO ENGLAND FOR A BETTER LIFE and was unsure if she would coming back. She promised to keep in touch, which she did by calling and checking on us often. Things were going good for her, she had enrolled in college, her intention was to continue her nursing, she was also working. She had taken her daughter with her and in no time, she was able send for my older sister and one of my younger brother. When she migrated, she left her house in Church Pen, filled with furniture. I stayed there and was alone in the house for some time, and for quite a while, I even brought one of my kids to live with me and keep my company. I planted a few peppers and others stuff around the yard, the yard was filled with rich soil. Anything you planted in the yard grew fast and flourished. Sometimes I would visit my cousins in Clarendon. If they had anything doing, like digging a pit and packing it, I would help them. The pit once done and packed was used for a toilet. When all the hard work was done, I decided to leave because I had some important business to attend to. I was sorting out myself to make a move shortly and hopefully join my sister Remi. I had been waiting for this day for a long time, I really can't see myself sitting here any longer. I needed to prepare myself and make arrangements to leave this place. I really wanted to leave here because my intention was to help myself and my family by providing a better life for them.

I wanted to be a better uncle, a better brother, and most importantly, a better father for my children and help anyone I can help. I always try to help my family, that's all I have ever done, my heart is clean and filled with nothing but love for my family and friends. But for some reason, the love and kindness I showed them or even how I treated them was never reciprocated. I didn't get this types of treatment from them in return, which is very sad. But such was life, unfair as it might seems. We always hear that from our elderly parents. They also told us manners will carry you through the world. Its only recently that I understood that saying, now that I was an adult. I really saw what it meant especially with these kids today. I'm on a journey, one of reflection and self-growth. My destination is a straightforward, I have no intentions of going backwards. My purpose is to make myself a better man, a father my kids will look up to and a son my parents can be proud of.

At last, the time came for me to elevate myself. I now had the opportunity to be what I wanted to be; the ball was in my corner. My sister kept calling and checking up on me, talking and coaching me with questions, I must expect whenever I reached my destination. I had limited time, so I needed to move as fast as I can, making last minute preparations for my departure. I didn't want to be late, so I had do what I had to do quickly and I mean very, very quickly.

The iron bird was on its way, I set myself to take a long rest after packing, helping digging the pit, plus all the last minute run around, putting a few things in place prior to leaving was tiring. I was moving on to a place of sweetness, which I should be arriving in a short while. As a matter of fact, it was only hours away. In my mind I was thinking what was going to happen next, or how this was going to work out, but I was still trodden on to my destination, which was about nine to ten hours away. For me this was a dream, one where eyes were wide opened, I could see what's going on around me clearly. It was a bittersweet moment, because even though I was happy, I was sad also. I was headed somewhere I didn't know or been before, plus I was leaving my three kids behind, and I loved them world without end. I felt like I was leaving my joy and happiness behind, but I had a purpose and it was to give them a better life. I wondered if I should leave them, or if this was really worth it, I kept asking myself. I could be really wrong but I hope the decision to leave will change all our lives for the better. Seated on this Iron bird, I have plenty of time to reflect. I thought about how gladly my cousin packed my stuff and wishing me the best. I thought about how excited I was and how excited they were for me. I can still remember the looks on my cousins 's face, she was so proud of me. I remember the two old ladies that were in the yard, they were sisters. One was blind in both eyes; the other sister suffers from asthma. Their names were Mrs Norlean and Mrs avill. Both are dead now, they loved me to bits, they were two nice old ladies.

They were both crying when I was leaving, wondering what they were going to do when I'm gone. I think everyone will still hold the fourth same way. Things will get even better for all of us, the future was looking brighter. We were all family, so I'll do what I can, while also still look out for the old ladies. Noting changes, nothing was different. If I could help the old ladies in anyway at all, I would do. Mrs Avill had cataract on her eyes, It cost a certain amount to do a surgery to scrape her eyes and it was s a substantial amount as well. She didn't have the money, but knew that once done, then she would be able to see again, which would be nice. Everyone in the yard would love for this to happen. However it's been a few years since this happen, and the two lovely old are resting peacefully.

Fast forward in time and I've have landed in a new country. I could hardly wait to see my mother, Remi, my older sister and my brother. Outside in the arrivals lounge, I spotted my family waiting for me. As soon as I approached them, they all embraced me, hugging me tightly. I was so happy to see them, after not seeing them for a while. We made our way to the car park, to begin the journey home. Looking through the car window, I looked at the scenery, noticing how different it looked from where I was coming from. At first it was just roads, motorway, traffic signs indicating to go this way or that way. Although the journey to their house was very long, we passed the time by reminiscing on old time, and with them filling me in on current situations. After driving for an hour, the scenery began to change. I saw lush green grass, I was thinking to myself, yes the grass was literally greener, I'm definitely in the right place. I saw plenty houses, most of which were made of bricks. It was a total contrast from where I was coming from. I was looking forward to walking outside and touring my new surroundings, that I will be calling home, for the time being. I can hardly wait to get settled into a routine, to reacquaint myself with the rest of the family and see where this life takes me. My mother was overjoyed with me being here, she has been living here years before my sister came to the country. Once I get to where I'll be staying, I will be calling back home in Clarendon to let them know the outcome of my travel and that I arrived safely.

The following day, I was taken on a tour around London. The first place I visited was Buckingham Palace. I was curious because I have never seen a Palace before. Upon seeing it, it didn't match the image of what I had in mind for a place, but it was impressive non the less. However, I did get to see the guards wearing their bearskin cap, dressed in black and Red and standing sentry around the palace grounds and huge black and gold gate. I have heard about this place when I was younger, now it was right in front of me. After we left the Palace we headed to Oxford circus, where I went shopping, was treated to a late lunch before we headed back home. It's been a long time since I felt such contentment. Not to mention, but my belly has never been so filled. I drank milk like it was water, ate cakes like it was going out of style. I was given all different kinds of food both from my culture and others, and I ate and drank it all, everything. I was give delicious fried chicken, curry goat and white rice, sometimes served with hard food. Such as yam, green bananas and dumplings or something with rice and peas. I was introduced to Turkish, Chinese, Indian and many other cuisine but the kebab was my favourite. A month in this country and I was a different person. When I came here, I was skinny as hell and looked as if I was starving. Now I could feel the fat on me like it was extra garment. I know I was gaining weight on me; I was getting fatter and fatter by the day. I know this sounds greedy, but my mother was giving food to me like no body's business, and I ate it all like craving bugger. I thought about nothing else, I just ate as I got the food, nonstop. My mother kept telling everyone she knew that her son was here. I was home a lot, because I hadn't found a job yet, so I was home everyday day, weekend also. At first, I wasn't so disheartened, I thought it was the norm for jobs to be harder to find. Especially as I knew to the country and wasn't a citizen, and didn't have the rights to work. But as the days turned weeks, weeks into months, I slowly realised that it wasn't at all filled with opportunities, and easy money. Back home in Jamaica, people believed that because you live in a foreign country, you are better off financially, or that money is easy to come by. But I was proof of the fact that, that was incorrect.

Finally after a few months I got a little cash in hand job, cleaning bricks on a construction site, along with some other task. The pay was very cheap, but it was better than nothing. I had a little money for myself to buy what I wanted. Moreover, I felt more comfortable knowing that I didn't have to rely on my family and was able to contribute to some of the house hold expenses. I was also able to send some money back home for my kids. I wasn't a person that went partying, I didn't drink or smoke, so even though my wages wasn't a lot, I was able to save a little. Being independent has always been important for me. For the first couple of months in the country without a job, just staying home and sitting down. I felt like a fish out of water. I have heard and seen how sometimes, living with family whilst not working can result in the them taking liberties. The added pressure of being responsible for another person are all contributing factors. Personally, I have never experienced anything of the sorts from my family, but things like this is a regular occurrence in foreign countries.

My sister Remi called to inform me that my father will be coming here soon. She told me that she was making the necessary arrangements for him, as he will be living with her while he was here. I was excited for my father, because he and I had always had a close relationship. I could hardly wait to see him; I love reasoning with him on a range of topics and enjoy being in his company. As time passes, I began settling into a routine, now that I was working and doing something to occupy my time, I didn't feel so unsettled. I began enquiring about enrolling myself in a college, I wanted to learn new skills and gain experiences working with computers. I found a college, but it was located in Brixton. The journey from where I was living, to where the college in Brixton was, too far away to travel. I had met up with a couple of friends I knew from back home and had gotten a single room to rent from one of them. I stayed closer to the college during the week but on weekends, I went to see my family. Keeping up with the little cash in hand job was a bit of a challenge, because I was given shifts on days that I'm supposed to go college. Plus, the money I would save was becoming less, because I had rent plus weekly travel tickets that I had to purchase. I decided to start looking in the area that I was staying for another job. I manage to get a cleaning job, cleaning office building after hours. A few months into college and I realise that the college wasn't at all what it seems.

The college that I was attending was located near the train station in a well-known multi-cultural community. It had a huge marketplace, where everything was sold, from food, clothes, household items to souvenirs. Anything you can think of was sold there. Many people from the Caribbean visited that community. Just by walking around, you will encounter a lot of people you knew from back home. I can tell you this, Brixton was like back home in Jamaica, anything Caribbean related was found in abundance there. I don't know if it was the area, or the people that attended the college, but the collage was under surveillance by officials. This was not a good look for the school. There were a lot of speculations, arguments going around that students attending school were involved in things of the criminal variety. Also, that they were attending for immigration reasons. They rumours were many, but after thorough investigation the officials had the proof that they needed, and the college was shut down.

Once again, I found myself in a situation, I didn't want to be in. With the college closed, I had a lot of free time, because I was only working part-time. I was already missing my kids, but with this much time spent doing hardly anything, I had time to reflect. I thought about my life here and compared it to the life I life I had back home. And to be honest, this supposedly greener grass country was not living up to my expectations. My mind was unsettled and the yearning to be with my kids became unbearable. With my mind made up, I decided to return home, to reunite with my children and be in a place where certainty wasn't so uncertain.

The police officer that sold herself to my brother

MY YOUNGER BROTHER LARRY WAS USED TO HAVING LOADS OF DIFFERENT female companions, on his WhatsApp profile. I noticed he changes them regularly. I found it strange, that he was so blatant about his proclivities and posting it. Thinking to myself what's wrong with this brother and wondering if his girlfriend didn't see them on his DP. I was just being nosey, wanting to know what was going on with him and these ladies. So, I kept watching his profile as it changed daily, without saying anything to him. These women varied and were had different nationalities. My brother liked having plenty women. I know this because every time I saw him, he had a different woman, other than the one he lived with. I was thinking, what was his girlfriend's saying about this, I want to ask him, but at the same time I didn't want him to think I was prying too much in his business. I always wanted to ask him this question, if they were just his friends or were they having intercourse. I just hope whatever the situation between them was, that he was being safe and covering his dick. Deciding to let this go, I kept quiet and waited, because this was happening quite regularly. But it was only a matter of time before his actions caught up to him. I don't know how he kept this up, or manage this many women, but I will continue watching, without saying anything at all to him or anyone. I was even trying to see some of these women for real, no lie. The thing about curiosity is, it's like a disease, once you have it, it spreads. The only cure is to find the answers to what made you become curious in the first place. So, I began feeding this curiosity, wondering how and where he knew and found all these ladies from. I find it really odd, my mind was just creating all these different scenarios, to come up with something to soothe my curiosity. I even wondered what his girlfriend had to say about all these different women he kept displaying on his profile or if she cared. I thought maybe it could be some of his and her friends. I didn't know who they were but a few of them were really pretty. I did have a look at them because they were on his DP, and I wanted to see them clearly. This appears as though he lacks respect for his woman. Maybe he didn't care whether or not she knew what he was getting up to. Either way, that was their business to sort, to each his own, I will still be here to watch the fall out.

For months I observed his behaviour, watching and waiting not doing or saying anything. Just checking to see what more he was going to put out there, what next was going to pop-up. Just so I could get a good laughed as usual, and that was something I enjoyed doing, laughing because some of the things he posted were funny. I was bursting to ask him about this for a long time, but never bothered. I wanted to give him time, hoping he could open that line of conversation between us. However, he never did, and this habit of watching his DP went on for months. By this point many were aware of his behaviour, some even had the audacity to call me to try get information regarding his lifestyle. I told them I was Just a silent observer, much as they were, we were all in the dark. Like me, they too will have to wait for whatever, because I was certain this was going to blow up in his face. I knew his woman had a temper, so if she was oblivious to what was happening, the minute the wool is pulled from her eyes, shits going to hit the fan. Especially if she found out that, this has been happening behind her back for ages. How he kept this a secret from her for so long was a mystery to me. I watched for months as things escalated, his apartment literally became a like a brothel. I honestly don't know what else to call it, because women kept going and coming minutely and hourly. The minute one departed, another took her place. I sometimes had to wonder if he was getting them off the internet or from some kind of on like dating app. I knew if I asked he wouldn't be honest about where these women came from he won't tell the truth either. Maybe he thought he was fooling everyone, but not me. I wondered if he was trying to prove something to me, or to anyone who could see, because we had many conversations about loads of different things, but this has never pop up, not once. I thought to myself, I might as well just leave him alone, and not bring up the subject. To just be prepare for when things come to light, or when things at breaking point. I know he will definitely talk then. I became aware that, not only were they on his WhatsApp but they were all over his Instagram platform too. I asked myself, why the hell was he putting up all these women on his profile, what was he getting from this. Why was he doing this, it was bad enough that he was the way he is, but to be flaunting it like this, was another thing entirely. I kept scanning the myriad, of faces, trying to see if I knew any of the women. Unfortunately, they didn't look familiar, not one of them. So I kept doing, what I started out doing, and that was watching his Watts app profile and now I was watching his Instagram too. Every so often I notice a new face was added to his collection, it's becoming a thing where I'm convinced this must be one elaborate joke, or he was doing this thing for fun.

One day I went to visit him, we were both sitting down in the house, when a lady walked right through the front door and entered the sitting room. She said hello, and I answered her in the same way, saying hello too, and carried on with what I was doing before. I thought to myself should I ask her any questions, but I didn't want to seem as if I was being invasive. This was the perfect opportunity to watch the interaction between them. I was fine with what was going on, she is my brother's girl, plus it was their business. I thought nothing of it, other than why does she have access to the placed he lived with his woman. I have always been mindful of situation like this, because I know how these ladies are now a days. I just didn't understand how he kept doing this, with no regards to the what ifs. I wondered what gave him such confidence to be so brazen, for him to be entertaining this behaviour in his residence. I could tell from his relaxed posture that he was comfortable doing this and not on edge like a person sneaking around. Clearly he didn't mind what his woman thinks, he showed no signs of concern about her finding another woman in their home. I had to seriously wonder if she knew what he got up to and turn a blind eye. If that was the case, what was she gaining from this, or maybe they were in it together. I this point I'm thinking anything was possible. If she didn't have an issue with it, then all I can say is that she was definitely a one of a kind type woman. Normally, things like this would irate another woman, making them more volatile and prone to violence. So with this in mind, I had to contemplate what was truly going on. Some women only needed to suspect their partners of cheating and the would raise the roof, of this I am sure. I wanted to pull him aside and have a good talk with him, letting him know that what I was seeing was disrespectful. Again, I said to myself just chill Byron just chill, just watch and see what happens. It didn't take long for me to notice a pattern, because the next day I saw a different woman in the yard. This one was an Indian woman. She had a straight face, nice, pointed nose. She wasn't that tall, she was about five feet seven inches in height. She wasn't too slim; she had a little meat on her body and had small feet. She was pleasing to the eyes, nice figure, long hair and a pretty smile. She looked the part of the perfect women, for a lot of men. But for me, those weren't what I looked for in a partner. Although, it didn't hurt if she was a good-looking woman.

My curiosity was driving me wild as hell. I was observing all these females go in and out, no doubt wishing it was me. Especially with the one I just describe, she fits the criteria, but I'm leaving that alone and focus all my energy on myself. I need more time to get myself together properly. This was crazy because this house was looking more like a show room for women. All types of women running in and out of the house. After a few days of watching this, I realised that his girlfriend knew about the whole thing. She was even present a couple time when the other women showed up. What really took me by surprise, was that she said nothing, did nothing. That really grabbed my attention, because in all my years of living, I have never come across a situation like this. Furthermore, what woman in her right mind allowed other women to run rampant in her home and remained unaffected by it. Something was definitely up with this, and I wanted to know what it was. I thought they are all friends, but I just came back home so I wouldn't know what was really going on here, after only staying for such a short while. I tried to talk to him, telling him that he needed to be careful, but he said he knew what he was doing. He told me I shouldn't worry myself, that I needed to chill, because he knew what he was doing and had been doing it for years. I noticed that there was this one lady in particular that stood out to me. This woman carried herself well. From her mannerism, to how well she dressed, to how she styled her hair and her overall appearance, was off. Something was not adding up, what was she doing here. I observed how she moved different from all the others that passes through the house. She didn't talk as much, like me she observed. I noticed that if there was any form of drinking, she would only have a little glass and it would be wine or something light. Another thing was that the one drink lasted her for the whole night, she never refills. While all the other women indulged in hard-core liquor like rum, brandy and so on. She only spoke if it was in greeting like to say Hi, hello or good morning. She didn't conversed with the her fellow concubines, that's the only word I can think of to call them. I don't know where he met her or how, she was very pretty but something was telling me, trouble was brewing where she stood.

I watched her carefully while trying not to make her aware that I was watching her. But something told me this woman saw everything. I was sure this woman was very different from the rest of them, and I knew she was in a different class, I could see it clearly. I made a conscious decision, to finally asked my brother the question, I really wanted to asked him. His girlfriend Arlene will be leaving us shortly to go visit her mother somewhere in Kingston. I told myself that this was the perfect time, to address this madness. The first thing I did was made breakfast. I prepared some nice fried dumplings with tin Mackerels with some fever grass tea. This tea is a really good drink in the morning, it loosens up the tension, and I wanted Larry to be relaxed for my enquiry. He was getting ready to drop his girlfriend Arlene, to her mother's house in Kingston. I decided to accompany him, so that I will be able to question him on the way back. We all ate together, he even thanked me for making breakfast and said he enjoyed it. When we were all ready, we exited the house and took our places in the car. We were travelling from a place in Old Harbour in St Catherine, to her mother's house somewhere in Kingston. The journey will takes us about forty five minutes to an hour depending on traffic.

Larry had a habit of checking the car thoroughly, before going anywhere. He made sure to check the oil, the engine and the tyres too before going out on the road. After he made his checks, he took his seat behind the wheel as he was the driver. Arlene sat in the front with him, I was seated at the back. This gave me an opportunity to really look at her, not that I haven't noticed, but she was not pretty at all, in fact she was far from it, opposite to be exact. She was quite short, with a big round face and an even bigger head. Her nose has a weird shape, it reminds me of a snout. Her ass was a flat as a sheet of paper and she dresses like a man. She made it very hard to distinguish her sex. The only feminine thing I have ever seen her in was a skirt, and she didn't even wear it with a blouse. She wore it over her breasts by pulling the waist of the skirt up to her chest, when she is in the yard. She was a just different breed of woman, and she loved arguing with Larry for money. Maybe she wasn't confident in her womanhood, that why she was ok, with all these females running loose in her yard. After driving for a little distance, he forgot that he left his wallet, with his driving licence and money. This slowed us down a little, but I had no problem. I had nowhere to be, so I wasn't worried about the time we reach. It was Arlene that seems to be in a hurry. I only wanted her to reach where she was going and out the car so I could ask the question. But I'm a patient man, I allowed very little to bother me. After retrieving his wallet, we continued our journey again. We listen to music to fill the silence in the car, which made the journey goes by quicker. There was nothing like silence to relax the mind. I use that time to watch both Larry and Arlene, to see if I can see any connection between them. It took no more than five minutes to realise a few things about them for myself, which I will explain to you shortly.

Larry was driving really fast, like he was in a race with someone else. That was how he and his girlfriend liked to drive anywhere they were going. The car he was driving was a nice black sports car, it drives very well, I like the work he had done to it. He takes pride in his car; it runs well and he keeps it in good condition. Inside the car was spotless and smells of expensive air fresheners. I took note of the place as we drove. I haven't been here for a while, so I'm not that familiar with some of these roads he was driving on, which wasn't problem. I barely recognise some of the places, it only when I came across a particular land mark or something that was inherently familiar that I'd know where I was. Other unfamiliar places I'd just asked about them, but sometimes I could pinpoint where we were. Larry seemed a bit restless, he informed me that he was tired and felt real sleepy. He asked me if I wanted to drive the rest of the journey. Clearly the driving wasn't a problem, but the knowing where I was heading was. I told him that I didn't wish to, at this point, it was too soon. Moreover, I hated how they drove, everyone was always in a rush to get to their destination, it appears that safety wasn't a concern. I declined, so he asked Arlene if she wanted to drive. Looking at her responding to him, it was like she eager for him to ask her. He pulled over on the side of the road and they swapped over. This is not a joke what I'm about to say, but I taught he never leave the steering wheel because she drove even faster than him. I was clenching my toes and even pressing my feet, like I was trying to break the speed from the back, and I wasn't even the one driving. I disliked driving fast, friend and family always commented on my driving. They say that I drive too slow but I don't listen to them, I like to think of my driving as being careful on the road.

I begged her to slow down, but they both thought it was funny, or that I was a coward. I didn't care what they thought, I just didn't like the fast driving, I got sick from the motion. She was driving like a maniac; this woman was dam crazy. I thought about the journey we still have left, and checking how long I will have to endure this drive before we reached the address. I hated this kind of driving and from what I remember speeds kills. I have seen this way too many times, over and over, from all around the world for me not to be cautious. Unfortunately, innocent people who respect the road code get caught up in it most of the times and that's so sad. Anyway, we were still on our way, when we got caught in a bit of traffic. It was so bad we ended up in a standstill for nearly an hour. Everyone was frustrated at this point, we all showed our mutual frustration by hissing our teeth. I for one was extra pissed because I couldn't wait to be alone with Larry, to finally ask him somethings. It became apparent the further we progressed into traffic, than an accident had occurred. It's been almost four hours and still we haven't made it to our destination. It seems as if this car trip, will likely be an whole day thing. Finally, we passed through the accident and saw that three cars collided with each other in a massive crash. There were debris and shattered glass scattered across the roads. On both sides of the road, there were passengers who were traveling in the vehicles laying down on the ground injured. Bystanders and other people who abandoned their vehicle to see what was happening crowded around the crash site. I could hear people saying that, one of the three cars was speeding and the driver lost control of the vehicle and it resulted in a collisions. My mood instantly changed, It was only a moment ago, that I was thinking that speed kills. Low and behold, the evidence of what I was thinking only moments ago. I hated seeing things like this, if only people would follow the speed limit, then most of these accidents wouldn't occur.

The traffic began to flow freely, it was a bit slow but we were moving again and could see where we going. Not long after we were like minutes away from her mother's house. I knew her mother lives in Kingston but I wasn't aware that It was in the Barbican area. We turned onto the road that leads towards the house, once outside the gate, we waited for her mother to come let us insider her home. Here comes this lady, smiling from ear to ear. She greeted Arlene with a hug, then after saying hello, she welcomed us all in her home. Looking at her I can see that her daughter resembles her a lot. They were like carbon copies of each other. Same big head, broad face, flared nose, down to the height and the same flat backside. They look to be the same size, even their walk was alike. This was really her mother, there was no denying that. I was meeting her for the first time, she ask me if I am Byron, I answered yes. She told heard a lot about me, and that it was good to finally meet me. She asked if I wanted a drink or a cup of tea. I accepted a cup of tea and thanked her for it. We stayed for a while, even had something to eat, shortly after it was time to leave. We said our goodbyes, went back to the car to make our way back to Old Harbour, but this time it was only Larry and I.

I was thrilled that we were finally on our own, it will give us the opportunity to speak openly. But as soon as we were in the car his phone rang. Hoping that he wouldn't take forever on the phone, I listen to the one-sided conversation while watching him as he spoke. I realized quickly that he was speaking with the fancy lady, the one I meet by the house. I think she was his favourite. Whenever she would visit him, it took her about two hours to get to the house. She was polite and really nice, I preferred her to the other girls. I had previously noticed that when she was by the house she always has her handbag which she clutched tightly, never putting it down. As soon as Larry was done talking to her, I said to him, this lady where did you meet her. Where is she from. He looked at me and simply stated off face book. I was surprised, so I said to him, she is a face book friend, just to be clear. He said yes, I said okay. I asked him where she lives. He told me same Barbican where we are coming from. I said what, he replied to same place where we are coming from. It wasn't funny but I had to smile. He was eager to get back to his house, so he began driving faster because he wanted to meet up with this woman. Plus, Arlene wasn't around to cramp his style. I asked him who she is and confessed to him that I have been watching all the women on his Watts app profile and on his Instagram. He laughed, then he began telling me how he met her and for how long they been in contact with each other.

He told me that she did whatever he wanted. I asked him, what does whatever entails but he just smiled to himself. I told him I like how quiet she was, always chilling by herself and watching television. I noticed that she only watches series movies and trials, anything to do with court room drama. I told him I like her but not in the way he I like her. I have my own girlfriend; I just mean that I like how she carried herself and how she behaves differently from the others. He looked at me and told me straight-up that she sells pussy. My word, I could hardly believe this, so I just went quiet and stopped talking. I sat back in the car seat wondering if all the others were pussy sellers too. Oblivious that I had stop speaking Larry continued to divulge details about their arrangement. I listened as he went into details, telling me the prices she charged for a particular activity. He said she charges a set price for sex only, but with oral sex the prices varies depending on what he wanted. For example if he wanted a little suck off without finish, then the price would be less. However, if he wanted her to bring him to release, then the price would increase especially if he wanted it on her face or on her chest. Curious, I asked, so how much would she charge to swallow. He laughed and hit the steering wheel. He said B, I never asked her to swallow anything yet, I can't afford swallowing price. She charges separate for everything, he said if wanted his balls suck, it's still for a price. But if he wanted her to suck his balls from behind, then its double the price. I started to laugh and said this can't be serious. He swore that he was telling the truth. He said fantasies and group act cost a lot. It was in a price league called money man category. He said if he wanted a threesome that price wasn't so bad, but if he wanted a foursome, with her and two of her girlfriends from work, then that price broke pockets. That price was fixed, no bargain because the money had to split between her and her friends. I can't even believe what I was hearing. The shocker was when he said, prices started from ten thousand Jamaican dollars and only if you were her regular.

I shouted, "are you serious". He replied deadly. I began thinking to myself, no wonder she dresses so good, she was making cheddar. Whether she did this part time, full time or as a side hustle, I knew he wasn't her only client. Plus, her body looked good and she was pretty, so men must be lining up to tap it. I believed him. Now I understood why he had so many girlfriends, if you can call them that, it was because they were being paid for their services. When I said I was going to asked him what was going on, I never expected he would confessed, to basically running a one man whore house. I asked him if he knew her name. He said Byron, just leave that alone, but I was too curious to just do as he asked. I still wanted to know her name, because she didn't look at all like the person, he was telling me about. This woman looked too prim and proper, to be doing all the nasty. I was thinking looks was really deceiving. I have nothing against how a woman chooses to make her living. If she can get top dollars for marketing her body, then good luck to her. This lady, any man would take her home and put a ring on her finger. Not just because she was attractive but because she was intelligent and smart, met meets the wife criteria. So, this was why I was baffled by her actions. I hate to say this but she was a decent whore, if she was anything like what Larry was saying. Regardless of what anyone might think, she was a professional, according to Larry. He says that she really knows her trade, and that the tricks she could do with her tongue, would turn a man into an addict. He said she had a few tongue rings, some have different ball size, while some had different textures. He said his favourite was the one with the small spikes. I could tell that he was enjoying telling this story. He laughed and said bredda, "if you know how it feels, when she wears the spike tongue rings, and uses it to massage the underside of your dick, while sucking on the tip. He rocked back and forth in the driver seat, then he said B that will make your ass twitch. I laugh and say I can only imagine. After he was done laughing, he said to me that she was business minded and don't play when it comes to her money. I said to him, do you have to pay her cash upfront before she starts. He said something like that and began explaining the payment process. He said if he calls her and arrange for a meet up, she will then ask him what he was after. He said he always choose a combo. I said to him, hold on, wait a minute, what is a combo. He laughed and said Byron you are a novice. He said a combo was when you combine two acts, like if you wanted sex and a blow job, it was classed as a combo. I said who called it that, he said she did. I said cool, so how do you pay for this combo. He said when he calls her he would tell her he's in the mood for a combo. After they talked about specific and agreed on the cost, then he had to make a thirty percent deposit into an account. I ask why so much; he said booking fee was included. I said fucking hell, she is serious about business. He was like, yeah, so even if you cancelled, she still gets paid. He said once she received the first payment, then they would arrange the date and time. Once she arrives at the house, she expects another thirty percent and when the act is done, she gets the rest. This was something unheard of, I said to him wow, she is running a proper pussy business. He said yes and once you pay up; she delivers.

With all the information he has given me, and knowing she was on her way to the house. I couldn't wait to see her. As soon as she enters the house her eyes and mine, met. The way she looked at me, it was like she knew, Larry had told me what's happening. She was wearing a nice neon-coloured shorts and even had the same neon coloured handbag to match. She carried it to the bathroom with her, it was something that I noticed with her. She never leaves her handbag unattended, not even for a second. I wanted to ask her name, but I just didn't bother because, it's not like we were friends. She had an air of formality about her, she even calls Larry by his surname. Whenever she addresses him, she would say "Mr Needle." I sometimes feel her eyes on me, she was always mindful of her surroundings. Either way, it didn't bother me, she was doing her thing. I was okay with her moving around the house, she was no threat to me or any other persons inside the house, she fitted in properly. I observed how she knows inside the house Very well, it would appear that she even knows it more than me. Her movements tells that she was no stranger, I only came here a few weeks ago. I'm just watching her keenly, just like how, she watches me. I realized that she was very vigilant and observant. I also noticed that she was cautious, how she moved and talked to him and everyone in the yard. I don't know if that's how she behave, when they get down to business. I asked him how she got here, when she visits, he said he doesn't know. Again, I asked, if he had ever met anyone of her family, anyone at all, he answered no. The only thing he knew about her, was that she was from Barbican. Plus, he was not entirely sure about that either. This lady was a mystery to him, I am sure. He wasn't interested in finding things about her background. He wasn't watching her like me, I found her behaviour off. I thought to asked her some questions about herself. But before I got the chance to asked, she approached me to asked if I had a phone charger to lend. She said, she phone is dying, and she left her charger outside. I said what, outside where, but before I could ask anything more, she changed her speech. Correcting herself, saying she left her charger at home. I pretend as if I didn't realised that she back tracked on what she said. I asked her the type of phone she was using; it was the same as mine, a Samsung. I didn't know the year or model; I just know they uses the same charger. I gave her the charger and ask her if she wanted anything from the shop. She said not really, but she could do with a charger. I agree to get one for her. When I walked out the house, heading towards the shops, I saw a strange car parked a little way down from the house. This car was not from around the area and the colour stood out. It was the only bright yellow mini car I noticed since I've been here.

The car definitely fits a woman or a small person. I wondered to myself if the car belongs to her and why she parked so far away from the house. Maybe she didn't want him knowing that she drives and was also collecting taxi fares from him. I went to have a thorough look at the car and the license plate. I made a mental note to asked Larry about this. For some this car matches her, from the bright coloured to the neat small size. I walked pass it but decided to try and see inside the windows when I was on my way back. Once I got the charger and a few other things, I made my back. I stopped beside the car and looked inside, it was clean as a whistle, not even a scrap of paper insight. There was nothing to see so I just walked back to the house and gave her the charger and a drink. She thanked me but didn't say much after. I didn't have a problem with that, I was a man of few words, but I watched her behaviour very keenly. I started looking out for car keys or something that might belong to her, but she was very meticulous, she even takes the handbags to the toilet. She did this for the entire time she was there, I noticed that while she was there the car was still in the same spot.

I still carried on with my investigation, I said nothing at all to him. He still believed she was taking the bus or taxi to come here over three the years that she has been visiting, according to him. I didn't believe at no point that this lady, looking like she did took public transport all this time. This lady looked like she has never taken a bus from the day she was born. I did noticed however, that since I bought the charger for her, she started paying me a little more attention not much but she acknowledged me in passing. I can also see changes in her movements with me, she acts more friendly, but I could see that she still remains vigilant around me. One day she was moving about as usual, charging her phone in the sitting room. She said that she was going outside and that she will be back soon, she just wants to stretch her legs. She came back clutching her handbag, she smiles and asked if I was okay. I replied to her, then asked what about you. She said, fine Byron. Now this was the move I wanted all along, it was time to up this game. I said to her how comes you know my name and I don't know yours. She answered in a cool respectable way. Her response was "it not my fault, the same way I know yours you should know mine".

The way she repeated, "it's my brother, Byron", indicating that my brother told her my name. She even emphasised on that too, not only she address me as Byron but as Mr Needle too. Letting me know she was aware of my full name. I said to her seeing as you know my name, why don't you tell me yours. She smiled cheekily and said, "sorry Mr Needle, go and asked the person that told me your my name, mine". She went as far as to say if I wanted I could call her Mrs Needle, she would be cool with that too. I could see that she was trying to play smart, it was clear. We were both laughing, my brother didn't even pick up on this mind game that was being played right in front him. I laughed and said cool Mrs Needle, she smiled again before making her way to the shower. This was what I wanted, her being comfortable enough around me, so she wouldn't be so guarded with her things. While in the shower she asked Larry to get her a towel and the things she left out, so she could get dress in the bathroom. After he retrieved the things she asked for, he handed them to her and left her in the bathroom to finish getting ready. Larry had left the room door slightly ajar and I could hear her moving around in there getting ready. She stayed in the bathroom applying her make up. I was in the room opposite, so I glimpse her walking in and out the bathroom with a towel wrapped around her. The room was set up with the bed facing the door, I saw that she left her handbag on the bed open. For the first time she didn't have her handbag on her person, it was just left open on the edge of the bed. She has never ever done this. I don't know what happens behind closed door between them, to know if she leaves her bag, but it was the first time I'm witnessing it. To say she made a huge mistake was an understatement.

Larry came back in the room where I was to get a drink before returning in his room and closing the door. I could hear them playing and laughing with each other but I continued with what I was doing. I thought to myself, she really put down the bag, she has never left her bags it was always under her arms clutched so tightly, like her life depended on it. It would have been better if she had left the bag in the sitting area where I was, but that was just wishful thinking. She was undress and playing games with Larry, this must have been what happen. While they were playing with each other, the bag fell off the bed, and everything from inside the bag scattered out all over the floor. My brother looked down and saw the contents that came out of the bag, and he nearly pissed himself. By this time, I had gotten up to go fix something to eat. Out of nowhere, I heard Larry shouting my name. "Byron, Byron, come here, come here. Come look at this, come quick, come quickly Breda. I hear all that commotion and the franticness in his voice, it piqued my interest. I ran to the room, which was only a few doors down, my speed breaking instantly and my eyes popping out my head, when I view what was on the floor in front of me. It took me a minute to gather myself. I looked at her, then I looked at him before asking what the fuck is this. I knew there was something off with this woman, my curiosity was not wrong. On the floor in front of me and my brother were two fucking handguns. One Glock pistol and a Revolver, with loads of bullets and three magazines.

Larry was shitting himself, he started to panic. Speaking all jumbled sentences, a mile a minute, I couldn't even make sense of it. His eyes were so wide with fright, and he was sweating profusely. I didn't know my brother had a stutter, but he was stuttering. I asked him Larry what's going on, what is this who is this person and what is she doing here. I have been suspicious of her for a while and had been asking him who she was, and he couldn't tell me anything about this lady. The only thing he knows was that she is from Barbican, and at this point even that was questionable. I looked at her, she was trying hard to remain calm, but I saw that she too was panicking, because the guns were no longer in her possession. I could tell she was scared. I stoop to the floor, to take a closer look through her things. I was in for some real surprise. The first things I picked up was a set of car keys, that had the same sign that matched the yellow car parked a few houses down. I simply never trust her to begin with, because her behaviour aroused suspicion. For one she was meticulous, very observant, choosing not to speak, but to listen to others conversed and she was just too well put together. Even though she wore those brightly coloured clothes, it was only when she was inside the house. Whenever she arrived at the house, she always dressed smart, and that was what caught my attention and made me start watching her closely. She wasn't flirty and all over the place like the others, she was different. She spoke and acted like a person, with a lot of responsibilities like a manager or something, instead of a prostitute, the profession she claims to be in. She was naked as the day she was born, standing and crying herself. Larry was beside himself, he taught she was on a mission to hurt him. He was shouting out what she is doing with the two firearms, Byron. I told him to let me deal with this, because he was not acting rationally, he wasn't handling whatever this was too well.

I let her know, that I know that the yellow car outside belongs to her. She looked like she wanted to scream, I looked her in the eyes, shook my head and told her, it's for the best, if you didn't, I just want some answers. What is your purpose here, did someone send you, are you going to rob him, do you plan on hurting him. I told her I just want to understand what's happening, so she need to tell me so we can sort things out as adults. She stared in my eyes, I knew that look, the eye-to-eye contact, she thought I was going to hurt her or do something to her. I told her I was going to ask her some questions and I wanted her to answer honestly. I asked her for her address, I told don't say Barbican, because that might just upset me. She said, please why are you doing this. I said, I'm not doing anything but asking a simple question to show my little brother that you are deceiving him. She said to me if she talked, if I will give her guns back. I said no, and she screamed, Jesus Christ, Jesus. At this point she was trying to cover her vagina and her breasts with her hands. I know how women are with their private parts. I could see that she was embarrassed by this, her being naked in this situation. I told her to put her clothes on, she immediately sprang into action, grabbed her pant and putting it on without her panties. I instructed her not to do that. I told her to dress herself as she normal would. I ensured her, that she was safe, that one was going to hurt her, we were only after the truth. My mind instantly recall this movie I had seen about an undercover police officer, who form a relationship with a drug dealer, to take down his operation.

I have seen many movies, over the years and seeing under, covers police officer infiltrating gang and befriend criminals just to bring them down. Now that she was dressed, I voiced what I was thinking. I said to her, your operation just got busted. She shook her head wildly, say no, no, no, she tried to assure me she was not on an operation. I told her to stay where she was, while I continued going through her things on the bedroom floor. I say a little black book and I opened it, it turned out to be her diary. I saw that she had written down her office number, and extension to reach her on, she also written down a number under the name hubby. I saw her kids school number, because that was how she wrote it down. She had a number for a supervisor at the station she works. In this little book I found information, that I'm sure she didn't want me to find, it even had contact details for her parents and siblings. After I was done going through the book, I scan the other things on the floor, most of it was trivial, so I took the bag and began searching it. Inside the pocket of the bag, I found her passport, I flick through the pages and saw that she had two different visa and had multiple stamps from all her travels. I wasn't interested in what type of visa she holds. I found a picture of a man in an inspector uniform, when I asked her about the picture, she said it was her husband. I could see this was starting to freak her the fuck out, because I said I was going to call him. She began telling me, that she will give me anything I wanted, but I am not stupid, plus I didn't want anything from her. I told her that the only will I wanted from her was the truth, then she could be on your way with all her belongings. She said to me, promise not to call my husband. I told her that I am not promising anything, so the quicker she tells me what's happening the quicker she could leave. This appeared to worry her, she started looking at Larry, watching his movements, like she was afraid of what his reaction might be. Even with everything that I found, she still didn't confess, still didn't want to talk. I said to her, in a stern tone that this was not a joke, stop watching Larry and speak. I don't know if it was the seriousness in my voice, but she broke down in tears, and said okay, she will tell me the truth.

She said her friend told her about Larry. That he loves women and will pay good money for women to come sleep with him and other women, even his girlfriend Arlene. My brother eyes nearly drop out of his head, it got big and bright like a car headlamp. I ask her how she knew it was him and not another person called Larry. She said her friend gave her the link and said she could get in touch with him on face book. She pointed at him and told me, he asked her to get girls a few times, which she did, and he paid all of them. She showed me two of her friends that she brought to him and told me he paid them eighteen thousand dollars, which they split for the three of them. I asked him if that was true, but he refused to answer me. His behaviour was starting to piss me off, he was up in her personal space, acting like he wanted to rough her up. Which I had to let him know was not happening, so he should chill the fuck out and be quiet, so we could get to the bottom of this. I said to him if he didn't calm himself, I was going to leave him alone with her, but I knew definitely he didn't want that to happen. She started telling me about myself, personal things, and said he told her. She said he borrows her cars all the time, that she leaves here with him. That the silver Benz and a black Toyota Corolla Moto car that I see are cars that she lent him.

She told me that he takes her to do loads of transaction for him. I knew then that she wasn't lying, she was telling the truth. I also realize that she doesn't means him or anyone harm. I could see that clearly. After she was fully ready, looking like she wanted to leave, I said to come have a look at this. I showed her herself naked, her guns, her driving licence and everything she had in the bag. I also showed her picture of her car license plate and the car. I showed her all these pictures I had taken. She must have not realised that I was doing so, because of how much she was panicking. I had even gone through the trouble of dialling her husband in my phone. She looked like she was going to combust. I told her not to worry, it was evidence. I said to her as long as you're good we are good too. I put the three magazines back in her handbag, all tied together in a blue plastic bag with the bullets in it as well. I told her, I was going to follow her to the car. When Larry heard this, he began looking at me like no car was out there still. I know from his attitude, that he didn't want me to know half the things she disclosed. From the expression on her face, I could tell she didn't give a fuck. She just wanted her handbag and things to leave. On top of all that she was embarrassed. I took a good look at her, still confused as to why a woman in her position would do what she was doing, if not to send him to prison. I even saw that that the paint on her fingers matched her hand bag and shoes. I had to shake my head; how could he believe this woman was a prostitute. She has been taking his money off him. He was slow so the ladies, so they work on him and send him in a circle. They used him as their feeding tree as old people would say.

I took her outside, open the car with the same key. She got in her car as he watched. I handed her the keys and told her to wind down the window and placed her handbag on the back seat on the passenger side. I knew she would have to stretch to reach, because she was a bit short so the driver's seat was pulled a bit closer to the steering wheel. By the time she picks up the bag I was inside the gates. She looked relieved; I could see her loading back her things. I told him to go and pay her, even though she was begging me to take that money and let her go. I instructed him to pay her, she should get seven thousand dollars off him, he went back outside and gave it to her. I wasn't the person in this predicament, and I was so ashamed about it, so just imagine how she felt. She told me about one thousand thanks in the house before I let her go.

After Larry came back inside, we were talking about the situation, thinking about the what ifs. Imagine my surprise when I saw the little yellow car, pulled up at the gate. Larry went to find out what she wanted but spoke to her through the grill. He came back to say, that she wanted to thank me. I told him to tell her it's okay, she already did. He went to tell her it was okay, but she insisted that she wanted to thank me again in person. He was telling me I should go and hear her out. I look at him good and ask him if he his right in his damn head. I got up from the sofa and went to stand by the door, she was no longer seated in her car but standing behind the gates. I shout out my phone number, and told her anything you have to say, you can say over the phone. She must be crazy to think that I would go outside to talk to her. With her having two guns and after what just went down inside the house with her, she must be having laugh. She called and said that she just wanted to thank me for how I handled the situation, and for keeping Larry from escalating things, because she knew things could had ended differently. I didn't want to prolong this conversation because I still didn't trust her and I wasn't sure if I was being recorded. I told her she was welcome and that I have no problems as long as she upholds her ends of the deal. She told me that if there is I need, I should let her know. I told her I just wanted her to go in peace. Until this day my brother Larry still keeps in touch with her, but that's their business. I am glad things worked out the way it did. People have to be vigilant and not just in Jamaica, but anywhere when they are handling money. This could have been worse. It could have been a police operation, or one of the other women could have set him up to be robbed. In the same way we must always be careful of people we let in our circle and our surroundings, be that friend or foe. Be cautious of new people, you are introduce to, not everyone has good intentions. Remember this saying, not everything that glitter is gold.

She still gives me a call every now and then, she also told me that she still speaks to her friend. I still remain cautious when talking to her, allowing her to do most of the talking. She told me that she still working as a police officer, and that she was recently promotion from

Sargent to inspector. She still talked about that day and thanked me for how I handled the situation, letting me know that she owed me one. She told me that in spite of how things ended at the house, she used to enjoy the time she spent there. She also mentioned that she really loved my cooking, of curry goat, turkey neck, fried dumplings and tin Mackerels. Those were the meals I often prepared. She said to me that to how observant I was, I could be in the same job as her, that I would make an outstanding officer. I simply thanked her for the compliment on the food but no thanks to the invitation for the job.

The Selena and the English man obeah story

OVER THE YEARS I HAVE ALWAYS BEEN FRIEND WITH SELENA AND HER two brothers, as well as her two sisters. They all lived in a place called Signam, which is located in Spanish town St Catherine. One of her brother Milton, who is the eldest works for the Jamaica defence force (JDF). The other one is called Denton; he was the youngest of them all and made furniture for a living. He was self-employed and owned his own furniture business. He had a shop that specialises in making beds, headboards, dressers, wardrobes, centre tables, bed side tables, and chairs. Her sisters are called Sharon and Sheela. Selena was younger than her sisters and was a massive party fan. She like going parties, loved clubbing and loud music playing in the house, every time she was at home. Selena was an attractive young woman, she has brown complexion, not too tall or short, average in height. She wore a lot of gold jewellery, and bleached her skin, to have a fairer complexion, even though she already had fair skin. She was what Jamaicans would call red skin. She was a person that I'd call high maintenance. She changes her wigs regularly and wore her hair in all kinds of different colours. She never kept one style for more than a week, plus she was friends with all the hairdressers in and around the area. She always has her nails done to match her toes. Her handbags, clothes and shoes were all designer brands. She wore her jewellery in sets, meaning the necklace, earrings and bracelet were matched. Most of the earrings she wore were big, she didn't do subtle, everything with her was over the top. Her ears were pierced multiple times on each side, she had a nose piercing, and her face was very pretty. She was a looker; she often attracts any and many men.

Quite often she can be seen coming out of all kinds of flashy cars, picking her up and dropping her exactly in front of her house. She loved wearing ex-rated clothes. Shorts that leaves her cheeks hanging out, and her vagina printing out, showing its shape and size and fullness. She had no shame about it either. This was her attire when she was walking on the road or going shopping in Spanish town to buy groceries, which was most of the time or every weekend. She is very attractive, always looking good, like one of those video vixens. Not going to lie, she was hot, real hot gal as we would call her. She has a nice big ass well rounded, like it was made in a mould, two ample size pair of tits. Her hips were wide and had that curved shape, when she walks, it was with a certain sway, like she was flaunting her shape. She had what a Jamaican would call a "boom shape" which means she was curvy. She had the kind of body that people had surgery to get. She did nothing halfway, she was a temptress. When she steps out on the road, the men in and around the Signam community, went wild when they saw her. Most places she went, she got that type of reaction, and she loved it. She had a style to tell any man she met and talk with, that she had no boyfriend or man in her life. She was always single, even when there was someone. Any man, she spoke to in the street would want to kiss those nice pair of tits, and those red cherry lips. Yes, there was nothing wrong with wanting to kiss them, you could kiss them of course, both tits and lips. It wasn't a problem but just remember they came with a price, and a hefty one too. She was a very friendly person; I know this for sure. She was just easy going and knew how to operate. Whenever she saw a man, she liked or her spirit takes, meaning if she likes him, her attitude would change straight away. As my old lady would say, her skin catches fire whenever she saw a man. She only liked men that had money and who were a lot older than she was, for some reason I don't know. Men just couldn't help themselves whenever they saw her, even if they were walking and talking or even driving with their partners, they would still wave or stared at her from head to toe, in a seductive way. This happened quite often and caused really bad argument between men and their partners, it even happened with other women. She was known for this, and the reason for all that was because she was very sexy and men were attracted to her. Some men can't help themselves when it comes to women and sex, she knew this and used it to her advantage.

Men always lusts after and continuously watched her, she made this worse by always walking around half naked, drawing even more attention to herself. Even in the back of her yard, she would walk around in this state of undress, parading around in the area where she lived with no shame. She would purchase jeans from the stores, then go home and cut them into tiny shorts called pussy printer. A very vulgar term men used, for the shorts that erotic dancers wore. To how smaller they were, half her ass cheeks, that us Jamaicans called batty jaw, would be on display. She was only interested in foreigners, old pensioners to be exact, or maybe they were the ones drawn to her. Her ways made her well known to everyone all over Spanish town, Libya gardens, Signam, and Old Harbour Road. People knew who she was related to as soon as they saw her anywhere around the adjoining communities. Selina's daily routine consists of her going to the bars nearby and shops hanging out there for the whole day, conversing with the owners and staff. She ensured that she had a good relationship with them, so she could get things to credit whenever she had no money.

Another habit she had was, she loved to beg. It didn't matter who the person was, they were eligible for begging. Oftentimes it would be the same bar owners and shop keepers, whom she had befriended she begs money from. That begging also extended to random men, that she met, but knew they were attracted to her. She made it her point of duty to know who who was. Meaning, she knew all the men that runs taxi, drives a bus and truck for a living around the area. She also knew all the police officers, that works in Spanish town and in the Spanish town police station very well. They also knew her and of her reputation well. Her and I would chat from time to time whenever she passed by where I worked if she spotted me standing alone. She visits the shops near my workplace, looking good and always smelling really nice. I think it's because of the younger guys that hangs out in that area. She likes younger men, I could see that for myself but as you, she was into older men because of the money.

She was kind to each and every one of the youths in the community. They all spoke to her regularly, sometimes you could even hear them when they are passing her yard, and shouting out her name Selena, Selena, they all loved her. Not all felt the same way, especially the females. Some women had gone out her way to let her know, she didn't like her one bit. She told Selena that she was pretty, but worthless with her beauty. Telling her straight up, that she doesn't want to see her around her husband. That she is not joking, because all she does is cause everyone problem with their relationship, in and around Signam. She made it clear to Selena and warned her about staying away from her husband. Stating that she heard it in the community, that she was seeing her husband. She told, if she doesn't listen to her and avoid her husband, stop seeing him, she is going to cut her in her face and spoiled it up. She informed Selena that she has a big kitchen knife with her name on it in her house, and that if she thinks she is playing games, continue to see her husband and find out what will happen.

This did not only happen with that one woman, Selena and many of the ladies around Signam have had these types of violent conversation before. Over and over and it doesn't stop her behaviour, and won't stop there either in my opinion. Women have problems with her all the times, just from seeing her around they feeling threatened by her presence around their boyfriends, baby father, fiancé and husband. Selena is the type of woman that will even see another woman with their husband or boyfriend, and blatantly called to him in front of the ladies. She found it funny, but none of these women don't find it funny at all. There is an old saying that what is joke to you means, death to another person. Some people say she is barefaced and daring, while others say she is effing rude and out of order. Selena didn't care about what they were saying, she loved the attention she was receiving from both men and women. From time to time, she could be seeing dancing in her yard, to the loud music she played every so often. My house was a few doors away from hers and whenever she passes my house, she would shout out my name Byron, Byron letting me know she was going out. Sometimes she even asked me to walk with her down the road in the night when it was dark.

Selena was a very funny woman, always giving plenty of jokes and loves to have a laugh with anyone especially men. Sometimes out of town men in strange cars will be driving around the area and asking for her and directions to her house more than once. Her mother was an older woman that I respect a lot, I always talk with her regularly. Her mother sometimes sold food in her yard on weekends. She sold anything from cigarettes, alcohol, Guinness, beers, Heinekens, and other drinks like, Pepsi and coca colas among other things. She often sold peanut porridge every Friday and Saturdays morning and roast and steam fish, in the night. She started cooking from early in the morning, so that by evening everything will be ready for customers. Selena had two sisters that I mentioned before, they were also good looking women, really nice and way more conservative and more easy going to me than Selena was. They all resemble and looking similar in their faces to each other, especially the sisters. Their resemblance was stronger with each other, than it was with their brothers. Once you saw them you knew that they were siblings. Their father was called Mr Moorland, his kids called him daddy, but outside of their household, and in the community, everyone called him Moorland. He was a nice man, very humble and respectful, the only fault I can think of about him, was he drank alcohol a lot. He drank plenty rum and was always drunk on the weekend, when he was home and not working. He worked as a driver for a well-known company in Kingston, he drives and deliver goods all over the parish. He delivered goods like bottle drinks, boxes juices, sometimes ground provision, and crates of beers plus loads of other food kind to supermarket all over the island.

Mr Moorland was a popular man around the community where he lived, and everyone had the uttermost respect for him around the area. He was a kind hearted gentleman, who gave money and food to anyone that was in need if they asked him. He gave away anything as long as he could afford it, the children around the area loved him very much, that was the type of person Mr Moorland was. When he was driving out to work in the morning, the kids would jump on the back of the van from his gate and jumped off at the end of the road. Although he was a well-respected man in the community, he had no respect in his own home. His children had no manners at all not one bit, they spoke to him in a way that was disrespectful. I found it very strange that all his kids were all grown men and women and still living at home except for Milton. Sometimes you could hear him shouting at them and them shouting at him too. They stole from him, they would go in his pocket and take away his money and left him with nothing, that made him upset. They didn't only steal from him but stole from their mother as well, and make her cry. That was not acceptable behaviour and that was how they were with their parents. Denton and Milton would speak to the girls about taking their parents money away, but they all denied the allegation. They all say they don't know anything about it, and perhaps he lost or spend it all on the rum he drank, but they took his money away for real he wasn't lying.

Mrs Moorland, their mother she was my good friend. We would talk about everything, she likes it when I tell her jokes and made her laugh, she enjoyed every moment with me. Mrs Moorland was the splitting image of her daughters, you could hardly tell them different. The only thing that was different was the age that showed on their mother. Sometimes when I go to their yard, I would see her sitting on the veranda. I always shout out to her, saying good morning or good night according to the time. I'm always in a good mood whenever I am around her. She would laugh and talk with me but on a few occasion, she didn't looking too nice or friendly in her face. She was a very nice woman, she treated me no different from her own kids I would say honestly. I keep a close link with her daughter Selena, I asked her every time if her mother was ok, she said her mom was fine most of the time. I also asked about the rest of the family, she informed me that everyone was well.

Fast forward in time, I saw Selena do something suspicious one day when I was chatting to her. I didn't say anything to her, but her action raised my eye brows. I saw her throwing away some money in a bag, it looked like only silvers coins in the middle of a cross roads near our yard. I was wondering what the hell was that she was throwing away, but I'd only glimpsed it, so I would now wait for a while this could happen again. It could also be a genuine mistake, but she was throwing away money, that shit didn't make sense coins or no coins, but let's wait and see. I was still curious about it, I don't know how she could to be throwing away money, when she loves money too much. Plus, I don't know of anyone who has ever done it, even me I don't have it to throw away myself. This was money, it didn't matter how small it was, it was strange. She wasn't rich in no way, I was sure of this, plus since I have known her, she was always begging.

I was honestly perplexed by this, why was what I wanted to know. What reason could there be to throw away money. I thought that was strange, how the hell she throwing away money and she was always begging, she did nothing but beg all throughout the day, day in day out, this didn't make any sense to me. I must see why, she was she throwing away money, nobody throws away money these days or ever. The evidence was clear this was looking suspicious to me, hell something wasn't right. I began watching her, every move she makes, I was searching for answers. I saw her with an old man, he looked to be well up in age, and could pass for her grandfather. He was of brown complexion, and also, he was very tall, about six feet in height. He was also very muscular, it showed that he took care of himself. He had a very big baldhead, full eyes and wore only short foot khaki-coloured pants, big steel cap boots with white t shirts or white vest. He was a big man in age and body. I heard he was in the British army. Most of the time, he can be seen wearing big, tall boots that covers his ankles that was laced up on his leg, it almost reaches halfway to his knees and looked to be about like size fourteen. He looked like a giant, he was always walking really fast. I've seen him up close and he always has sweats on his nose and his forehead, even when the time was cold he was still sweating. I had to wonder if he was on something. I thought to myself where she found this one now, only God knows. This man was new to the area, other than the few times I've seen him, it was the only time I've seen him around the area, I was positive of that. I wasn't a hundred percent sure that he served in the British army like people were saying. However, what I do know for certain was that he must be a pensioner or had money for Selena to have him up in arms. There is a saying that ants always follow fat, it is true. In this scenario he was the fat and Selena was the ant following. It didn't even matter that he was very old, he had something she wanted, and she would get it by any means necessary.

All around the community there were talks of Selena and her new old man, everyone was talking about it. Was this a joke thing or what, just by knowing who she was, but it was not even a joke. This man was living with his wife, on the same street as Selena, and come out looking for younger girls on the same road. Things was about to become a lot more interesting. I asked her about him repeatedly, after I went in her yard to buy a drink, and saw him in the yard. I also saw him with her mother speaking on her veranda, she gave him a drink and something to eat, that expected. I started to notice that she was washing his clothes, and hanging them ups on her clothes line around the back of her yard. His wife passed and saw them hanging, and ask her husband about them, he told her that he paid her Mrs Moorland to wash them, she was his friend. He told his wife that he didn't want to put any pressure on her, but his wife didn't believe him one bit. I'm sure she heard the rumours too. She didn't say anything much about it, according to Selena. My view was, maybe she was waiting to catch him red handed with Selena. Selena didn't care about him or her one bit, she cares only about the money. That was what she was on at the moment, to get his money every month from him out of the pension payment that comes in for him from England.

This went on for two days, and from days, into week then months, with led to years. No respect or consideration shown for his wife from either of them. I'm my yard just noticing him and her lots of time, they didn't 't even notice that I was watching when they met up, in opened lands or in half-finished houses besides both of our homes. Just by chance I happened to see them more than once on the roadside in Signam. They met each other over and over, all around area at various times night and day. She carried on with this act, just to con him out of his money, that was her sole interest, taking his money off him. She didn't even saw me watching them sometimes. She was just doing her thing, it was obvious that she was only doing what she was doing for the money, if he gave it to her, then everything was okay. She grabbed at anything he had believed me, she was very greedy when it came to money, no lie. She didn't care about him or nothing else, and that's for real. Selena and her sisters were always falling out over money too. I can see clearly where this behaviour was coming from with her. Everyone knew it well and kept telling her about it, especially the ladies who was not fond of her around the area. They were saying, she took all her bad ways from her mother. People would say this about her all the time, this was the behaviour of her mother when she was much younger, she was that type of a person, everyone said so.

It was hard to believe how Selena was behaving, knowing the man's wife lived just few hundred yards away from hers. Her behaviour annoyed me, I'm looking at this girl and watching her every move. She had potential to make something of her life, yet this was how she chose to live. She still say hello to me sometimes, even buys me a Guinness out the blues, I thank her to for that, you know me already forever grateful. On occasion I will I buy her drinks too, she uses that opportunity to beg me money all the time. I would just hear her shouting my name Byron, Byron waah gwaan. Meaning what's going on, and come over and chat with me for a little while, before moving off again, heading towards the shop or her yard. Again, I saw her talking to the English man, he gave her a small bag that contains dirty clothing and plates he had recently received food in from her few days ago. I thought to myself, he's giving her dirty clothes to wash weekly, so that's normal. She opened the bag, looked inside and asked, if any shirts and underwear were in the bag. He replied that there were no dirty shirt or underwear in the bag this time. I found it strange, why was she insisting on washing his dirty shirt and underpants, why was she asking for those specifically to wash. The man gave her what he had dirty to wash, yet she was telling him what she wanted to wash, this was beyond strange. I thought seriously. She spoke to him with no respect like he wasn't a big man. I didn't like that either the way she talks to him. He loved her very much, you could see it on him, but little did he know what's going on in her head. He was in for a real rough ride of his life with this girl. Selena and I spoke regularly, and I listen to her very carefully. She wasn't the match for him, I could see that he was an elderly man. He was way older than her by about forty-five years. He could even be older too. He might be looking at her with stars in his eyes, thinking how pretty and young she was, he could believe his luck. But this young beauty that he loved might cost him more than his money. Selena was on a very different mission with him. Her level of thinking, what she had planned for him was nasty, horrible and cold, she meant him no good.

He didn't even understand or know what these young girls were like in Jamaica. He recently came back from England to lived here. He migrated from Jamaica when he was young with his mother. Some people had it harder than others, so they migrate to a different country for a better life. Selena quickly gave him a child by telling him she was pregnant for him. This got even more deeper and more interesting. This made me want to asked her what was going on, but I prefer to wait a bit, while her tummy got bigger and bigger. She was using thus pregnancy thing to pressure him harder and harder for money. She went as far as to tell him she was going to abort the baby, just to get more money off him. What she was doing was horrid, she was doing some real bad things to him. The way she his treating him, any man would walk away, or even Knock her out long time. But no matter what he just couldn't leave off his own. No matter what she did to him or says to him, or how bad it was, he didn't care, he took it like it was nothing. Maybe there was something holding him back. It was unusual for a person to be treated a certain way and be disrespected without any form of reaction. I'm telling you, no matter what she did or says it's like nothing was said and done that was how he operates. She did and said the worse things to this poor man, she wasn't even apologetic for her terrible behaviour. To make things worse, she chose the nastiest set of words to tell him in front of people. She even threatened to slap him in his face more than once. I disliked how she talks to him, but it wasn't my business to get myself involved. I told her not to do it around me or where I am. She said she won't do it again, but she just gave it sometime and start all over again. She went back to being horrible, her normal way of treating him, it got even worse. The words were dirtier and her behaviour was worse than before, it was like she was making up for lost time. Has for me, I hold my position as usual, just watching her carefully and discreetly.

I noticed some of the moves she made very carefully, like every time she cooked and offered him food, she take out his and put it aside. She hid it so no one could come close to it either. Whenever she Cooked anything and gave it to him, she watched him while he ate, ensuring he ate it all. Even if he wasn't hungry and refused the food, she told him he had to eat because she put time and effort in preparing it. I've seen her done this to him multiple times. She even had the audacity to bring food for him at his home, even if his wife was present. She knew her way around him home very well, because he had taken her there to spend time with him when the wife wasn't about. Selena only accompanied to his house because she wants to steal something, or used the opportunity to search through their belongings. I know of this, because she told me with other people present and listening. She bragged about stealing lots of money from the English man and his wife house, she said anytime she goes there, she steals some of his wife most loved and expensive jewellery. She stole anything she got a chance to steal from his house, that could hide in her pocket or hold in her handbag. She told me she even hid things in her panties or her bra as long as it can fit, she is taking it. I had to take a good look at her whenever she was telling me these things. I saw this girl as someone who has capable doing some serious damage, she was more dangerous than I thought. She dresses a certain way just to attract men, she definitely knows what she was doing all this time. You will see and hear clearly what I'm about to tell you shortly.

I found this really strange that she treated him so poorly, yet he kept coming back. I don't think she even loved her father, to have the heart to treat another man, a father this way. I thought he would have leave long ago, I even wondered if he didn't have anyone, his kids or anybody to talks to him. He hid from his wife and met Selena all over Spanish Town, just to gives her money when he collects his pension that comes in from England monthly. You could tell when it was pay day, she could see her well dress for head to toe waiting on him outside the bank.

Once I caught her doing some weird things, she noticed me watching. By this point I was sure that she knew I've been watching her and the English man carefully. She caught me watching her and she laughed out saying, Byron you know you're not easy, with a smirk on her face. I responded by telling her, no, you're the one not easy. She asked why I said that to her. I said to her you have the big man on lock, meaning she have him her way controlling him. She just smiled and said to me I will talk to you soon my brother. I told her whenever she's ready I'm here, she said okay later we'll talk. She came over my house, I saw her approaching and met her on the veranda. I said what's up Selena, she said her belly was hurting her really bad, I asked her if she had breakfast already or if she ate something bad that goes against her stomach. I even suggested she had something hot to drink. I thought maybe it gas or she was hungry, I was thinking something along those line. She immediately told me it was nothing like that, that she was on her monthly. I told her I don't want to hear about that or anything like that either, that's too much information. I swear, I'm about to hear something even worse off than that, which was really disturbing and nasty it more sickening to hear this from her. She was about to tell me this shit out of her own mouth, which I wanted to hear because it was about the English man. I decided to cut to the chase, I didn't want her dragging out the subject, so I asked her what was going on with the

English man. She said he's good, I have him lock in some reason. I don't know what's her lock means, but I suspect it had something to do with some form of rituals or voodoo. I don't know nothing about these types of things, but I really want to know what was going on with this man and woman, because something wasn't adding up. Again, she said, I have his head lock, he's under my control. It still wasn't clear to me, I'm missing something, because she kept on repeating this remark over and over. I was like you have in lock. I was dying to ask her questions like, where you know him from, how long you knew him, and where was he getting all that money from to give you like that. I even asked her if she didn't let him gives his wife money. She said she don't care about his wife or anyone. I said OK carry on, then whispered to myself, you fucking good for nothing woman.

I asked her about the baby she had and told people it was the old men. She started telling me about a boy she met from countryside, who gives her lots of money. She told me how the boy can grind, meaning he can fuck really good and how his dicks was good. This girl was on some different shit, a whole other mission. I asked her again about the baby, she said she wasn't repeating herself to me, because she told me already, that it's the boy from country that breed her. She said to me, let me tell you something Mr Byron. I don't love the English man, and I don't want him either, is tie I tie him. I asked her straight away, what you really mean by you tie him. She said I make it so he can't go nowhere, he can leave me, no matter what I do or say to him. How I miss treat him or run him away, he wasn't leaving, he's stuck here. She began telling me how she holds him and how the magic works that she uses and how the trick goes. The trick that she uses to hold him is (obeah). I asked her, so how do this go. Her response was fucking shocking, and this was straight from her mouth in her own words. I can't believe what I'm about to hear from her, I was beyond flabbergasted. She said Byron, promise me you won't talk about this with anyone. I said yes, I promise you, I won't say a word, you've known me a long time, you should know me better than that. With the promise made, she began by telling me, she goes to the shop and purchase everything to cook stew peas and puts it down in her room, not in her kitchen. She said for it to work, her alone must have access to these things she purchased. That

257

includes the rice, red peas and chicken and any other piece of salt meat, like pigtails or salt beef it can be mixed.

She said she knows the date when her period was due. On that day when it reaches that's the day, she will be cooking the stew peas. She said her belly cramps badly, so she knows when its nearby. She told me she would cook and do everything in the night when everyone in the house was sleeping. That was the time she always starts the doing the magic (obeah). Selena said she put a pot on the stove to get hot, before it boils up and start steaming, she said she took the pot off the fire while it is steaming up. She told me while doing this she'd wore only a skirt without panties. She said she was dripping blood like a burst pipe because, she wasn't wearing a pad, all this was in her own words. I scrunch my face and ask, are you serious. She said you think I'm play with him. She said she stood over the pot that is steaming and steam herself over the pot, making sure all the steam going in her weeping vagina. She said that part with a whisper. She told me that the steam made underneath her started sweating like hell. I felt like I was about to throw up, my stomach was sick, but I carried on listening as she continues talking. She said she called out his entire name three times, his full government name while squatting over the pot. She said she did this to make sure some of the blood drips in the pot and repeat a certain psalm over the pot. She said she could see the blood in the pot clogs up and change colour, but the warm water melts out the colts. She said you could smell it all over because it had a kind of raw smell. She said she had to open the kitchen Windows to let some of the smell outside the house. She said even her couldn't take the smell of it sometimes and that it took a while for the scent to wear off. I could no longer hold back the bad feeling and I just started throwing up. She just laughed and said Byron your stomach weak. I couldn't take this no more, I wanted her to stop talking but she continues, to say she wiped herself down properly, with the dirty panty she wore for about a week before her period came. She said she kept that panty on for a long while and didn't wash it either just to do this ritual. She then used the same panty to collect some of the blood. She said once she was satisfied, she put the sweaty, blood soaked dirty panty into the pot of water until it was drenched. She said she let it soak for a little, then she removed it, then squeezed the excess water out, back into the pot of hot water thoroughly.

Selena says that when she put it back on the stove to boil, the water changes colour to a reddish-brown look. She said she season the pot just like normal, then put the peas in to boil, put the rice in then let it cook with the meat and everything. She then used the panty to cover the top of the rice and leave it to dry down. Like when you're cooking and put a plastic bag or foil to cover the rice to let the top of the rice steam and cooked properly, that's what she did with the panties. Then put the lid on the pot with the panties covering the rice and leave it to steam down and dry out the rice further. She explained that she gave him something red to drink at all times like syrup or carrot juice with some of the menstrual in it. She saw me scrunch up my face again and said Byron, why are you making your face like that, I'm not telling you anything more. I told her to stop carry on like that because, I wanted to hear every single thing. She also told me about a different occasion, where she used a different method, but she insisted that the one with the blood was stronger. She says that when he gives her his dirty clothes to wash she uses his shirts or underpants with his sweat in it, she would boiled it in a pot of hot water repeating his name over the pot of water. She then proceeds to whisper a certain palms and past it through her legs three times when the pot was steaming.

She explained that she puts two silver coins in the Pot to boil. Then after everything was finished, she put the coins in a bag and throw it in the nearest crossroads to her yard. She said she turned around and walked away, as soon as she thrown the bag away, not looking back. Not even if her mother, father or child was dying behind her and calling out her name. I realized then, that was what I saw her doing the day when she threw the money away at the crossroad. This means that she must not or can't look back after throwing it for no reason. She was serious about this and believed in this so much. I asked her if I could ask a question, she said yeah man, feel free. I asked her how she knew to do this, who teaches her these things. She looked straight in my face and said her mother. In a previous conversation I had with her father, I recalled him telling me a woman had done something to him, but he never gave or mentioned the name. I nearly drop dead, the way I was frighten, I was totally lost for words. They are people I've been around eating and drinking from them. I can't see myself eating or drinking from these people ever again. The mother was a lady, I have love and respect for and her father too, which I still do. Never in a million year would I have ever expected something like this. For them to be so firmly grounded in their belief of obeah, that they would do something so abominable, to another person was just disgusting. Knowing what I know, I worked out who had done it to the father. The minute she said this to me about her mother teaching her. It was then I realised that her mother was a dangerous woman. I don't want to judge her, but what her daughter had just revealed, it implicated her straight away after remembering what her father had said to me earlier.

Life has many ways to show us signs. This means you don't know who to trust when it comes to food and eating from some people. Especially ones you don't known sometimes it can be your very own wife, fiancée, girlfriend or baby mother. Your very own partner could be your down fall, or the cost of your illness because, if you give a person something like that to eat or drink that will definitely make him or her sick. How could a mother do something like this to someone else's child, and even assisting her child in such an act. People can't be trusted these days, we have to be careful with what goes down our bellies. Furthermore, we have to be cautious of where and who we decide to eat from, and who we sleep with. As men we can't think with only our dicks or make our dick lead us. We live in a world that is filled with evil and wickedness. This is a fact not an opinion, from what we can see happening all around the world today. I think the Bible is definitely fulfilling.

Selena still lives in Spanish town today doing her thing, nothing changes with her. The English man told her he wants a blood, test to be done on the child, and wants the result asap. Sadly, that's never going to happen, she recently told me that the English man had passed away from terminal Cancer. He never gets to find out if the child was really his or knew what Selena had done to him either. He later died at the age seventy-five, his wife still remains in the house in Signam. Selena's father also passed away from terminal cancer rip in respect of both men. As for her she mother she still remains in Signam, she continues to cook on weekends, selling her food in the back of her yard as usual. Her two brothers are still doing their same jobs respectively and remain in Signam also. Her two sisters both have kids of their own and still living in Signam, with their mother. Selena has had another baby by another man, who she still continues to say gives her a lot of money, yet she still gave the child to the English man and registered the child in his name. She recently told me this in the same conversation we had, when she told he had passed away. She then asked me if I knew his name. I told her no because we weren't familiar like that, so I never knew his name, all that time I've seen him. Now was the time she chose to tell me about his full name after his passing. She told his name was Mr Rupert Davian Alfonzo Ecuador Theodor Philador Broadmoor.

The story of the police and soldier arguing

I WILL BE TRAVELING WITH MY FRIEND LINCOLN, BETTER KNOWN TO everyone else as Red. We were travelling from Portmore Waterford, in St Catherine, heading towards Linstead that's also in St Catherine, a little further out of Spanish Town. We were going there to meet with a *gentle* man, known to me as Mr Manley. Reds was going there to sort out some very important business, pertaining to a property. Reds owned a property in Kingston that he intended to sell, and Mr Manley was interested in the property. Reds made a call to his nephew, telling him we were traveling to Linstead, and ask if he wanted to come for the ride. He said yes, he was off working today, and he definitely wanted to come with us. He asked Reds if he could pick him up at his house. He lived in Portmore, which was only a few minutes away from where we were. He told his uncle that he was off for the next three days, so he didn't mind hanging out with us. We quickly head to his house, to grab him as he asked. When we reached his house, we saw him outside standing, waiting patiently on us. He invited us inside the house and offers us a cool drink which we gladly accepted and thanked him because the sun was very hot. My friend Reds drove a pickup truck that can only carry two persons inside the front, and he wanted all three of us to travel together in one vehicle. Red's nephew then called one of his friends and informed him that we will be travelling to Linstead with his uncle and one of his uncle's friend. He asked if he could come along, and if it was okay to pick him up. He lived close to where we were at the time, so we went and got him straight away. When we arrived at the house, we noticed he had two vehicles park outside his yard, and he was standing beside them waiting for us. He told us he wanted to use one of the two vehicles, a big Toyota SUV, it looks brand new. It also looked like it's a government vehicle. I say this because of the colour of the licensed plate the other one was a Honda Crv. He told us he worked for the Jamaica defence force (JDF) that means he was solider. Reds introduced us all to each other. Once the introduction was out the way, we all board the SUV and drove off. We were leaving from Waterford and making our way to Linstead. We all knew each other by names now, so we continued talking with each other while making our way. We stopped and bought something cool to drink, as you know the day was scorching hot. We also bought some sugar cane and some oranges and continued our journey. Everyone was at ease and knew each other by name. On board the vehicle was Marcel, he worked for the JDF and was called Sogie. Owen that's Red's nephew he works the Jcf as a police officer. Next was Reds as you know he worked in construction, and me Byron the author. That makes four of us in the vehicle.

We started listening to some music on the radio along the way and talking about singers and deejays, rappers and artistes all over the world living and dead. We talked about a lot of different topics, we even talked about foreign and foreigners. Meaning people that lived and resides in America, Canada, English nationals, also Europe other Caribbean islands residents. We basically talked about all kinds of things, we started talking about kites and bikes and car. At one point we found ourselves talking about even the roads abroad. Debating that the worse sets of roads in England and America was better than the best road in the whole island of Jamaica. This caused a big discussion that prolong for a while. Marcel told us not to wind the Van windows down, because he was going to drive fast. He knows why he said this, maybe he didn't want the dust or the little flies to come inside while he was driving. The vehicle will be moving fast, and this happens all the time. Reds began telling us that he is a building contractor, and he works all over the island, but most of the jobs he was doing at present was in Kingston and St Thomas. We carried on driving and chatting all kinds of funny things, the conversation was getting even more interesting. we stop on the side of the road again to purchase some cool coconut water alongside the road way. We bought some east Indian and Julie mongos and start eating them straight away. Both types of mongos were very sweet and delicious when they are ripe properly. I love both mangoes they were my favourite out of all the mangoes grown in Jamaica. They are very sweet I love eating them, but before I eats them, I washed them properly because sometimes I eat even the skin on them and that's the truth.

After we've all finished eating our mangoes, we returned to the vehicle to continue our journey. We drove until we reached an intersection where there was a school. Now, the conversation changed again from mangoes to school. The conversation turns to a serious school dilemma. The JDF man the soldier, was adamant that his school was better than the Jcf guys, that was the police officer's school. The police guy wasn't having it, he said, that his school teachers were better and have better rating. He told the solider to look it up. Both men were saying that their respective school from primary up to high school and even collage were better that the other. This was a joke; I was laughing all the way to Linstead. Reds being Reds, started mouthing them, setting them up on each other adding fuel to the fire, but not in a bad way I must say. He was fuelling the fire and they were blazing up. The conversation and the argument steam up and Reds was killing himself with laughter. The JDF guy was saying he can play football very well, and he scored many goals in high school, in the under sixteen competitions. I don't know what that was, but the JCF guy still saying he was a better footballer, and he still have quite a few medals from his last school, and he wasn't joking. For some reason they seem to be competing with each other.

The argument continued all the way to a place called Damhead. That's still in the old capital heading towards flat bridge, going through the Gorged Road towards Bog Walk. This argument sounded as if it could carry on for the whole day, neither of them would relent. I am good with these three men, I'm comfortable in their company. They were talking about all kinds of things, I still haven't heard the half of it, more was yet to come. This was just a chip off the iceberg. The JDF man, who was the solider, said he had money in his account, that his mother bought him cars and he has assets, and he has Money and properties. He started talking all kinds of things just to wind the JCF guy, the police officer up again. The police officer name was Owen and the solider was Marcel aka (Sogie). Owen was about six feet tall, slim with straight face. His complexion was a course black, he had full eyes, wore his hair in a low haircut. He had long limbs, wore about size eleven in shoes. He lived with his girlfriend of twenty-five years, and she was soon to be wife. Sogie was married for seven years and had a son. He was teasing Owen, telling him, that he didn't have any kids and he was barren. Meaning he was infertile and could get any woman pregnant. This was getting more intense, I told them I had five kids, four boys one girl. He said Byron, you are leading on that front, but I didn't want to get involved in their little competition they had going. Reds said he had eight kids, now reds was leading the kids competition. It still didn't stop they're it's going to be getting even more interesting further down in this conversation.

We've now crossed Flat bridge heading onto the Gorge Road, minutes away from bog walk. It was a long drive so stopped again to buys more fruits, right in the corner, just before entering the bridge. Flat bridge was known for loads of Travel accidents over the years even from I was a small. They were also selling jerk chicken, roast yam and salt fish with festival, roast and fried fish on the corner. We bought some jerk chicken, roast yam and festival. The food was good, we are going in really cosy today. Now Sogie had already talked his part about money and all the assets he had, it was now Owen's turn. He started talking about his little money he was earning and that his monthly salary was hand to mouth. In this area you know the solider has one up on him, the soldier was leading the competition because the policeman had no kids or assets to talked about. It was Pure jokes in the car, this looked to me like it was a drama show. Owen has no kids and little money, but he was not giving up or accept defeat. He was still thinking about what to say, before stating he was a better chef than Sogie, and he cooks real good food. Boasting about his curry chicken with white rice and other food such as rice and peas and a variety of soups, plus much more dishes, he was saying with confidence. Then the solider starts saying he can cook stew peas and white rice also. Now the police man that's Owen, he wants to asked a question and he needed silence to ask this one. He said the question was for everyone and he wanted an answer. Listen this question, he was asking if anyone in the van had ever eaten dog before. This argument takes a different turn, Reds said he thinks dogs tasted good and not confirming if he had ever eaten dogs before. The questions and all the attention were on Reds but wasn't confirming or denying anything. He wasn't giving a definite response, not saying yes or no. He was funny, he had just fucked the argument right there because everyone wanted to hear a yes or a no from him out his mouth, but he wasn't saying nothing.

Everyone was telling him to make himself clear, but he wasn't doing that either, it was pure laughing again. Reds was saying he can more than the two of them together, he said he can eat two pounds of rice or dumplings plus yam banana and around the same amount of meat. He said he can a chicken weighing up to five or six pounds, and he can also eat a whole goat weighing up to forty pounds, when cooked in curry. He said he has done it before and was serious about it too. These men are jokers until now no one was holding up their hands to eating dog meat. Then Reds changed his tune, saying he ate dog, because Reds said that, Owen started saying he eats cat meat and all kinds of cats things. I don't understand that one, he was saying he means every kind cat. This was veering to another level, I don't know when or if these guys were serious, because it's pure jokes all the way. The solider didn't want to be left out of the conversation, piped up saying he eats rat, just because the police said he eats cat. The argument get even more ridiculous. I don't know if what they're saying was true or if it's making any sense, but the police started saying he eats snakes and vultures, that Jamaicans called John crow and even crocodiles.

They were talking about all sorts of nasty things and didn't care. I was just listening and enjoying the jokes, all I know was that these men were good. They are uncle, nephew and friend. Heading into Bog Walk we reached a bridge where loads of coconut, tangerine, melon, pineapples and grapefruits, were being sold, clothing too. We saw a Rasta man selling some fruits, we stopped and started speaking to him. The Rasta man began talking about the emperor Selassie, for a while the conversation took a different turn again. They started talking about the creator and the creation of earth with the Rasta man and wasn't going their way. The Rasta man got steam up the argument and started preaching, you know the Rastafarian ways already. He started telling them his woman must not work for no one but him, and he meant it. The man started taking this thing to another level. The Rasta man started telling them when his woman his on her period, he was the one that runs the kitchen at his house. She had to back off, that women were unclean when they are on their period, and he was being serious. He told us that no other man, that didn't smoke couldn't touch his chalice, or his herbs. He went on to say he didn't want anyone who deals with obeah in his yard either.

We bought some stuff from him and told him we were leaving then said our goodbyes to the Rasta man. We drove off heading into Linstead, the weather was good, and we reach the place where we are going. It was located near Linstead police station. I can remember the meeting was sets up just outside, in the station yard. The police officer that's Owen, met a few of his friends and squaddies that he knew from training school, or the police academy at the Linstead police station. They greeted and talked with each other while the business gets on the way. We were outside waiting on Reds and Mr Manley for about two hours, for them to complete their business transaction. Reds went straight into business mode, and did what he came here to do, while we walked around waiting in the marketplace. He told us he needed some season for his home. Things like tomato scallion, onions, scotch Barnet peppers, bell peppers and pimento seeds to take back to his house in Portmore. We all purchased somethings from the market for ourselves to take home. After Reds was done with is business, we headed to the nearest petrol station to filled up the tank with petrol. Reds attempts to give Sogie some money, but he gives it back, saying thanks but refused to take it, but Reds insist on paying for the petrol.

Once we filled up on petrol, we decided to head back home. They started talking about foreign countries, the USA, Canada and England even Europe. None of the two ever travelled, Reds lived in America. He began telling us about the fifty-two states. he was at it again and telling us About the houses in USA. Nobody can compete with him on that one. He started talking about the weapon he used to handle in USA and that he owns over five firearms in the states. He said he owns a few Glock pistols in different sizes. This stirred up the argument in to a steam house again, he was saying he loved Glock 45 Cal. The two lawmen just listening to him carefully, before letting him know they loves Glocks too. This was going to be a Glock conversation; Reds was saying he knows how to take a part a Glock. I was thinking if he did, then the other two must know, how to as well, after all they were in law enforcement. I was just listening to them until it turns into a Glock and a shooting exhibition.

Reds suddenly took out his Glock 19 pistol, brandishing it. Informing us that it was licensed. The police that's Owen also brandished a Glock pistol; it was a bigger pistol according to him. It was a Glock 34, he stated that it has a longer barrel, it too was a licensed firearm. From what I could see It was definitely a bigger gun than the Glock 19. Now the JDF guys Sogie, as he is called, went into his waist band and retrieved a Glock 19 pistol too, he said it was a licensed firearm as well. I was there driving with these three men all this time, and was unaware that they were all harmed, I was totally surprised. The two lawmen were now determined to shoot at some form of target and were looking for a shooting range. They began talking about a Chinese man in Twickenham Park, who has a range and sold ammo. I was just listening carefully and learning as much as I can. They were telling me that it wasn't too late for me to obtain a licensed firearm. They started telling me about the process of getting a licence firearm, saying that I just need to sort myself out, then I could get one as a business man. I told them yes and started thinking about the procedure to get one straight away with no delay.

All three men were now eager to fire their weapon, this was even more serious. The soldier insisted he was the best shooter among them, that he excelled in that department when he was in training. The police not one to let things slide, was saying the same thing. Reds defending himself told them both that he held that spot as best shooter, I found this entire ordeal so funny. They carried on bickering all the way. Heading into Spanish town they saw a sexy lady all three men were looking, even I was looking. Now hear this, the conversation changes from who was the best shooter, to who could handle the woman sexually. Both the soldier and the police were saying that Reds couldn't manage her because he was old. They event old me that I couldn't manage her either, for what reason I don't know. Sogie said he could manage because that lady was his type and sized woman, the police can't. Even though he never gives a reason as to why he thought neither of us could manage. We all want this lady, so the competition starts all over again. I wasn't competing with anyone; I appreciated the fact that she was a sexy woman. Again, the three men were arguing, saying they could fuck her well. I'm thinking what the hell was happening. Sogie stopped the car and all three then called out to the lady. She started smiling, Sogie told her he wanted to go home with her and cook her dinner. When it was

Reds time to speak, he told her that he will wash her draws meaning her panties. Laughing spoil, everyone within earshot of the conversation was in fits of laughter. Now it was the police time to talk, he told the woman that he can iron the panties after Reds washes them, then he would fold them and put them away in her panty draw. That made the woman burst out laughing. Sogie wanted the woman's attention back on him, told her he wanted to lift her up and carry her home on his back. This was getting really funny.

None of these men wanted to be the loser of this competition, So Sogie came up with a different tactics. He stated with confidence that none of them can eat pussy like him, I'm laughing like hell. The police that's Owen said no one can eats pum pum like him, meaning pussy. Reds saying, he can do his thing. Sogie saying how he puts honey on the clit and suck on it, chewing it like a bubble gum. The police said he sucks on it, until women legs trembles and they can't stand up. He told us that the first time he ate pussy was on his eighteenth birthday and hasn't stopped eating it since, and he was now thirty-six-year-old. He said he likes the smell of pussy on his finger, when he his patrolling with his colleagues. He said when he was on the road after eating pussy, he didn't like washing his face properly. He liked to leave a little whiff of the smell on his nose, so that he can wipe his fingers across his nose while he is patrolling and can smell his fingers all day. He was saying all he wanted to do was to go home and eat his wife's pussy. Reds asked both men how pussy taste, they both had different answer. The police man that's Owen, says it tastes a bit salty, he laughed he told us it had a ocean breeze smell. Sogie too agreed that it tasted a bit salty but also have an onions taste and smells. He said he also liked when the pussy was well shaved, because sometimes the hairs from it will get stuck in your teeth or your throat and caused problems making you cough. Owen was telling Sogie that he doesn't know what kind of pussy he was eating, but it's not supposed to smell like onions. Sogie was said he didn't care; he just likes the salty taste.

Owen was saying he is a professional when it comes to eating pussy, that he takes this role serious. He said when he gets home after a hard day of work, if he was tired sometimes or feeling sleepy, and his wife wanted sex. Then he would tell her to just sit on his face, as long has her batty was clean, meaning her ass and she just had a shower. He said she could sit on his face and do her thing, the only thing she must not do was fart in his face, because that was a violation. He was saying that when the fart was that close to the face, and it hits you from the naked bottom at close range, he can feel small bits hitting him in his face. He was saying it could be shit or something from the ass and that won't let him sleep. At this point I laughed until I had tears running down my face. He said he lets her ride his face until she comes, then he would wipe it off when she was done because licking pussy was a joy. Sogie now trying to steal the spotlight in this competition, he says he like biting the clit and pulling it, like he wants to pull it out of its place. He said he too like chewing it, but preferred to put his mouth over the entire pussy and just suck. He admitted that he was a scholar at pussy eating, saying he satisfied his woman every time and very well. He said he can't have sex without eating his woman pussy, he said if that didn't happen, it wasn't proper romancing. He was telling us, that he loved getting his dick suck, especially if she didn't have a gag reflex. He told us that he loves to fuck, and he was willing to do anything for his girl. Owen drawing the attention back to him, said he don't mind the smell of pussy on his nose and his forehead, but he can't stand the shitty or batty smell on him. I wondered what he meant by that, I didn't want to interrupt what he was saying so I didn't ask. He said that it happened to him before, and he didn't like the smell of ass in his nose. Sogie confirmed was Owen was saying. He said he and his wife was in a sixty-nine position and she accidentally done a silent fart in his face. He said he was so mad because the smell went right up in his nose and lingers, he said he could smell it for the whole day, and the smell was awful. Owen said to him, you should have bitten her in it. I nearly died laughing, these men were too funny. Sogie was saying that, some women when there were coming, they fart and jook on his face and he didn't like them ones to do sixty nine with. He thinks they are dangerous because his nose was long and pointed, so when they brace back on his face his nose was touching their batty hole.

Marcel was too funny, he said whenever you are making love to a woman and she lies down dead, meaning inactive. He said if that happens to you, he knows how to make lazy women move, especially the fat ones. He said in bed, if they're lazy worse if the woman was fat, fat. He would stick his middle finger in her asshole, and she would vibrate like a jackhammer and whine nonstop. He even said he knows how to test the pussy if it can eat, meaning if it's fit and also if it sick. He said you must get some cow's milk and put some in a glass or any container stick your finger in her pussy, then put it in the milk. He said, you should take it out and looks at it. If the milks runs smoothly it's good to go, meaning fit to eat but if the milk curdles and don't runs, that means that pussy cannot eat. He also mentions that he likes ladies that goes with other ladies and he loves threesomes. It was pure laughing, Reds asked Sogie, what happened after he takes his fingers out her ass. He laughed and said the fingers looking like it stuck it in mud, he said she walked and jook for the whole day, asking him to do it again, because she like the feel of his finger in her ass. Reds and I said gave him the winnings, he deserves the winner position for the day for his outlandish tales. Both of them did their thing, but Marcel was in a class by himself, he decided to win by any tale necessary. Reds and I were drop back at his vehicle, we all shook hands and bid each other farewell. We all took our bags with the seasonings and other items we purchased from the market. Marcel said he would drop Owen back to his house. That was a day filled with fun, laughter and jokes every one enjoy themselves. I enjoyed being around these men the whole day. Two of them I was seeing for the first time, although they say looks are deceiving, I had good impression of the two men. I've since built-up trust in Marcel and Owen. The things both men said today about themselves other men in Jamaica will hurt or even kill you for even suggesting that they suck pussy. Everyone did things differently to enjoy themselves. The thing about oral sex and other sexual preferences is that it's a taboo subject in Jamaica. No one wants to associate themselves doing these acts, yet in private they enjoy themselves to the fullest. The fact is, in this day and age people whatever they wanted to with their partners and their lives. No one has the right to dictation how a person should live. People have their preferences, what they like and don't like. What people do in the privacy of the homes, shouldn't impact others, so long as they are not forcing it on others or breaking the law.

Reds secured a good deal for the house he sold in Kingston. We boarded back his pickup and was headed laughing. Life was not only about sadness, but there were also time when you can find happiness with your friends and family. It also depends on you and the person understanding of the relationship. People can be really fucked up, but there are still good people out there in the world. You can have bad experiences with anyone, such as your children, your siblings, aunts, uncles even your parents, but it's how you handle the situation. Sometimes you have family that will fail you, most of the time it's your children trust me on that one. Trust is a very valuable and rare commodity. It hard to put your trust in people, especially with things you are eating and the people you are eating from, even something as simple as that, you can't trust sometimes. I've seen this happen to families and friends all around the it's not good.

Looking on social media today, you can see how it's common. How families are living and doing horrible things to each other, like sisters killing sisters and nieces assisting in the killing of their aunts. They are doing these types of cruelty and wickedness over money and properties. Brothers and sons killing their parents and grandparents. Just recently, I came across a similar situation in the news, where a granddaughter killed her grandmother and threw her body behind a chicken coop. Some people are living very badly over property, they make it difficult to believe that there are still good person left on earth, which is not true. I have a few friends from as far back as kindergarten and primary school, that I'm still friends with. We still love and respect each other since we were small, from about six years old or even younger. At present, we are all fifty year old men and women, and we still have love and maximum respect for each other. That love also extends to their children until today nothing has changed.

In all my years of living, since I've been old enough to understand life, I have found myself in peculiar situations. I have encountered and been in the company of some dangerous people. With each circumstances I came away with a life lesson, it has though me things I didn't even knew about myself. I learnt how to be patient, I have learnt how to be grateful and not take things for granted. That waking up each day was a blessing. Most importantly I have learnt to be caution